DEREK PARKER

# FAMILIAR TO ALL

*William Lilly and Astrology in the Seventeenth Century*

JONATHAN CAPE
THIRTY BEDFORD SQUARE LONDON

FIRST PUBLISHED 1975


JONATHAN CAPE LTD, 30 BEDFORD SQUARE, LONDON WC1

ISBN 0 224 01112 X

SET IN 12PT BEMBO 270 1PT LEADED

PRINTED AND BOUND IN GREAT BRITAIN
BY COX & WYMAN LTD
LONDON, FAKENHAM AND READING

For
Julia

# Contents

# Illustrations

*'Be humane, curtius, familiar to*
*all, easie of accesse: afflict*
*not the miserable with terrour of*
*a harsh judgement ... let no worldly*
*worth procure an erronious judgement*
*from thee, or such as may dishonour*
*the art ...'*

WILLIAM LILLY, Epistle to the Student in Astrology, 1647

# Foreword

For one reason or another—chiefly, one suspects, because of lingering prejudice against the whole subject—historians have sadly neglected to study the effect astrology has had on the social and political life of man over at least three thousand years of history. This is true not only of ages when that influence is difficult to trace (the medieval age, for instance) but of ages such as those of Imperial Rome and Elizabethan England, when it played an enormously important role.

William Lilly is one of the few astrologers to leave enough material behind him to enable one to look fairly fully at his life and work. As much as the priest, or later the psychologist, an astrologer was inevitably in touch with the complete fabric of his time. Ordinary men and women visited Lilly for advice on the most intimate problems; both Royalist and Commonwealth leaders approached him for advice on the conduct of the war, as well as on more personal matters. Lilly claims that Cromwell himself was interested in his work (if only for its unquestionable value as propaganda), and certainly Charles II later consulted his friend Elias Ashmole. It may surprise many readers to discover the extent to which such men as Clarendon relied on astrological advice, or at the least took cognizance of what astrologers said.

Lilly was the leading astrologer of the last great age of astrology, when it was still possible for an astrologer to make a very good living indeed by practising his art (or science); when he could be respected by at least a reasonable number of reputable and intelligent contemporaries. Soon after his death, the age of enlightenment was to give astrology a blow from which it was never to recover—although there are at present signs that meteorologists, psychologists and doctors are finding facets of ancient astrological theory worth investigation.

The autobiography which Lilly wrote at the suggestion of

Ashmole has the reputation of being one of the most amusing memoirs of the Stuart age. It has been out of print for a hundred and fifty years. It is perhaps less amusing than its reputation claims; but when it is read in combination with the letters Lilly wrote to Ashmole, and with extracts from his always lively and frequently splenetic almanacs (and the almanacs of his rivals), and when Ashmole's diaries are used to fill in some detail, a story emerges which gives a picture of a man curious enough and interesting enough to engage our attention.

He cannot be compared with that marvellous gossip John Aubrey as an entertainer; but his mind was a remarkable compendium of natural wisdom and quick-wittedness, folly and superstition, nervousness and nerve. And his astrological and later medical practice shows some facets of Stuart life which, glimpsed at in other contemporary journals, still repay study. There is also the part astrology played during the Civil War, when it was used calculatingly by people who rejected the astrological theory; but had its effect on those who, like the majority of Elizabethans, would never have dreamed of questioning the proposition that the planets affected terrestrial life.

The chronology of this book has not been easy to arrange satisfactorily: I have thought it best to deal with Lilly's private practice, his almanac-publication, and his work for the Army, substantially in separate chapters, which inevitably overlap somewhat in time. The brief chronology of Lilly's life which follows should clear up any difficulty.

A list of my main sources will be found in an Appendix. In transcribing material, I have taken the view that a retention of the original spelling often preserves atmosphere and adds colour, but must obviously not be allowed to interfere with the easy understanding of a passage, or to become tedious. In Lilly's narrative, which is relatively straightforward, and from which I have sometimes quoted at length, I have modernized the spelling and punctuation. In other cases (Ashmole's diary and letters, Lilly's letters to his friend, and the texts of his almanac and the almanacs of his contemporaries), I have retained the seventeenth-century spelling and capitalization, and have only modified the punctuation when it has seemed to obscure the sense of the text.

I am grateful to a number of institutions and individuals for help in preparing this book. The staff of the British Museum Reading Room, the London Library, the Bodleian, the Library of the London Museum, the Public Record Office, the Society of Genealogists, and the Astrological Association have all been extremely forbearing and helpful in guiding me to sources of which I had not previously been aware.

Mr Robert Latham (Fellow of Madgalene College, Cambridge, and editor of Pepys's diary) kindly made available some notes of his own regarding the part astrology played in the Civil War and Interregnum. Mr E. Freeman, Librarian of the Wellcome Institute of the History of Medicine, Mr J. Steven Watson, Principal of the University of St Andrew's, and Miss Marguerite Gollancz, Surrey County Archivist, have all been of help; Mrs Frances Heywood kindly allowed me to look around Lilly's birthplace at Diseworth, and to photograph it; Dr and Mrs Norman Heatley kindly gave me hospitality. Mr John Shephard, now at work on a major bibliography of astrology, kindly read my MS, and offered invaluable help and advice. Like so many authors, I also owe a debt to the late William Plomer, that civilized writer, kindly man and good poet, without whose encouragement this book would not have been written.

Finally, my wife has borne with her customary good humour months of my preoccupation with William Lilly and his contemporaries; has enabled me to interpret many technical astrological allusions which would otherwise have escaped me; and has made many suggestions about the text. I am, as always, grateful to her.

D.P.

# A Brief Chronology

| | | |
|---|---|---|
| 1602 | April 30, William Lilly born at Diseworth, Leicestershire. | Shakespeare's *Merry Wives of Windsor.* |
| 1603 | | Elizabeth I d. April 10. James VI proclaimed King of England as James I. |
| 1605 | | Gunpowder Plot discovered. |
| 1613 | Lilly joins the Grammar School, Ashby-de-la-Zouch. | Beginning of building of Bodleian Library, Oxford. |
| 1616 | | William Shakespeare d. |
| 1620 | Lilly leaves school; teaches at Diseworth; April 3rd, travels to London to become servant to Gilbert Wright, in the Strand. | Pilgrim Fathers leave Plymouth in the *Mayflower.* |
| 1622 | Lilly nurses Wright's second wife through terminal cancer. | |
| 1624 | | England declares war on France. |
| 1625 | Lilly guards his master's goods during the plague; Wright marries Ellen Whitehaire. | James I d. Charles I succeeds. |
| 1627 | Wright d. May 22nd. September 8th, Lilly m. Mrs Wright. | |

| | | |
|---|---|---|
| 1632 | takes lessons in astrology from John Evans. | |
| 1633 | Mrs Lilly d. | Galileo Galilei forced to abjure theories of Copernicus. |
| 1634 | Lilly searches for treasure in Westminster Abbey; November 18th, m. Jane Rowley. | |
| 1635 | begins to teach and practise astrology. | |
| 1636 | takes a house at Hersham, Surrey. | |
| 1642 | | Beginning of English Civil War. |
| 1643 | established practice puts him in touch with influential men. | |
| 1644 | April: first almanac published. *Prophesy of the White King* plunges Lilly into political astrology. | July 2nd: Royalists defeated at Marston Moor. Milton's *Areopagitica*. |
| 1645 | The exchange of invective with Sir George Wharton, the Cavalier astrologer, begins. June 14th: predicts Roundhead victory at Naseby. Examined by Parliamentary committee. | June 14th: Royalist defeat at Naseby. |
| 1646 | first meeting with Elias Ashmole. | Charles I surrenders to Scots. |
| 1647 | *Christian Astrology* published. Lilly accused of plotting the marriage of a rich client. Consulted | |

| | | |
|---|---|---|
| | by Mrs Whorewood on behalf of Charles I. His portrait painted. | |
| 1648 | supplies hacksaw to facilitate Charles I's escape from Carisbrooke Castle. Granted a pension of £100 by Parliament. Sent with John Booker to the siege of Colchester. | Beginning and end of second Civil War. |
| 1649 | Attends trial of Charles I; procures release from prison of Wharton. | Trial and execution of Charles I. |
| 1651 | Summoned before Committee for Plundered Ministers; imprisoned. | |
| 1652 | buys Hurst Wood, Hersham. | |
| 1654 | February 16th, Mrs Lilly d. October: m. Ruth Needham. | |
| 1655 | indicted for fortune-telling. | |
| 1658 | | Oliver Cromwell d. |
| 1659 | Lilly receives gold chain and gift of money from King of Sweden. | Pepys begins his diary. |
| 1660 | Examined by Parliamentary Committee enquiring into execution of Charles I. | Restoration of monarchy; Charles II crowned. |
| 1661 | arrested by mistake; swears allegiance to Charles II. | |

| | | |
|---|---|---|
| 1663–78 | | Samuel Butler's *Hudibras.* |
| 1665 | at Hersham during the plague; churchwarden of Walton-upon-Thames. | The Great Plague. |
| 1666 | October, examined by Parliamentary Committee enquiring into cause of the Fire of London. | The Great Fire. |
| 1670 | acquires a licence to practise medicine. | |
| 1677 | increasingly poor eyesight; the astrologer Henry Coley becomes his amanuensis. Friendship with Elias Ashmole and his wife deepens. | |
| 1681 | d. June 9th. | |

# 1
# Leicestershire to London

*Do not the Hist'ries of all Ages*
*Relate mysterious Presages*
*Of strange Turns in the World's Affairs*
*Foreseen b'Astrologers, Soothsayers,*
*Chaldeans, learn'd Genethliacks,*
*And some that have writ Almanacks?*

SAMUEL BUTLER, *Hudibras* (II,III:685)

William Lilly was born in the little village of Diseworth, in Leicestershire, on April 30th, 1602, in a timber-framed thatched cottage which still stands beneath the steeple of the largely fourteenth-century church of St Michael. He was the son of a yeoman farmer.

An unpropitious birth? Many years later, a rival of Lilly's referred to him as being 'the son of a labourer or ditcher', and certainly to have been born to such a man in the last year of Elizabeth's reign would not have offered much in the way of a possible education. But Lilly's rival was wrong; though for some time confusion over what precisely was meant by the term 'a yeoman farmer' (Lilly's own description of his father) obscured the true circumstances of his birth and childhood.

In fact, his family had been reasonably comfortably situated for some time—at the beginning of his autobiography, Lilly tells us that Diseworth was 'of great rudeness, wherein it is not remembered that any of the farmers thereof did ever educate any of their sons to learning, only my grandfather sent his younger son to Cambridge, whose name was Robert

Lilly, and died Vicar of Cambden in Gloucestershire, about 1640.'

Lilly's father, William, perhaps felt that there was more money (and, at a time when contention often made religious practice embarrassing for men of conscience, more safety) in working the land than in joining the church. And his father would no doubt have encouraged him to continue the family's traditional occupation—the cottage in which Lilly was born had housed several generations of yeomen of his family.

The word 'cottage' suggests something unambitious, but in fact this was a substantial house of its time. It stands on a road which leads from Diseworth south-west to Ashby-de-la-Zouch, and even without the later wing which grows out of it to the east, it remains sizeable, with several rooms rather larger than one might expect in a mere labourer's house.

The family lived in some comfort. When Lilly's father died, in November 1635, an inventory of his cottage's contents was taken, and survives to show that even after bankruptcy and some years of relative poverty, he was a man of comfortable means, with, for instance, three candlesticks of brass and three of pewter, and a good supply of kitchen utensils ('two brasse pots and a posnet; one broad brasse pan one great Caldron three kettles two skillets and a skimmer; four spits one paire of Cobyrons 2 Cressets and a fryinge pan; twoe double salts one single salt one pestel and a morter 2 basons 4 smal dishes and one quart pott . . .' and so on).

The linen left in the house was also a mark of respectable living: not only coverlets, blankets, curtains, but cushions, flaxen sheets, towels, napkins. The house's contents, together with a few outdoor items and livestock—'three kyne, one other cowe and a yereling calfe; one sowe 2 hogs & 3 weaninge pig; one fillye; two sheepe'—were valued at £62 15s 10d, and when young Lilly was growing up, playing in the garden among the hum of bees, and scratching his initials and the outline of his hands on the new plaster inside the front door (the marks are still to be seen), life must have been at least as comfortable as in any other house in the parish.

William Lilly senior was a leading member of his village community, as his father had been before him. Though Diseworth, like any other place of its size in Elizabethan England, appeared to have an egalitarian structure (the squire's son attending the village school with his husbandmen's children), in fact there were sharp social divisions, on an economic basis. There was a group of yeomen families of middling income, about a quarter of the families of the village, owning half or more of its wealth. Beneath them in the social scale were their less wealthy social equals, then the husbandmen, craftsmen, cottagers and labourers.

The fact that Lilly's father owned his own land sets him apart from most of his contemporaries: even recognizably prosperous yeomen farmers did not necessarily own their own land—frequently it was leased from a local squire or religious house. Lilly owned *and* leased—from Christ's College, Cambridge, which owned most of Diseworth and the surrounding area, presented to the College by Henry VII's mother, the Countess of Richmond.

The comparative luxury of the cottage in which the elder Lilly lived with his wife Alice (daughter of an Edward Barham, who originally came from Norwich, but at the time of her marriage lived at Fiskerton Mills, Newark, twenty-five miles or so from Diseworth) underlines his position in his little community, for it had only been in his own time, or in his father's, that the richer yeomen of the country had begun to build themselves half-timbered houses of a size and style previously unknown in the small villages of England. In the middle of the sixteenth century whole villages were virtually rebuilt as yeomen began to spare money for comfort and even for show.

The value of farmers' goods rose during the sixteenth century: between 1500 and 1588 the general level of prices doubled, and in the same period the average value of Leicestershire farmers' goods more than trebled. Since in the last quarter of the sixteenth century William Lilly was farming, with his father, 150 or 200 acres at least, one might expect him to have consolidated his position, and built up a considerable fortune. Young Lilly might have been born to a very comfortable inheritance. The Rev.

William Harrison, a parson who toured England at the end of the sixteenth century, looked somewhat enviously at the prosperous yeomen of England:

> For the most part the yeomen are farmers to gentlemen, and with grazing, frequenting of markets and keeping of servants (not idle servants such as gentlemen do, but such as get their own and part of their master's living) so come to great wealth, in so much that many of them are able and do buy the lands of unthrifty gentlemen, and often setting their sons to the schools and to the universities and to the Inns of Court; or otherwise leaving them sufficient lands whereupon they may live without labour, do make them by those means to become gentlemen.

That was a heritage to be envied. But by the time Alice was carrying her eldest son, her husband was already in some financial difficulty; by the time young William was of school age, his mother was pointedly referring to his father's 'back-slidings in the world, with no hopes by plain husbandry to recruit a decayed estate'. And by 1620, the elder Lilly was in Leicester Gaol for debt. What caused his downfall? One can only conjecture: but it seems most likely that he was simply a poor businessman, a bad manager—and unable in particular to cope with the sudden change in the distribution of crops which took place towards the end of the sixteenth century in Leicestershire, and confused many small farmers.

Peas, barley and wheat were the most important crops grown by the farmers of that county during the first half of the sixteenth century; but for no appreciable reason, by the 1580s all three showed a decline in importance, and wheat in particular showed a spectacular fall in popularity—from 13·8 per cent of the arable area of the county to a mere 8·6 per cent, and with worse to come. By the turn of the century, many farmers grew no wheat at all, or just a half-acre or so. The elder Lilly (and perhaps his father before him) may simply have failed to adjust, and gone on cultivating crops he could not profitably sell. His 'plain husbandry', in other words, was insufficient to keep the farm going. If it seems unjust to blame the poverty of the family on Alice Lilly's husband, it must be remembered that in fifty years' time—when the astrologer Lilly was writing his autobiography—his younger brother had managed to build up the farm once again to a point at which (though all the land was leased from Christ's, Lilly's father having sold his freehold acres) it was 'of the value of forty pounds per annum'.

So young William Lilly grew up in the atmosphere of tightening belts—to the extent, even, that his mother had to cut down on food, and the wheaten loaf vanished from their table (one of the boy's delights, when he reached London in 1620, was to 'eat good white bread, contrary to our diet in Leicestershire'). But Alice Lilly refused to give up the idea that her eldest son should better himself. He was 'put to learn at such schools, and of such matters, as the rudeness of the place and country afforded'. He was probably about seven years old: most boys went to their first school at about that age.

While educational standards were being radically improved in the grammar and public schools, schooling in small towns and villages was rudimentary. Children would often arrive at grammar school without knowing so much as their ABC, so that the Master had to waste his time teaching ten- or eleven-year-olds to read; there was some pressure for an entrance examination, which would reject any boy unable to read a passage of scripture.

There is no indication of the quality of the primary school Lilly attended; a few years later he was to return to it to teach there for a while himself, and the standard may well have improved, considering the training he had by then received. As it was, he passed his time there for three years or so, and then moved on to a much more rigorous and rewarding school.

Despite the financial difficulties which by now were pressing on the family, Mrs Lilly was determined to make of her son something other than a farmer—particularly, one supposes, because it was by now fairly clear to her that her husband would have little in the way of land to leave him; he had started to sell his land to pay his debts. He could have done with young

William's help, no doubt. Instead, on Trinity Sunday, 1613, he took the boy the ten miles or so to Ashby-de-la-Zouch, and the Grammar School there. It was one of the most fortunate things to happen to William Lilly in his long life, for the Master at the school was one of the finest teachers of his time—John Brinsley.

It seems more than likely that Mrs Lilly had heard of Brinsley and his reputation, and determined to put her son under his care. That she was able to do so was also a matter of luck for her son: had he been born a century earlier, his education would have been too costly to contemplate. As it was, an enormous amount of wealth had been made over to the endowment of education between 1560 and the end of the century, at the beginning of a period which saw education in England expand faster and with better results than in any other century, up to and including the present one. The grammar schools flourished, and much attention was given to theories of education. John Brinsley was a distinguished theorist.

Lilly describes him as 'very severe in his life and conversation'; but he was far less so than most schoolmasters of the period. Brinsley had been appointed Master and 'Minister of the word' at Ashby in 1574; the fact that he had a little earlier married the sister of the Bishop of Norwich can hardly have hindered him. The year before Lilly arrived at his school, Brinsley had published his *Ludus Literarius: or, the Grammar Schoole; shewing how to proceede from the first entrance into learning to the highest perfection required in the Grammar Schooles*. It is perhaps the most comprehensive educational treatise of its time.

Lilly tells us little in his autobiography about his years at Ashby, except that when he was fourteen he almost had his right eye knocked out during a playground game, and that he fell into a fever, the same year, after eating beechnuts. But the gaps are amply filled by Brinsley's own account, based as it was on the regime at his own school.

The first and most important thing about Brinsley is that he was a convinced vocationalist; his whole life was his pupils. He writes:

> I can take ordinarily more true delight and pleasure in following my children (by observing the earnest strife and emulation which is amongst them, which of them shall doe the best, and in the sensible increase of their learning and towardness) than anie one can take in following hawkes and hounds, or in anie other the pleasantest recreation, as I verily perswade myselfe.

He was obviously fond of children, and showed very considerable kindness and care in dealing with them; he could certainly have taught a lesson to many Victorian schoolmasters, let alone his contemporaries. He was horrified, for instance, by 'that extreme severitie whereby all things are done in very many schooles, and the whole government maintained only by continuall and terrible whipping', and when he set out his picture of the ideal schoolmaster must have been painting a self-portrait, even if an idealized one. The master

> should be of a loving and gentle disposition with gravitie; or such a one as will frame himselfe unto it; and to incourage his schollers by due praise, rewards, and an honest emulation; who also dislikes utterly all severity, more than for necessity; yet so, as that he be quicke and cheerful to put life into all, and who cannot indure to see sluggishnesse or idlenesse in any, much lesse any ungraciousnesse; and therefore can use not onely sharpenesse, but even severety with discretion where neede it.

The school day at Ashby began at six in the morning, and went on until half past five in the evening. After three hours of copying Latin exercises there was a break of fifteen minutes for breakfast; then work until eleven, and a generous break of two hours for lunch and play. The afternoon was interrupted only by a quarter or half-hour's break for 'drinking and necessities', and school broke up after a Bible reading, psalm and prayer. Brinsley was a puritan—a notable one, like Dr Beard, who at Huntingdon Grammar School had implanted puritan ideals in Oliver Cromwell's young head. Brinsley especially disliked 'the popish schoolemasters ... who make [religion] the very chiefe marke at which they aime, in all their teaching, to powre in superstition at the beginning, first to corrupt and deceive the tender minds.' But he imposed, of course, a religious regime, making the Sunday sermon the focus of much of the week's learning, for the boys had to précis it, translate it into Latin, learn it by heart, and even offer a reasoned critique of it.

The two hours of playtime were carefully supervised so that the boys only occupied themselves with games 'meet for Gentlemen. Clownish sports, or perilous, or yet playing for money, are no way to be admitted'. King's School, Worcester, put it even more strongly: the boys there were allowed 'to play and sport together, not wandering about here and there, lest they incur loss of character, and their minds become set upon other things, and estranged from learning.'

Brinsley, though a great deal kinder than many of his contemporaries, was in no doubt that it was his duty to ensure that his pupils learned as much as possible while under his care; and he went about his duty soberly and with great attention to detail, intent not simply on knocking a few facts into the boys' heads, but giving them some notion of what the process of learning was about. Scholars, he believed, should be

> taught to do all things with understanding; and to be able to give a reason of every matter which they learne ... To reade and not to understand what we reade, or not to know how to make good use of it, is nothing else but a neglect of all good learning, and a meere abuse of the meanes and helps to attaine the same. It is no other thing but a very losse of our precious time, and of all our labour and cost bestowed therein.

His methods of keeping order and discipline seem admirable: he did not completely eschew corporal punishment, though he obviously disliked it intensely.

> What father is there; nay which of us is there who is a father, who would not have our own children rather trained up by

> all loving meanes of gentle incouragement, praise and faire dealing, then with buffeting and blowes, or continuall and cruell whipping, scorning and reviling? Or which of us could but indure to see that indignitie done to our owne children, before our faces?

He taught mainly, then, by encouragement and praise; and for discipline relied largely on a Black Book, in which names of the lazy or disobedient were entered. They were not allowed to play 'untill they shew themselves truly sorry for their faults, and doe amend, becomming as dutiful and submisse as any other'.

Two or three blows of the birch were all Brinsley allowed himself for the most serious offenders—and even then he was 'very wary for smiting them over the backes, in any case, or such sort as in any way to hurt or indanger them'. 'Having the rodde always in our hands, if we be of hostile natures,' he concludes, 'I take it to be as for a furious man to carrie ever a naked sword in his hand. It will make us to strike many a time, when wee will bee sorry for it after, if it fall not out worse.'

When Lilly left Ashby, he claimed he could speak Latin as freely as English, and extemporize verses on any theme (this occupation often took the place of games, when the weather was wet or there was any other reason for keeping the boys indoors). He was always put up by Brinsley to argue or dispute with visiting examiners. He seems, in fact, to have been a showpiece of the school—if one takes him at his own valuation. But even if one does not, there was certainly one thing he learned from Brinsley which was to be of inestimable value to him for the rest of his life: the love and use of the English language. His knowledge of Latin too was to be extremely useful, for virtually all astrological textbooks were published in that language.

Many masters of the time considered Latin and Greek more important than English. Brinsley disagreed, and concentrated steadily on English:

> Because that language which all sorts and conditions of men amongst us are to have most use of, both in speech and

> writing, is our owne native tongue. The puritie and elegancie of our own language is to be esteemed a chiefe part of the honour of our Nation: which we all ought to advance as much as in us lieth.

So the boys practised oratory in English; and were also made to attempt some style in their English writing, 'striving to expresse whatsoever they construe, not onely in proprietie, but in varietie of the finest phrase, who can give the best'. Good handwriting, too, was encouraged, and Lilly could write handsomely, as the manuscript of his autobiography proves; his jotted notes and letters are, however, less legible.

By the time they reached the highest form in the school, the boys were allowed and encouraged to help Brinsley and his single usher to teach the smallest pupils: and it was assumed that they would go on to Cambridge, and possibly into the teaching profession. As it happened, Lilly was an exception. 'All and every of those scholars who were of my form and standing went to Cambridge,' he writes in his autobiography; 'and proved excellent divines, only poor I, William Lilly, was not so happy; fortune then frowning upon father's present condition, he not in any capacity to maintain me at the university.'

He left school in 1619, just after Brinsley himself had been forced to give up his post there. The reasons for Brinsley's departure are obscure: Lilly simply says that his master 'was enforced from keeping school, being persecuted by the Bishop's officers'. It is fairly easy to guess at the reason. Brinsley was a great friend of the Vicar of Ashby, Arthur Hildersham, a famous puritan who had originally been intended for the Roman Catholic priesthood, and had been disinherited for his conversion to protestantism. Hildersham was in constant trouble with the authorities. In 1598, he preached a protestant sermon before the Assize Judge, Sir Edmund Anderson, which upset the latter so much that he rose to leave the church, and later invited a grand jury to indict the Vicar. (The jury declined.) In the very year Lilly arrived at school, Hildersham was suspended by the High Commission, and a couple of years later found himself in the

Fleet Prison, prosecuted by the new Vicar of Ashby, one Hacket, for refusing to kneel to receive communion.

Brinsley was of much the same religious temperament and furious independence of mind; it is unsurprising that he too should have suffered for his faith, at a time when religious questions were so unsettled and unsettling. Lilly himself perhaps caught something of the independent spirit of his master; certainly, however able he found himself to twist and turn between, for instance, Roundhead and Cavalier, he maintained a certain basic honesty, and was a naturally religious man (not for nothing was his most substantial work called *Christian Astrology*).

One seems to catch, in the autobiography, a lingering regret that he was unable to go into the Church; though there is no evidence that he was ever intended for it, his uncle's example may have impressed him. When he was sixteen he went through a not uncommon stage of religious morbidity: 'I was exceedingly troubled in my dreams concerning my salvation and damnation, and also concerning the safety and destruction of the souls of my father and mother; in the nights I frequently wept, prayed, and mourned, for fear my sins might offend God.'

There is no hint, however, that Lilly regarded his sudden removal from Ashby, and the final extinction of his hopes of a university education, as the intervention of the hand of God (unless divine displeasure were to be regarded as applied via the misfortunes of his earthly father). Back he went to Diseworth, where he lived in very considerable penury for a year, teaching for part of that time at the little village school where he himself had been a pupil. (Years later he was to receive a petition from the Vicar of Diseworth for financial assistance to support a new grammar school there: it was signed by—among others—William Lillye and Rowland Lilly, two relatives.)

His father was in the last stages of staving off the final degradation of arrest for debt, and making much use of his lawyer, one Samuel Smatty. Young William was naturally used as messenger between them. Smatty recognized that he was a bright boy who had had a good education, and one day told Lilly that recently, in London, he (Smatty) had come across a gentleman who was on the look-out for a youth to act as a secretary and general servant. It was a fairly promising position: there was always the chance of preferment for someone who could read and write, even if all that could really be hoped for was a position as secretary or writer in a wealthier household.

William told his father. The latter had, in his difficulties, completely lost patience with his son, who instead of helping him save the farm, had been engaged in studying Johann Scapula's *Lexicon Graeco-Latinum* and improvising iambic hexameters. He 'was very willing to be rid of me', wrote Lilly; 'for I could not work, drive the plough, or endure any country labour; my father oft would say, that I was good for nothing.'

So the boy prepared for adventure. He had scraped together twenty shillings, with which he bought a new suit, hose and doublet ('my doublet was fustian,' he writes rather sadly: it was a coarse, uncomfortable cloth of cotton and flax). Smatty gave him a letter of recommendation to his new master, and on Monday April 3rd, 1620, the eighteen-year-old set out, walking alongside Bradshaw's carrier's cart all the way to London. The weather was stormy and wet; his clothes were soon soaked through, and he had no others to change into. He had very little money—he had briefly said farewell to his father, finally subdued by his creditors, in Leicester Gaol—and a few friends had clubbed together and contributed ten shillings to his pocket.

Bradshaw's cart reached Smithfield on Palm Sunday, after almost a week's hard tramping. Lilly tipped the carrier two-and-six for his trouble (the trouble, simply, of showing him the way, though also of providing vestigial protection against footpads), and made his way towards the Strand. 'I had... one suit of clothes upon my back, two shirts, three bands, one pair of shoes, and as many stockings,' he tells us.

Very little can be discovered about Lilly's master other than what Lilly himself tells us. His name was Gilbert Wright, and he had been born at Market Bosworth in Leicestershire. For some years he had been the servant of a Lady Pawlet, in Hertfordshire; but then had become an upper servant to Sir John Puckering, the Lord Keeper of the Great Seal, sometimes Speaker of the House of Commons, and a great favourite of Queen Elizabeth, with whom he curried favour by entertaining her grandiloquently at Kew, and flattering her incessantly.

Wright lived in Puckering's house between Charing Cross and the Temple—Russell House; and when Puckering died, in 1596, became Lord Keeper to Sir Thomas Egerton, the Lord Chancellor, another favourite of the Queen's (but highly thought of as a man of the greatest probity). It was Egerton who introduced Wright into the Company of Salters, which had been founded in the fourteenth century, and was engaged in the business of bringing in salt from Droitwich and Cheshire, the Biscay coast, and along the French coast south of La Rochelle, for salting down meat, pickling fish, and other uses.

His membership of the Company did not mean that Wright was in the salt business: from its beginning (as in other cases) the social element in its composition was as strong as the commercial, and politics too played a part. A man interested in local government or municipal power (and Wright was certainly that) had to make his way through one of the Companies, and would choose one which was easy to enter—because he had relatives, or friends, or an employer connected with it—rather than, necessarily, one close to his own trade or profession.

By the early seventeenth century, the Salters' Company was in its heyday, and Wright (Lilly tells us) became its master in 1624—though the Company's records do not show his name. He was evidently a man of some moment, but though he was a good speaker, could neither read nor write. Lilly, then, was in a favourable position to make himself indispensable, and did so. He was expected to make himself generally useful, however; a quiet life taking dictation, if that was what he had expected, was certainly not to be his. He had to clean Wright's shoes, sweep the street in front of his house in the Strand, carry water from the Thames to the house ('I have helped to carry eighteen tubs of water in one morning'); he weeded the garden, emptied the slops, and ceremonially walked before his master to Church on Sundays.

Lilly was to live in Wright's house—'the corner house in the

Strand'—for many more years than he can have suspected at first. The Corner House (sometimes Lilly notes that it is 'over against Strand Bridge') is not marked on any extant map, but would have stood at the east end of the Strand, and probably on the north side, since John Stowe in his 1603 *Survey* notes all the large houses as being on the south side, whereas on the north there was only 'a large Middle Rowe of houses'. Looking at Norden's plan of 1593, and comparing it to an earlier map *circa* 1563, one sees a passage, Drury Court, running from the bottom end of Drury Lane (opposite Drury House) to join the Strand just opposite the east end of Somerset House. On the corner is a house from which it would have been easy to cross to the end of Strand Lane, leading down to the Thames whence Lilly collected his tubs of water.

It would have been a pleasant enough place to live, away from the hugger-mugger of the city itself. A small village originally stood on the site of the Strand between the city of London and the area of Westminster. By the fourteenth century a highway had grown up, with a few 'great houses', their gardens running down to the river, masked by tenements abutting the road itself. Gradually, more and more land was granted for building along the line of the road, so that by 1560 it could be called 'a street', though a 1560 map (probably largely conjectural) shows only a single line of houses running on the north side from Charing Cross to the junction with Drury Lane, and on the south another single line of houses, with, between them and the river, Arundel House (where Thomas Seymour, Lord High Admiral, when it was called Seymour Place, had made those unwise advances to the young Princess Elizabeth), and Somerset House (in which the same girl was occasionally to stay as Queen).

To compare the 1560 map with Norden's is to appreciate how quickly London was growing; yet how leanly, still, the area outside the City itself—that is, the line of the city walls—was built upon. To the north, beyond Covent Garden, fields stretched away to the little village of St Giles, the road to Holbourne, and up to the north-west, the Oxford Road. West of Charing Cross were Hedge Lane and the Hay Market, with not a house near them;

and to the east of Drury Lane, again open fields until a scattering of houses marked Fetter and Shoe Lanes.

Wright's house, then, had some space around it—enough to save it, with Arundel, Essex and Somerset Houses, from the Great Fire, years later; and there were pleasant public walks down by the river, not only a wonderful spectacle as a highway to the court, but also useful for travel. There were, however, certain penalties: the road was indescribably rough, with irregular and treacherous pavements; the kennel, or water-channel, in the centre of the way was frequently choked with the offal, dust and rubbish servants threw into it, and overflowed until it made the road slippery to horses and pedestrians; and when it was wet one walked in a foot of water while more water fell on to one from the gutters discharging from the houses on either side.

The Corner House was not a particularly happy one, during Lilly's first years in it. Wright had married his second wife Margery for her money, and she had married him (being seventy years old—his senior by four years) for quite other reasons: 'for considerations he performed not', says Lilly slyly, adding in parentheses 'nocturnal society'. She was fanatically jealous, and made Lilly's life a burden to him by constantly questioning him about his master's activities when out of doors.

When Lilly had been with the Wrights for two years, his mistress began to complain of a pain in her left breast, where 'a hard knob no bigger than a small pea' had appeared. It was a cancer, and it enlarged rapidly, despite the 'oils, sear-cloths, plates of lead, and what not' applied to it. By 1623 it was obviously incurable. Lilly, in his autobiography, gives a detailed and nasty description of it. Evidently he was fascinated, and in a strange way enjoyed the experience of nursing the poor woman, who would have no one but him to change the dressings and generally nurse her. It was the beginning of an interest in medicine which was to culminate years later in his actually becoming a practising physician.

He was kind and attentive, getting up often three or four times a night to comfort his patient. Finally, he even performed surgery: 'In 1624 by degrees with scissors I cut all the whole breast away—I mean the sinews, nerves, &c.' Unsurprisingly, the patient died not long afterwards. There was nothing anyone could have done, and no reason to suppose that Lilly's attentions made her illness or death any more painful (or indeed much more comfortable) than it would have been in any event.

On her death-bed she gave him five pounds, and told him to go to a trunk at a friend's house, where he would find a hundred pounds in gold. He did so—but the trunk was empty, a kinsman having got there first. Mrs Wright was so infuriated to hear this that she told Lilly to help himself to anything in the house when she had died (her husband was away at the time). Wisely, the young man declined, simply seeing to her burial. Preparing her for this, he found beneath her arm a small scarlet bag containing all sorts of talismen, 'some of iron, and one of gold, of pure angel-gold, of the bigness of a thirty-three-shilling piece of King James' coin', Lilly recalled years later. This latter had been designed for her by Simon Forman, one of the best-known Elizabethan astrologers. Lilly sold it for thirty-two shillings. One can hardly blame him: he had earned the right.

Gilbert Wright now had ample proof of Lilly's faithfulness and honesty; and, perhaps also relieved that a wife for whom he had not much affection was no longer available to rail at him, treated the young man with great kindness, and trusted him implicitly—so much so that when, in 1625, the plague attacked the city, he left for the relative safety of the country, giving Lilly charge not only of his household goods, but a large stock of money and plate, his own and other people's property.

Lilly's duties were very light: apart from keeping an eye on the house and its contents, his only regular task seems to have been to pay out, weekly, alms from a fund administered by Wright. The rest of his time was his own:

> My master was no sooner gone down, but I bought a bass-viol, and got a master to instruct me; the intervals of time I spent in bowling in Lincoln's-Inn-Fields, with Wat the cobbler, Dick the blacksmith, and such like companions: We have sometimes been at our work at six in the morning,

and so continued till three or four in the afternoon, many times without bread or drink all that while.

Meanwhile, however, the virulence of the plague grew worse. This was the first time a really serious outbreak had hit London (the precursor of the massive attack of 1665), and by midsummer it was clear that it was the most serious since the days of the Black Death. In one London parish (St Dunstan's) where normally only twenty or thirty people died during a month, there were 23 burials in June, 87 in July, and 337 in August. In September 210 people perished, and then as winter drew on the disease began to abate, with 52 burials in October, 23 in November, 20 in December. And by January, when only 12 burials were recorded—lower than the average, the weak and aged having all been carried off—it was clear that the outbreak was at last over.

John Donne, Dean of St Paul's, and at the height of his powers as a preacher, wrote to Sir Thomas Roe, British Ambassador in Constantinople:

> Your number of 2,000 a day was so far attempted by us that in the City of London, and in a mile compass, I believed there dyed 1,000 a day ... the Citizens fled away, as out of a house on fire, and stuff'd theyr pockets with their best ware, and threw themselves into the highways, and were not receyvd, so much as into barnes, and perish'd so, some of them with more money about them than would have bought the villadge where they died.

London was indeed deserted by all except those who were bound, either by contract or conscience or self-interest, to remain there. 'No habit of a gentleman or woman continued,' Lilly wrote; 'the woeful calamity of that year was grievous, people dying in the open fields and in the open streets.'

> At last, in August, the bills of mortality so increased that very few people had thoughts of surviving the contagion. The Sunday before the great bill came forth, which was of five

> thousand and odd hundreds, there was appointed a sacrament at Clement Dane's, during the distributing whereof I do very well remember we sang thirteen parts of the one hundred and nineteenth Psalm. One Jacob, one minister (for we had three that day, the communion was so great), fell sick as he was giving the sacrament, went home, and was buried of the plague the Thursday following. Mr James, another of the ministers, fell sick ere he had quite finished, had the plague, and was thirteen weeks ere he recovered. Mr Whiteacre, the last of the three, escaped not only then, but all the contagion following, without any sickness at all, though he officiated at every funeral, and buried all manner of people, whether they died of the plague or not. He was given to drink, seldom could preach more than one quarter of an hour at a time ...

Lilly was a regular church-goer—more regular during the plague, it seems, than before. (He writes in his life of Charles I: 'I do well remember ... that going in July, 1625, about half an hour after six in the morning to St Antholin's Church, I met only three persons in the way, and no more, from my house over against Strand-bridge, till I came there; so few people were then alive, and the streets so unfrequented.') Twice at least he visited St Dunstan's-in-the-West, close to the corner of Fleet Street and Chancery Lane, where on January 15th Dr Donne, the Vicar, reviewed the progress of the contagion, now over:

> Even in this City, no doubt but the hand of God fell upon thousands in this deadly infection, who were no more affected with it than those Egyptians, to cry out We can but die, and we must die: And, Let us eat and drink, and take our pleasure, and make our profits, for tomorrow we shall die, and so were cut off by the hand of God, some even in their robberies, in half-empty houses; and in their drunkenness in voluptuous and riotous houses; and in their lusts and wantonness in licentious houses; and so took in infection and death, like Judas' sop, death dipt and soaked in sin. Men

> whose lust carried them into the jaws of infection in lewd houses, and seeking one sore perished with another; men whose rapine and covetousness broke into houses, and seeking the Wardrobes of others, found their own winding-sheet, in the infection of that house where they stole their own death; men who sought no other way to divert sadness, but strong drink in riotous houses, and there drank up David's cup of Malediction, the cup of condemned men, of Death, in the infection of that place ...

The nobility of Donne's language can scarcely have failed to impress his congregations, even those members who tended (as he certainly did not) to favour puritanism. He had already spoken of the 'intemperate use of the liberty of the Gospel, and sometimes the impotency of a satirical humour' which 'makes men preach freely, and over-freely, offensively, scandalously ...' Lilly, on the other hand, was at this time thoroughly puritan. Brinsley and Hildersham had taught well: their pupil, soon after he came to London, became a regular attender at St Anthony's Church, on the corner of Watling-street and Sise Lane, a little east of St Paul's.

Known familiarly as 'Antholin's', the Church was an old one, dating from 1513 (its last rebuilding), and with a beautiful modern gallery divided into fifty-two separate compartments, each with its coat-of-arms, which had been added in 1623. It was later to be burned down in the Fire, and though Wren designed the building which replaced it in 1682, that in turn was demolished at the end of the nineteenth century.

Antholin's was a source of some discontent in the area. Its puritan Rector, Charles Offspring, had helped to found and administer a series of famous lectures which made his church the centre of puritan social and religious activity in the London of the 1620s. Every morning for an hour, between five and six o'clock, the bells tolled to summon parishioners and others to lectures, to the great vexation of non-puritans in and out of the immediate vicinity. Clarendon points out in his *History* that 'there was so great a conflux and resort, by the citizens out of humour and faction, that from the first appearance of the day in the morning on every Sunday to the shutting of the light, the church was never empty.' Lilly went there to hear Mr Gouge of Blackfriars, Dr Micklethwait of the Temple, Dr Oldsworth, and other famous preachers and lecturers. He 'leaned more and more to Puritanism'.

Simultaneously, he began more and more to dislike Presbyterianism; his opinions on that subject were to strengthen as time went on, and were indeed to place him in a perilous position when the Presbyterians came to substantial power at the Restoration.

The Presbyterian problem was really a result of the return to England of the Marian exiles from Frankfurt soon after Elizabeth I succeeded to the throne. At first, the English Calvinists, more generally called Puritans, seemed likely to become extremely powerful; but after a defeat in the convocation and Parliament, they split into various factions, one of which consisted of those Puritans who favoured either Congregational or Presbyterian theology. Until Charles I's time, they more or less vanished within the Church of England, generally managing to find some accommodating parish which would accept a certain amount of quiet nonconformity. By the end of the sixteenth century, there was virtually no sign of them. But then, partly as a result of the pamphleteering of Thomas Cartright, the Presbyterian theorist, there came a new clamour for a change of policy in the Church of England, and nonconformity came into the open again.

Both Charles and Archbishop Laud were impatient, and visited the Presbyterians with considerable punishments, both physical and financial. But every punished Presbyterian encouraged ten others to protest, or so it seemed, and increasing bitterness made them more and more extreme. The Congregationalists and other nonconformists joined their voices to the general protest, of course; but the Presbyterians were the chief protesters.

Their position was not only religious, but political, and there was a certain type of political dissent which by the early years of the seventeenth century came to be called 'Presbyterianism'. It was a loose term which had little meaning in the strict sense of the term 'Presbyterian', though it is true that many people with political objections to the regimes of Elizabeth, James I, and Charles I, did support religious Presbyterianism, or at least some other branch of nonconformity. The majority of 'political' Presbyterians, however, were simply branded with the name. Lilly seems to have disliked Presbyterianism for religious, political and temperamental reasons. He was simply not that kind of Puritan, though it is difficult indeed to say just what kind of Puritan he was, for he was not a conventionally religious man: his interest in theology was minimal. Above all, he probably disliked Presbyterian extremism, even when it led to the Commonwealth whose ideals (at least at first) he supported.

After the plague had ceased, Lilly's master returned to London, and married again—a widow, Ellen Whitehaire. Grateful (and not without cause) for Lilly's devotion to duty, Wright settled £20 a year on him—which, considering that Lilly and his one fellow-servant had been living well on six shillings a week, was a very reasonable sum. But in May 1627 Wright died; and since his elder brother and his wife were both illiterate, it fell to Lilly to tidy up his affairs, administer the estate, pay the debts, and so on. Again, he proved completely trustworthy.

And now comes a delightful little comic set-piece: Lilly's courtship of his master's widow—or perhaps one should say, hers of him. He must be allowed to tell the story himself:

> My mistress had been twice married to old men, was now resolved to be cozened no more. She was of a brown, ruddy complexion, corpulent, of but mean stature, plain, no education, yet a very provident person, and of good condition. She had many suitors—old men, whom she declined; some gentlemen of decayed fortunes, whom she liked not, for she was covetous and sparing. By my fellow-servant she was observed frequently to say she cared not if she married a man that would love her, so that he had never a penny; and would ordinarily talk of me when she was in bed. This servant gave me encouragement to give the onset. I was much perplexed hereat, for should I attempt her and be slighted, she would never care for me afterwards; but again,

> I considered that if I should attempt and fail, she would never speak of it—or would any believe I durst be so audacious as to propound such a question, the disproportion of years and fortune being so great betwixt us.
>
> However, all her talk was of husbands, and in my presence saying one day after dinner she respected not wealth, but desired an honest man, I made answer I thought I could fit her with such a husband. She asked me, where? I made no more ado, but presently saluted her and told her myself was the man. She replied I was too young. I said nay—what I had not in wealth, I would supply in love—and saluted her frequently, which she accepted lovingly, and next day at dinner made me sit down at dinner with my hat on my head, and said she intended to make me her husband—for which I gave her many salutes, &c.

It was a nicely managed courtship; and Lilly was careful enough to persuade Mrs Wright to keep the proposed marriage secret, for any wealthy widow consulting her friends or relations about a proposed marriage to a 25-year-old servant would attract certain inevitable answers. On September 8th, 1627, Ellen Wright and William Lilly were married at St George's, Southwark, and for as long as two years afterwards the marriage was kept secret. They must have had tractable servants.

When the news eventually came out, there were recriminations and later lawsuits with Wright's relatives, which however went in the Lillys' favour. As for Mrs Lilly, she was quite happy: 'When it was divulged, and some people blamed her for it,' Lilly remarks, 'she constantly replied, that she had no kindred, if I proved kind and a good husband she would make me a man; if I proved otherwise, she only undid herself.' And indeed it was to be a happy and contented marriage, for all its six years.

For the first five years, Lilly revelled in the opportunity to live comfortably without the necessity of working. He fished in the Thames down by Somerset House, went to the theatres and to the fairs where acrobats walked on ropes, and fencers gave exhibitions; saw the archers shooting in Lincoln's Inn Fields, and watched (perhaps even joined in) the dancing around the great Maypole which stood only a few feet from his front door.

It must have been at this time that he got the taste for cards, which he played with his first and last wives (the second seems to have been above such trivialities); primero and basset occupied candlelight evenings in winter. Though he never indulged the national sport of hunting, he loved dogs, and always had one or two about the house—cats too.

Mr and Mrs Lilly were able to live well, to keep a servant, and to entertain their friends (if not her relations). Beef was only twopence a pound, a leg of mutton one-and-six, butter sixpence a pound, and eggs two shillings a hundred. A thousand pounds a year was riches: in fact a table of incomes towards the end of the seventeenth century placed the income of a baronet at only £880 a year, whereas a mere 'gentleman' would have an income of only £280.

Lilly's leisure activities—and life was, for this period of his life (and this only) entirely leisure—were not all flippant. He went a great deal to the religious lectures at Antholin's and elsewhere. He was also accepted as a member of the Salters' Company—no doubt they welcomed him as the husband of a former member's elderly widow: after all, it would help to avoid the possibility that the Company might have to provide for her, in her old age, in its almshouses. He dined occasionally at the Salter's Hall in Bread Street, near St Paul's Churchyard; but spent most of his evenings at home. 'We lived very lovingly,' he says, and there is no reason to disbelieve him.

One Sunday in 1632, Lilly was sitting in his place in Antholin's waiting for service to begin, and chatting to his neighbour, a Justices' Clerk. The latter happened to say, of someone whose name came up in conversation, that he was 'a great scholar, nay, so learned that he could make an Almanac'. It struck Lilly as very strange that this should be considered an attribute of great learning, and he seems indeed to have been in some doubt as to what the exercise consisted of. One thing led to another, and the Clerk suggested that he might take Lilly to meet an astrologer he happened to know. It has been thought that this was Rhys or

'Arise' Evans, a Welsh astrologer and hot-gospeller. It was in fact one John Evans, whom Lilly describes as being mainly occupied in preparing and selling antimonial cups—the seventeenth-century equivalent of Epsom salts.

In 1634, 'John Evans, Minister and Preacher of God's Word, dwelling neere Fetter-lane in Gunpowder Alley' published *The Universall Medicine: or the Vertues of the Antimoniall Cup.** This seems to have been literally a cup, made of brittle antimony, which one steeped in wine—claret or muscatel, or, best of all, malmsey. (If it broke, Evans would replace it for 10s.) In the *Ephemerides of Origanus,** which Evans brought out the following year, he placed an advertisement for it: 'Claret wine, or white wine, or new Ale, having stood in this cup twelve hours, and after taken fasting, purgeth the body from whatsoever is offensive to nature: the operation is gentle, and without any violence or danger, as hath beene oftentimes proved.' Those who read on might have taken the last words literally, but would still perhaps hesitate to send their money on reading that the liquid 'sometimes, and in some conditions, operateth by Vomit alone, in some others by Siedge† alone, in others by urine and sweat, but most commonly it worketh all these waies ...' However, even the busy hour or so resulting from taking the cup must have been worth while in view of the fact that it

> helpeth against all evill effects of the Stomacke; it cureth all intermitting Agues, and burning Fevers, it helpeth the swimming in the head, Madnesse, & Frenzie; cureth the Greene Sicknesse ... destroyeth Worms ... restoreth appetite lost ... aswageth the paine of the Gout ...

and in short dealt efficaciously with most ills known to man.

Lilly was not impressed by Evans at their first meeting: he found him suffering from a monumental hang-over, groaning

* I am indebted to Mr John Shephard for bringing these books to my attention.

† as a laxative.

on his bed ('if it be lawful to call that a bed whereon he then lay') in a sleazy house in Gunpowder Alley, a little turning off Shoe Lane. Evans was a squat little man, dark and beetle-browed, with splay-feet and a flattened nose: 'the most saturnine person my eyes ever beheld, either before I practised or since'.

He was 'much addicted to debauchery', Lilly noted, 'and when very abusive and quarrelsome, seldom without a black eye, or one mischief or other.' Lilly seems to have considered him a competent astrologer, and believed in his occult experiments—telling a tall story about Evans successfully raising the angel Salmon, who kindly stole the deeds of some land on behalf of a poor widow who was being defrauded. Later, Evans was to appear in a less admirable light. But as it was, Lilly was interested in learning about astrology, and Evans was glad of a pupil to eke out a living. The two got on well enough.

# 2

# Astrology and Society

*Were the stars only made to light*
*Robbers and Burglarers by night?*
*To wait on Drunkards, Thieves, Gold-finders,*
*And Lovers solacing behind doors,*
*Or giving one another Pledges*
*Of matrimony under Hedges?*

*Hudibras* (II,II:817)

It is difficult for a twentieth-century reader to understand the true position of an astrologer in sixteenth- or seventeenth-century society. We are so conditioned to the present popular reputation of astrology – founded on the Sun-sign newspaper columns which originated in the 1920s – that it is the common impression that astrology is too simple a system to have been taken seriously by an intelligent person for any historical period.

This is no place for an analysis of the niceties of that system; it need only be said, briefly, that the astrologers founded their attempts at character delineation and forecasting on much more complex and scientific considerations than the simple one of what astrological sign the Sun occupied when a man or woman was born. Their system entailed the calculation of the precise position of all the planets in all the signs at the moment and for the place of birth; unless he was born in the same room and within four minutes of another person, no single man could have a birth-chart identical with that of any other person ever born.

When the planetary positions had been calculated, the symbols representing the planets were placed in a birth-chart (or 'figure', or 'scheme', as the Elizabethan astrologers called it); and consideration of their relative positions and the angles they made with each other, and would make in the future as they changed position, enabled the astrologer to reach his conclusions. There were other factors to be taken into consideration also: the planets' positions within the Zodiacal signs and houses, for instance; and there was a sufficiently large number of possibilities (the critic would say) to enable the astrologer to produce evidence to support almost any prediction or contention he might make.

All the same, the system was a strict one, based on an empirical collection of information built up over at least four thousand years, with *written* evidence of astrological techniques from 500 BC onwards. There are now many books spelling out in detail the manner of calculation and interpretation of a birth-chart, which differs very little from the manner employed by Ptolemy, Petosiris or Nechepso of Egypt during the three hundred years before the birth of Christ; indeed, the documented history of the technique of astrology is as fascinating as the history of its effect on the social and political life of man. But we need not concern ourselves with it here.

What is important is to understand the climate of opinion about astrology in the sixteenth and seventeenth centuries; for that of course governed William Lilly's professional life entirely, after his decision to study the subject, and later to set up as a professional consultant astrologer. It is an area neglected by historians; until Dr A. L. Rowse's recent examinations of the papers of Simon Forman, an Elizabethan astrologer more or less in Lilly's own class, no serious historian had given much attention to astrology and astrologers—even to John Dee, one of the most truly remarkable men of the Elizabethan age—despite the fact that they had had a very considerable influence on their time.

It is difficult for a non-historian to speak authoritatively of this influence; but there is one source from which any intelligent reader can see quite clearly the average Elizabethan's attitude to the subject—the works of Shakespeare.

One does not need to be warned of the dangers of attributing to Shakespeare the opinions he gives his characters. On the other hand, there are certain conclusions to be drawn from the many astrological allusions in the plays and poems; and from them one can build up a picture of how the Elizabethan man-in-the-street (for Shakespeare, genius though he was, was also that) regarded the influence of the planets on terrestrial affairs.

The first thing to be said is that in general the Elizabethans accepted that influence as natural, and not seriously to be questioned. Shakespeare himself undoubtedly shared that view, and moreover makes it quite clear that it was not the silly view of the modern reader of the astrological columns in the newspapers, or indeed of many unthinking twentieth-century 'believers' in astrology. The position is very different, incidentally, for Lilly's great contemporary Milton, who was obviously totally uninterested in astrology. He only used astrological symbolism very sparingly in his work, though he knew enough about the subject to make an occasional pun, or an occasional semi-technical allusion:

> Among the constellations war were sprung,
> Two planets rushing from aspect malign
> Of fiercest opposition in mid sky . . .*

In Sonnet 14 (and in the sonnets he was surely speaking from his own heart) Shakespeare wrote:

> Not from the stars do I my judgment pluck,
> And yet methinks I have astronomy;
> But not to tell of good or evil luck,
> Of plagues, of dearths, or seasons' quality;
> Nor can I fortune to brief minutes tell,
> Pointing to each his thunder, rain, and wind

* *Paradise Lost*, VI: 313

> Or say with princes if it shall go well
> By oft predict that I in heaven find ...

Although he was aware of the value of astrology ('astronomy' and 'astrology' were often synonyms), the Elizabethan was not given to relying on 'the stars' (by which the planets were meant; the stars of course have nothing to do with astrology) for his decisions, much less to bring him good or bad luck, or to forecast plagues or famines or even the weather—though some work on astrological weather-forecasting had been going on for a thousand years or more. He did not see astrology as a means of 'fortune-telling' which could tell a man when his personal 'weather' would be good, bad or indifferent; nor was he interested in using the science (for so it was regarded) to tell great princes whether they would win battles.

That is what the Elizabethan did *not* feel about astrology. What, then, was it good for? There are various hints. In *Julius Caesar*, for instance, in a passage which has been much misunderstood, Cassius tells Brutus that

> Men at some time are masters of their fates.
> The fault, dear Brutus, is not in our stars,
> But in ourselves, that we are underlings.

That is, there are particular moments of time when men are best able to grasp the opportunities life gives them—are best able to be 'masters of their fates'. They should be careful to note these times (which any competent astrologer could tell them), and taking them at the flood, go on to fortune. In other words, if a man remained an 'underling', it was not because he was forced to do so by the planetary positions, the influence of 'the stars', but because he did not seize the moment when the planetary positions were most propitious for him.

The intelligent Elizabethan believed in such propitious moments, and was often careful to time his important affairs to chime in with them, as Prospero does in *The Tempest*, noting that the planets at the time of his enemies' wreck are most favourably placed for the accomplishment of his revenge:

> and by my prescience
> I find my zenith doth depend upon
> A most auspicious star, whose influence
> If now I court not, but omit, my fortunes
> Will ever after droop.

The history of this belief is long, going back at least to the time of the rise of Assyria, and even earlier. But that it was, during the sixteenth century, both general and firmly held can scarcely be questioned. Almost any contemporary author will confirm it. Raleigh, for instance, in his *History of the World*, speaks for his contemporaries in a noble passage which clearly shows how rash and foolish he would have considered anyone stupid enough to deny the astrological theory:

> And if we cannot deny but that God hath given virtues to spring and fountain, to cold earth, to plants and stones, minerals, and to the excremental parts of the basest living creatures, why should we rob the beautiful stars of their working powers? For, seeing they are many in number and of eminent beauty and magnitude, we may not think that in the treasury of his wisdom who is infinite, there can be wanting, even for every star, a peculiar virtue and operation; as every herb plant fruit and flower adorning the face of the earth hath the like. For as these were not created to beautify the earth alone and to cover and shadow her dusty face but otherwise for the use of man and beast to feed them and cure them; so were not those uncountable glorious bodies set in the firmaments to no other end than to adorn it but for instruments and organs of his divine providence, so far as it hath pleased his just will to determine?

Shakespeare, similarly, saw that 'men as plants increase/Cheered and checked even by the self-same sky', and his belief found expression again and again in his work, when he wished to comment on the governing forces that inclined men's lives this way or that. And in Sonnet 60, at a moment of pessimism:

> Nativity, once in the main of light,
> Crawls to maturity, wherewith being crowned,
> Crooked eclipses 'gainst his glory fight,
> And Time that gave doth now his gift confound.

Time, that is, having given certain propitious planetary attributes at the moment of birth, is later apt to confound them by the planets' progressions.

The fact that there are so many allusions in the plays (apart from glancing references, there are for instance eight specific astrological references in *A Winter's Tale*, six in *I Henry VI*, five in the sonnets, five in *King Lear*) demonstrates not only Shakespeare's recognition of astrology as an everyday influence on life, but the fact that the meanest member of his audience would understand his references. These can even, at times, be moderately technical: when, in *Twelfth Night*, Sir Toby says to Sir Andrew, 'Were we not born under Taurus?' Sir Andrew replies, 'Taurus; that's sides and heart.' 'No, Sir,' replies Toby, 'it is legs and thighs.' And the point of the exchange (lost to modern audiences) is that they are both wrong, and that the Elizabethan audience would recognize the fact. A few lines later on, Sir Andrew underlines the effect by launching into a gobble-de-gook semi-astrological reference: 'In sooth, thou wast in very gracious fooling last night, when thou spok'st of Pigrogromitus, of the Vapians passing the Equinoctial of Quebus.' (Shakespeare was by no means averse to sending up the over-serious astrological apologist, as when Launcelot Gobbo in *The Merchant of Venice* claims that 'it was not for nothing that my nose fell a-bleeding on Black Monday last at six o'clock i' th' morning, falling out that year on Ash Wednesday was four i' th' afternoon'.)

Astrology was a useful dramatic device (a point, again, lost by modern critics). The long speech of Edmund's in *King Lear*, often quoted as 'Shakespeare's attack on astrology', is a case in point.

Gloucester, it will be remembered, discovering that Edgar has apparently betrayed him, blames this and other discords in the state on 'these late eclipses in the sun and moon'. When he has left the stage, Edmund, the villain, laughs and launches into the beautifully poised, cynical speech about

> the excellent foppery of the world, that when we are sick in fortune, often the surfeits of our own behaviour, we make guilty of our disasters the sun, the moon, and stars; as if we were villains on necessity; fools by heavenly compulsion; knaves, thieves, and treachers by spherical predominance; drunkards, liars, and adulterers by an enforced obedience of planetary influence; and all that we are evil in, by a divine thrusting on.

'An admirable evasion of whoremaster man,' he continues, 'to lay his goatish disposition on the charge of a star.'

> My father compounded with my mother under the Dragon's Tail, and my nativity was under Ursa Major, so that it follows I am rough and lecherous. Fut! I should have been that I am, had the maidenliest star in the firmament twinkled on my bastardizing... Oh, these eclipses do portend these divisions. Fa, sol, la, mi!

The Elizabethan audience will have heard that speech with the increasing realization that Edmund was not to be trusted. How could one rely on the judgment, even the sanity, of a man who argued so against the natural state of things, the self-evident disposition of man under the planets? Instantly, the effect Shakespeare wanted—the establishment of Edmund's perversity—was achieved; and he reinforced it by inserting the high-flown allusions to the Dragon's Tail and Ursa Major, and by having Edmund, within a few lines, demonstrate his duplicity by turning about and taking the opposite view in conversation with Edgar, pretending to mirror Gloucester's attitudes.

Elsewhere in *Lear*, Shakespeare uses astrology respectfully, as when he makes Kent (wondering that Lear should have had three daughters so disparate in character as Goneril, Regan and Cordelia) say:

> It is the stars,
> The stars above us govern our conditions;
> Else one self mate and make could not beget
> Such different issue.

The differing planetary conditions at the time of their birth gave the three daughters their personalities, not the coupling of Lear and his wife.

Time and time again, in play after play, we find serious allusions to astrological forces as *naturally* exerting an influence on man; the Duke in *Measure for Measure*, the repository of all wisdom, tells Claudio, condemned, to 'be absolute for death', for he is merely

> a breath
> Servile to all the skyey influences
> That dost this habitation where thou keep'st
> Hourly afflict.

Yet if man must learn to accept with resignation certain astrological influences, there are others against which he can and must fight. Cassius pointed this out to Brutus, and Helena (a physician's daughter, and all physicians had some astrological training) says in *All's Well that Ends Well*:

> Our remedies oft in ourselves do lie,
> Which we ascribe to heaven. The fated sky
> Gives us free scope; only doth backward pull
> Our slow designs when we ourselves are dull.

Historians have consistently understated the fact that astrology was one of the very few generally recognized universal laws during the Elizabethan age. The astrological theory fitted soundly into the Elizabethan's general conception of the universe, with its great emphasis on *order*—an emphasis which stressed, certainly, the necessity for order within the State, an inflexible social order; but which reached out beyond man's life, or rather through it, to the easily discernible order within the observable universe: the order of the moving planets and the fixed stars, impressive by the fact that it seemed to regulate what otherwise would easily become a chaos, but also because it provided a paradigm by which man could learn about his place in the natural, universal order of things.

Raleigh emphasized this in his *History of the World*, and the idea appears again and again (implicitly as well as explicitly) in other Elizabethan literature. But Shakespeare puts it most memorably in Ulysses' great speech in *Troilus and Cressida*:

> The heavens themselves, the planets, and this centre,
> Observe degree, priority, and place,
> Insisture, course, proportion, season, form,
> Office, and custom, in all line of order:
> And therefore is the glorious planet Sol
> In noble eminence enthron'd and spher'd
> Amidst the other; whose med'cinable eye
> Corrects the ill aspects of planets evil,
> And posts, like the commandment of a king,
> Sans check, to good and bad: but when the planets
> In evil mixture, to disorder wander,
> What plagues and what portents! what mutiny!
> What raging of the sea! shaking of earth!
> Commotion in the winds! frights, changes, horrors,
> Divert and crack, rend and deracinate
> The unity and married calm of states
> Quite from their fixture!

The passage shows more vividly than any other easily accessible quotation the Elizabethan vision of a parallel system of heavenly and earthly order, and more important from our immediate point of view, of the palpable connection between them.

Astrology had too long been regarded as an immutable law for any but the strongest mind to ignore the fact. It would have taken as much single-minded courage for an Elizabethan positively to deny the planets their effect on man's life as for an early Victorian to deny God his influence.

The educated Elizabethan knew of the continuity of the astrological theory and its effect: of its general use in Babylonia and Egypt, and through the classics of its influence in Greece and, much more extensively, in Rome. In England, within the two hundred years before William Lilly's birth, an interest in the subject had been particular as well as general: Chaucer, whatever his own views on the subject, showed in the *Canterbury Tales* the popular view—the habit of most people of acting in accordance with the positions of the planets, if they knew them. *The Knight's Tale* shows characters acting in careful accordance with the astrological qualities of the separate hours of the day; the Wife of Bath excuses her lust by explaining how it was impressed upon her, or at least encouraged in her, by the positions of the planets at the time of her birth.

During the Renaissance, art and science continually made use of astrology and encouraged its study overtly as well as obliquely. It should be remembered that astronomers were invariably, until after Newton, also astrologers; and that the general desire for more and more accurate horoscopes was at least in part responsible for more accurate astronomical observation. Many astronomers began to suspect that astrological theory could not be as simplistic as unscientific people believed; but very few of them, even after a lifetime's study, concluded that the planets had no effect on terrestrial matters.

Tycho de Brahe, for instance, found himself (like Kepler, some years later) forced to become a court astrologer in order to maintain himself; he cast horoscopes for his patrons and their friends, and evidently did so with his tongue somewhat in his cheek, seeing the work of conventional social astrologers as quackery. But he remained until his death utterly convinced that the planets did influence man's personality and destiny, though the existing astrological techniques failed to reveal how.

England produced no really notable theoretical astrologer

during the sixteenth century; but a great many distinguished men practised astrology, some of them to political effect. Perhaps the most notable of these was John Dee, still known popularly as 'Queen Elizabeth's astrologer'. This is perhaps to give the astrological side of his work and personality too much importance, though there is some foundation for such a claim. One cannot, however, underestimate the interest of his character; he was a most remarkable man, and his influence on his contemporaries was enormous. He had befriended Elizabeth while she was still a prisoner at Woodstock, and when she found herself Queen, she engaged him to calculate a propitious date for her coronation. There was a period during her reign when she called on Dee almost every day; for years she asked from time to time for advice on specific events or people, inviting him to cast horoscopes for men she wished to trust or perhaps tended to suspect, to suggest cures for her toothache, to explain the significance of a comet, or to discuss the rumours that she was threatened by witchcraft.

Elizabeth was evidently not temperamentally hostile to astrology: in a letter to Mary Stuart in 1588 she rebuked Mary for her changeability, writing: 'if it were not that I consider that by nature we are composed of earthly elements and governed by heavenly, and that I am not igorant that our dispositions are caused in part by supernatural signs, which change every day, I could not believe that in so short a time such a change could take place.'

What astrologers tend to forget, in rightly claiming Dee as the foremost prognosticator of his time, is that ironically he was responsible to some degree, and despite himself, for the beginning of the desuetude of astrology. The rumours of sorcery and witchcraft that had first attached themselves to him during his Cambridge days persisted, and were used by his enemies. Shortly after Elizabeth's accession, Bishop Jewell preached a sermon before her which was obviously to some extent directed against Dee and others who showed an interest in witchcraft:

> It may please Your Grace to understand that this kind of people, within these last few years, are marvellously increased

> within your realm. These eyes have seen most evident and manifest marks of their wickedness. Your Grace's subjects pine away, even unto death, their colour fadeth, their flesh rotted, their speech is benumbed, their senses are bereft. Wherefore your poor subjects' most humble petition unto Your Highness is that the laws touching such malefactors be put into execution.

During Dee's own lifetime he was vehemently attacked by John Foxe, in his widely disseminated *Actes and Monuments*. In the 1563 edition, later ordered to be placed in every cathedral church, and displayed too in many parish churches, Foxe referred to 'Dr Dee the great Conjurer' as 'a caller of Divils'. Dee complained at this 'damnable sklaunder', and in 1576 issued a plea that Foxe should be refrained from calling him, among other things, 'the Arche Conjurer of England'. The plea evidently succeeded, for all references to him were cut out of the 1576 edition; but the damage was done. From then until our own day, Dee has been widely regarded as a 'magician' and sorcerer, and historians have until very recently dismissed him as 'extremely credulous, extravagantly vain, and a most deluded enthusiast' (to quote *Biographica Britannica*). If the most intelligent of Elizabethan astrologers could be dimissed in that way, what hope was there for the rest? And Dr Dee was the exception; most of them were far less intelligent than he, and were concerned mainly in acting as consultant psychologists to a wide variety of people—making astrology work for the ordinary man in the street, in the way in which Lilly was to use it. One such, certainly the best known, was Simon Forman, who was born at Quidhampton in 1552.

Left destitute by the death of his father when he was only twelve, Forman determinedly bettered himself, becoming an apprentice to a general dealer in Salisbury, but persuading a schoolboy who lodged with his master to teach him at night what he had been taught during the day. He was 'a person of indefatigable pains', as Lilly said. After some years of schoolmastering, he went to the Hague, where he studied astrology, in which he had been interested for some time. In 1583 he came to London, set up as a consultant astrologer, and remained there until his death in 1611. Among his enthusiasms was the theatre, and he has been chiefly known to historians as the man who left the earliest impressions of Shakespeare's plays by a contemporary member of the audience.

Dr A. L. Rowse's examinations of Forman's papers in the Bodleian Library reveal in some detail the kind of work Forman did (as well as, it is claimed, the identity of Shakespeare's Dark Lady, Emilia Bassano, whose favours were given as freely to the astrologer as to the playwright). Rowse names the Earl of Hertford, Frances Howard Countess of Essex, Vice-Admiral Sir William Monson, Sir Barrington Mullins, and Sir Thomas Shirley as regular clients of Forman; and he was asked a great number of varied questions, more or less important, more or less amusing. Dean Thomas Blague, of Rochester, a chaplain to the Queen, went to him to ask 'whether his wife be enchanted by Dean Wood or no,' while Mrs Blague gave Forman 26s. 8d. to look into the matter of Dean Wood's lovers, and to tell her what would become of them—and promised to pay him another five pounds 'when he [Wood] is a full friend to her'.

Forman was consulted about lawsuits, the sailing and safety of ships, the whereabouts of stolen articles; there seems to have been no question he would not answer. He took advantage of his position to make love to as many of his women clients as possible, and perhaps for this reason—as well as his tendency to get mixed up in various occult experiments—found his business gradually falling off; by the end of the sixteenth century he was practically bankrupt. But, certainly in our view, and perhaps in that of his contemporaries, he redeemed himself during the early 1590s, when he went to work as an amateur physician in the plague-stricken areas of London, even becoming infected himself.

He is sometimes described as a friend of Lilly's. Since the latter was only eight at the time of his death in 1611, this is not very likely; but certainly Lilly knew many stories about Forman, which he tells in his autobiography—one amusing and characteristic enough to quote, not only as evidence of the idiocy to which some astrologers pretended, but once again, of Lilly's racy style of narrative:

> One Coleman, clerk to Sir Thomas Beaumont of Leicestershire, having had some liberal favours both from his lady and her daughters, bragged of it, &c. The Knight brought him into the star-chamber, had his servant sentenced to be pilloried, whipped, and afterwards, during life, to be imprisoned. The sentence was executed in London, and was to be in Leicestershire: two keepers were to convey Coleman from the Fleet to Leicester. My mistress [that is, Mrs Wright, who evidently was a client of Forman's] taking consideration of Coleman and the miseries he was to suffer, went presently to Forman, acquainted him therewith; who, after consideration, swore Coleman had lain both with mother and daughters; and besides said that the old Lady being afflicted with fits of the mother, called him into her chamber to hold down the fits with his hands; and that he holding his hands about the breast, she said 'Lower, lower,' and put his hands below her belly; and then —— He also told my mistress in what posture he lay with the young ladies, &c., and said 'they intend in Leicester to whip him to death; but I assure thee, Margery, he shall never come there; yet they set forward tomorrow,' says he; and so his two keepers did, Coleman's legs being locked with an iron chain under the horse's belly.
>
> In this nature they travelled the first and second day; on the third day the two keepers, seeing their prisoner's civility the two preceding days, did not lock his chain under the horse's belly as formerly, but locked it only to one side. In this posture they rode some miles beyond Northampton, when on a sudden one of the keepers had a necessity to untruss, and so the other and Coleman stood still; by and by the other keeper desired Coleman to hold his horse, for he had occasion also; Coleman immediately took one of their swords, and ran through two of the horses, killing them stark dead; gets upon the other, with one of their swords;

'Farewell, gentlemen,' quoth he, 'tell my master I have no mind to be whipped in Leicestershire,' and so went his way. The two keepers in all haste went to a gentleman's house near at hand, complaining of their misfortune, and desired of him to pursue their prisoner, which he with much civility granted; but ere the horses could be got ready, the mistress of the house came down and enquired what the matter was, went to the stable, and commanded the horses to be unsaddled, with this sharp speech—'Let the Beaumont and her daughters live honestly, none of my horses shall go forth upon this occasion.'

The kind of astrology practised by Forman (and which was to be practised by Lilly) certainly did no good to what had always been considered a serious study. While Forman claimed to be able to tell Mrs Wright precisely in what postures Coleman coupled with his mistresses, to give her a charm to prevent her husband committing suicide, to be able to tell some housewife where a stolen jewel was, or when and how he himself would die, more serious theorists stressed that astrology could not be used to predict events; and the astronomers who were reaching out towards new conceptions of the way the universe worked, if they held to the astrological theory at all did so in the belief that it could not be used for the purposes of fortune-telling.

Their scepticism of the popular astrologer, and the ordinary man's tendency to regard him as a magician, somewhat damaged the reputation of astrology. Aubrey, many years, later, wrote of

> those darke times [when] Astrologer, Mathematician, and Conjurer were accounted the same things; and the vulgar did verily believe [Thomas Allen, the mathematician and astrologer] to be a Conjurer. He had a great many Mathematicall Instruments and Glasses in his Chamber, which did also confirme the ignorant in their opinion, and his servitor (to impose on Freshmen and simple people) would tell them that sometimes he should meet the Spirits comeing up his staires like Bees.

But the intelligent man's confidence in the astrologer remained unimpaired, and there was sufficient evidence to bolster it. Aubrey recorded that Allen had calculated the nativity of William Herbert, Earl of Pembroke, and that

> his death was foretold, which happened true at the time praedicted, at his House at Baynard's Castle, in London. He was very well in health; but because of the Fatal Direction which he lay under, he made a great Entertainment (a Supper) for his Friends: ate and dranke plentifully; went to bed, and died in his sleep.

The struggle between the opportunists who saw astrology as a means of earning a good living by playing on the credulous, and the serious theorists, had started some years before, but now became keener because there was more money about, and the very people whom it was easiest to deceive were able to pay more for the deceit. The theorists were fighting a losing battle, as far as publicity was concerned; though their work behind the scenes was much more interesting.

This focused on an attempt to make astrology more natural and scientific in nature, and to provide a bank of information on which astrologers could draw in their attempts to make personal horoscopes more accurate: to put astrological laws, in fact, on an experimental basis. The result was a growing pile of astrological books such as the *Tractatus Astrologicus* of Luce Gaurico, Bishop of Civitate. In several volumes, published in 1552, Gaurico published the horoscopes of a great number of well-known people, living and dead, and drew certain conclusions from them. He included seven popes, twenty-nine cardinals and prelates, thirty-four secular rulers, forty-one men of letters and learning, nine musicians, five artists, and forty-six men who had met violent deaths. The main result of publication, for Gaurico, was that he was attacked for libel, and had to flee his city. But his work was typical of, though more comprehensive than, several works of a similar kind.

Meanwhile astrologers, then as now, prepared and published

various papers arguing about such technical matters as the division of astrological houses, or the determination of the precise moment of birth. Then there were books written in moderately technical terms, but aimed at an intelligent lay public: such as the *Mantice ou discours de la verité de divination par astrologie* published in 1558 by Pontus de Tyard, a friend of Ronsard (who himself accepted the validity of astrology). This is a dialogue in which Le Curieux argues against astrology, Mantice defends it, and the author sums up, concluding that astrologers are inaccurate in their predictions only because past astrological tables did not give the true movements of the planets, and encouraging contemporary astronomers towards greater accuracy. And indeed men like Cyprian Leowitz were tireless in working out true planetary positions and publishing them in ephemerides.

Other astrologers were working out their own theories and elaborating them, dismissing or modifying earlier systems. Joannes Francus Offusius, for instance, found Ptolemaic astrology childish, and giving up a lucrative medical practice and refusing pleasant sinecures offered by various princes, lived in virtual isolation working on his own system, in which he attempted to measure quantitatively the influence of the planets, which he believed they exerted through the four qualities rather than by any occult power. The Sun warmed and dried, the Moon moistened and chilled somewhat, Saturn produced cold and dryness, Mars heat and dryness; Venus gave out moisture and heat, while Mercury dried. Convinced that nature followed a numerical, geometrical order, Offusius worked out a complicated system of calculation by which it could be discovered how much of a planet's particular quality was exuded at any one moment of its orbit. (Hot is to dry as the pyramid to the cube; hot to cold as the pyramid to the octahedron, and so on. A system related, of course, to the Pythagorean theories of relationships between numbers and forms, forms and emotions, linking, say, music to medicine in the same terms.)

Serious work was going on in relation to astrological influences in the field of medicine: in the *Astrological Medicine* of Cornelius Schylander, an Antwerp physician, published in 1570, one is taught diagnosis (without actually having to see the patient!), and how to prognosticate the degree of danger in an illness; and twenty-seven years later, amid a great number of similar works, was published Henri de Monantheuil's *Ludus Iatromathematicus*, in which he proved to his own, and many other doctors', satisfaction that (as Hippocrates had put it two thousand years earlier) 'a physician without a knowledge of astrology has no right to call himself a physician'.

So, though criticism was growing and the climate of belief changing, astrology was still largely respectable; and the astronomers, who eventually were to become most sceptical of all, still held to it, though they were beginning to modify their opinions. Most of them had to cast horoscopes as part of their professional work. Kepler, teaching mathematics and astronomy at Graz, capital of Styria, published an annual almanac of astrological forecasts (for a fee of twenty florins a year).

There was an example of why some astronomers clung to the astrological theory: partly for money—twenty florins was one-twelfth of Kepler's whole annual income!—but partly also because the theory seemed often to work. For instance, in his first almanac, Kepler promised a cold spell and a Turkish invasion. Six months later he wrote to his friend Michael Maestlin:

> By the way, so far the almanac's predictions are proving correct. There is an unheard-of cold in our land. In the Alpine farms people die of the cold. It is reliably reported that when they arrive home and blow their noses, the noses fall off ... As for the Turks, on January the first they devastated the whole country from Vienna to Neustadt, setting everything on fire and carrying off men and plunder.

Kepler ended his career as Court Astrologer to the Duke of Wallenstein. He called astrology 'the step-daughter of astronomy', and wrote that 'a mind accustomed to mathematical deduction, when confronted with the faulty foundations [of astrology] resists a long, long time, like an obstinate mule, until compelled by beating and curses to put its foot into that dirty puddle.' But, on the other hand, he wrote a series of wholly serious treatises on astrology, and warned his contemporaries that 'while justly rejecting the stargazers' superstitions, they should not throw out the baby with the bathwater.' 'Nothing exists,' he said elsewhere, 'nor happens in the visible sky that is not sensed in some hidden manner by the faculties of Earth and Nature: these faculties of the spirit here on earth are as much affected as the sky itself.' And, conclusively, 'the belief in the effect of the constellations derives in the first place from experience, which is so convincing that it can be denied only by people who have not examined it.'

It was the hope of Kepler and other serious-minded men that the tendency towards levity and quackery which they already discerned in the mid-sixteenth century could be stemmed. Hieronymus Wolf wrote to the astrologer Cyprian Leowitz in 1557 that astrology would never have been the object of so much envy and hatred if it had not been abused and prostituted by unscrupulous or unqualified men. He hoped that Leowitz and his colleague Girolamo Cardan would restore it to its pristine dignity and authority.

But the tide was against them. As popular belief in astrology grew, so intelligent belief in it waned. There were a number of swingeing attacks on astrologers round about the turn of the century: *A Treatise against Judicial Astrology* was published in 1601, for instance, by John Chamber, who objected to the theory on several grounds, notably that no-one could know the *precise* time of a birth (his other objections were properly regarded by astrologers as ignorant; so they are). Thomas Dekker parodied astrology in *The Raven's Almanacke* in 1609; John Cotts attacked medical astrology in 1612; Christopher Davenport and others argued on theological grounds, and indeed there had been a papal bull against astrology in 1586, and there was to be another in 1631. These had no discernible effect.

The tide was slow in turning. European publications during the first half of the seventeenth century were still largely pro-astrology, many of them serious and well argued. Ilario Altobelli, historian of the Franciscan Order, and an eminent astronomer (who was for some time in correspondence with Galileo) published a number of astrological works, as did Fr Redento Baranzani of Vercelli, Ferrante de Septem, Alexander Vicentinia, Giacomo Filippo Tomasini of Padua, and many other Italians.

In Germany, Spain, France and northern Europe the tendency, similarly, was to uphold and strengthen astrological beliefs. There were attacks, certainly, but these came almost invariably from those who had not studied the subject very closely: one thinks of Newton's alleged response to Halley, when the latter accused him of being silly enough to believe in astrology. 'Sir: I have studied the matter. You have not.' Antonia Merenda, for instance, whose attack (the title itself is long enough to be tedious) was published in 1640, was a professor of civil law at Pavia, and his arguments against astrology are as simplistic and easily refuted as those of St Augustine, which they resemble.

But in England at all events, such efforts were vain: the financial temptations were too great, and during the years when Lilly was learning and beginning to practise astrology, there were many more quacks than serious astrologers. He gives character-sketches of some of them in his autobiography.

There was Alexander Hart, for instance, who lived out at Houndsditch, and 'had been a soldier formerly, a comely old man, of good aspect'. He practised a little medical astrology, but seems mainly to have been concerned to tell young men when they might most profitably play at dice. Lilly says that he went to Hart several times to ask him various questions, and that he failed every time to give a satisfactory answer.

Then there was Captain Bubb,

> a proper handsome man, well spoken, but withal covetous, and of no honesty, as will appear by this story, for which he stood upon the pillory. A certain butcher was robbed, going to a fair, of forty pounds. He goes to Bubb, who for ten pounds in hand paid, would help him to the thief. Appoints the butcher such a night precisely, to watch at such a place, and the thief should come thither—commanded by any means to stop him. The butcher attends according to direction.

About twelve in the night there comes one riding very fiercely upon a full gallop, whom the butcher knocks down, and seized both upon man and horse. The butcher brings the man and horse to the next town, but then the person whom the butcher attacked was John, the servant of Dr Bubb; for which the Captain was indicted and suffered upon the pillory, and afterwards ended his days in great disgrace.

Jeffery Neve was scarcely more respectable, and had had an interesting career in local government before setting up as an astrologer. He had been a merchant and alderman at Great Yarmouth, and in 1626 was appointed deputy water-bailiff of Dover. He then got into trouble with the local aldermen for abusing his position as commissioner under Henry VIII's Bill to encourage archery: he made a small fortune by rigging the figures of the returns which entitled him to one shilling on every branch cut to make a bow.

He seems to have gone bankrupt; went to Holland to study medicine, graduated M.D. at Frankfurt, and set up in London as a quack astrologer. He put to Lilly a scheme for printing two hundred horoscopes set up to answer various questions, in an effort (modelled perhaps on Gaurico) to show astrology to be a science. But, says Lilly, 'when I had perused the first forty, I corrected thirty of them, would read over no more. I showed him how erroneous they were, desired his emendation of the rest, which he performed not.'

Then there were the downright comics, like William Poole, 'a nibbler at astrology', who had been gardener, drawer of linen, plasterer and bricklayer, and used to brag that he had 'been of seventeen professions'. He was very good company, a likeable fellow (Lilly gave away the bride at his wedding), who seems to have managed to keep out of trouble as far as predictions were concerned, though he was once accused by Sir Thomas Jay, J.P., of being suspiciously implicated in the theft of a silver cup. Perhaps he was, for he packed up and left the district;

but hearing some months after that the Justice was dead and buried, he came and enquired where the grave was; and after the discharge of his belly upon the grave, left these two verses upon it, which he swore he made himself:

> Here lieth buried Sir Thomas Jay, Knight,
> Who being dead, I upon his grave did shite.

When he died, in the 1650s, Poole left all his books to Dr Ardee, another astrologer; and 'one manuscript of my own worth one hundred of Lilly's *Introduction*'; with the note—'Item: if Dr Ardee give my wife any thing that is mine, I wish the devil may fetch him body and soul.' So the doctor gave all Poole's books to Lilly, who passed them on to the widow.

Dr Ardee, by the way, informed Lilly (several times) that 'an angel, one time, appeared unto him and offered him a lease of his life for one thousand years. He died about the age of four score years.' Presumably he had rejected the offer. He had been a friend of the Rev. William Bredon, Vicar of Thornton in Buckinghamshire, who was mildly interested in astrology but notoriously addicted to tobacco and drink—or rather to drinking and smoking, for when he had no tobacco, Lilly tells us, 'he would cut the bell-ropes and smoke them'.

And finally there was Nicholas Fiske, a doctor who became a friend of Lilly's soon after Lilly first became interested in astrology. Fiske was a well-educated man, who had been destined for the university, but instead had decided to give his time to privately studying medicine and astrology, both of which he practised in Colchester and later in London. Lilly admits to having learned much of literature from him; though he also accuses him, because he had Scorpio ascending, of being 'secretly envious to those he thought had more parts then himself'. He does not specify whether the 'parts' were intellectual or sexual; both in abundance fit the Scorpio personality.

There, then, was the astrological scene when Lilly came upon it. As far as England was concerned, scholarly and unscholarly attacks on the theory were increasing, and educated men were for the first time in history beginning to be persuaded that the most that could profitably be said of the subject was that it seemed likely that the positions of the planets had some effect upon terrestrial matters, but that astrologers were certainly not in complete command of the means of precisely stating that effect.

But these opinions, like the two papal Bulls, were to have very little effect upon the credulous middle class, which was now composed of men and women with a certain amount of money which they could afford to lay out upon so promising a possibility as knowing the future, forecasting good or evil luck. Jeffery Neve, Alexander Hart and Captain Bubb were the seventeenth century equivalent of the astrologers who, in the 1970s, make a reasonably lucrative living writing astrological columns for the daily press or the monthly magazines.

Lilly evidently always had a sympathetic eye for a rogue, provided he was an interesting, intelligent and amusing rogue. He was also, certainly, credulous in occult matters. He was to engage in a little fortune-telling himself, though always fairly discreetly; and he was always to maintain a much greater degree of wit, and a higher standard of literacy and often of honesty, than his colleagues.

# 3

# Some That Have Writ Almanacks

*For I assure you, for my Part,*
*I only deal by Rules of Art;*
*Such as are lawful, and judge by*
*Conclusions of Astrology:*
*But for the Devil, I know nothing by him,*
*But only this, that I defy him.*

*Hudibras* (II.II:581)

In 1633, not long after Lilly had started to study astrology with John Evans, Mrs Lilly died, and left him about £1,000. Most of it seems to have been inaccessible, for his first action was to borrow £530 on security, to buy thirteen houses in the Strand. He also had to buy the lease of the Corner House. He drew up an astrological chart, of course, to advise him; it was favourable—but according to *Christian Astrology*, published some years later,

> the truth of the matter is, I had a hard bargaine ... so did I doe myself injury by the Bargaine, I meane in matter of Money; but the love I bare to the House I now live in, wherein I lived happily with a good Master full seven years, and therein obtained my first Wife, and was bountifully blessed by God with the Goods of this World therein, made me neglect a small hindrance, nor now, I thank God, doe I repent it.

On November 18th, 1634, Lilly married a second time: the bride was Jane Rowley, of whom he says little, and of whom little can be discovered. She was a year younger than her husband, brought him £500 as a marriage portion, and was, he says dryly, 'of the nature of Mars'—in other words, sexy but cantankerous and even vicious. When she died, he was to say that he shed no tears; and the whole marriage seems to have been fairly disastrous.

While he had no great opinion of Evans as a man or an astrologer, Lilly did learn from him the basic techniques: how to set up and interpret a birth-chart and from it to draw certain conclusions about the character and personality of the man or woman it delineated. He also learned to draw up a chart for the moment an event took place (the arrival of an important letter, or even of an important idea) and to conclude from it the probable course of events to follow. Then there was the casting of a chart to decide a propitious moment for starting a business or beginning an enterprise; to answer a question of any kind (by drawing up a 'figure' for the moment it was asked); and to set up the 'annual revolution', or chart for the time when every year the Sun reached the same degree and minute of the Zodiac as it occupied in the chart for the moment of birth. This would reveal trends in the year ahead, and could be elaborated and improved on by other techniques.

All this was bolstered by Lilly's own reading. He read widely from the beginning, and never ceased to collect interesting new (and old) astrological books. Evans was less interested in improving his own technique: he only possessed two astrological books, and Lilly remarks that 'as often as I entered his house, I thought I was in the wilderness'. So while he learned something from Evans, he learned much more from his conversations with other astrologers, and from his own books—an *Ars Notoria* written in manuscript by Simon Forman, which a hard-up scholar pawned to him for forty shillings, and other books from the library of the late Arthur Bedwell, chaplain to Sir Henry Wotton, a great collector.

During his lifetime, Lilly was to build up a very considerable library of astrological books, as Dee had done before him; and it is sometimes forgotten what a feat it was to do so at a time when many books were printed in editions of about a hundred copies, and were expensive because of the high cost of hand-made rag paper, the hand-setting of type, and the time-consuming craft of binding by hand. Even half a century later, John Evelyn was able to write out with ease on a single sheet of paper the libraries of which he had personal knowledge—most of them belonging to members of the clergy.

Lilly's library was a workman's library: he was not interested in fine bindings, nor did he have the money to invest in the red, green or purple velvet bindings, embroidered with silk, or the red or white satin covers which dignified books in the library of, say, the Earl of Anglesey. Those of his books which have survived bear every mark of use in the study and at the consulting-room bench. Many of them were from Europe, and the value of the whole library (though it is impossible to value it in terms of the seventeenth century) was considerable.

Lilly made his way regularly to Gunpowder Alley through the narrow, cobbled, mucky streets, jostled on one side by pedestrians and on the other by the 'vile swaggering' of coaches, for some months. Eventually, however, the temperamental difference between him and his master boiled up into a positive quarrel.

The break with Evans came suddenly and predictably. A woman came to see him, and demanded the answer to a particular question. Evans drew up a chart, consulted it, gave her his answer, and she left. Lilly writes:

> I standing by all the while, and observing the figure, asked him why he gave the judgment he did, since the signification showed quite the contrary, and gave him my reasons; which when he had pondered, he called me Boy, and must he be contradicted by such a novice! But when his heat was over, he said, had he not so judged to please the woman, she would have given him nothing, and he had a wife and family to provide for; upon this we never came together after.

It was a lesson Lilly never forgot; fond though he was of prestige, and indeed of money, he became (as he put it in the Preface to

*Christian Astrology*) 'capable of knowing truth from falsehood, and perceived the vulgar astrologer that merely lived off the Art, was a knave'.

Within a year, Lilly felt confident enough of his own powers to teach astrology to other people; his first pupil was Sir George Peckham, to whom he claimed to have taught the astrology of medicine (which signs and planets were connected with which parts of the body, and which sicknesses, and how to use this knowledge to diagnose and treat illness) so well that 'in two or three months he would give a very true discovery of any disease, only by his figures'. (Sir George did not live long to profit by the knowledge: the following year, he stayed so long in the damp and chill of St Winifred's Well, in Wales, 'mumbling his *Pater Nosters* and *Sancta Winifrida ora pro me*', that he caught a chill and died.)

Astrology was still, in the early seventeenth century, very much aligned with occultism; unsurprisingly, Lilly began to cultivate an interest in ghosts and fairies, alchemy and communication with spirits. He was never to become as involved with the occult as John Dee had been before him; though others were later to defer to his knowledge, and refer special cases to him. For instance, after a very great deal of money had been spent on boring for coal in Surrey, the speculators employed the astrologer, who, examining the ground (Aubrey says) 'was quick to blame the subterranean Spirits: For as fast as the Irons were put in they would snap off.' And there was the more celebrated episode of the Apparition which, Aubrey recorded, was seen in 1670 'not far from Cyrencester' and which 'Being demanded, whether a good Spirit or a Bad? returned no answer, but disappeared with a curious Perfume and a most melodious Twang. Mr W. Lillie,' added Aubrey, 'believes it was a Fairie.'

Just as everyone, in the sixteenth century, had more or less believed in astrology, so everyone had more or less believed in magic. And the seventeenth century had not much dented this belief by the 1630s. It was still agreed by a very large number of intelligent men that certain magical effects could be provoked, if one had the necessary knowledge and used it accurately. A division was made, certainly, between natural and illicit magic. The latter, being used to injure, or for diabolical means, was actively discouraged. 'Natural' magic, however, was not, however much some churchmen (for instance) may have doubted the wisdom of using it.

But there was a connection between the two, for though 'natural' magic merely presupposed that man had a sufficient knowledge of occult forces to provoke marvellous effects without positive supernatural aid, demons themselves were often thought to work their miracles simply by a superior technical insight into the occult; so that the relationship between the demon and the practising magician was closer than was comfortable, however well-meaning the practitioner.

Some of the 'magic' practised provided, as we see it now, harmless fun. One reads Wolfgang Hildebrand's *Magia naturalis* of 1610 with delighted amusement, with its secret recipes to provoke marvellous dreams, prevent easy intoxication, to make men seem headless or to have the heads of animals, or to detect magical butter. Other magical recipes, in other books, are far less amusing; and there is of course the horror of the Elizabethan and Marian pursuit of witches, with its butchering of innocent or crazed old women.

At least astrology contributed little fuel to the medieval witch-hunter: only one astrologer was burned for his beliefs, as far as we know—and that in Spain. The notorious *Malleus Maleficarum*, or *Hammer of Witchcraft*, for so long the witch-hunters' handbook, specifically laid it down that witches had no power over 'the influence of the stars', and for very simple reasons:

> First, the stars are above them even in the region of punishment, which is the region of the lower mists; and this by reason of the duty which is assigned to them. The second reason is that the stars are governed by the good angels. Thirdly, it is on account of the general order and common good of the Universe, which would suffer general detriment if evil spirits were allowed to cause any alteration in the influence of the stars ...

The English law was not so kind. An Act of Henry VIII had stated quite firmly that 'It shall be felony to practise or cause to be practised, Cunjuration, Witchcraft, Enchantment or Sorcery, to get money;' astrology was all too often embraced by that Act, which later Acts were to reinforce.

The connection between magic and astrology was in some ways a natural one; no astrologer was necessarily interested in the occult, but it was a natural interest, for both were in a sense attempts to make a connection between man's inner life and the outward arrangement and phenomena of the universe. But for every astrologer who was genuinely interested in, say, the art of scrying (concentration on a crystal which made the subconscious mind more keenly receptive to thoughts and visions) or of conversation with spirits—two occupations which had much preoccupied Dr Dee—there were ten whose interest in the occult was far more keenly prompted by the fact that the mumbo-jumbo of magic easily impressed the gullible among their clients.

Sometimes astrology and the occult came together quite rationally (in the astrologers' eyes): Tomasso Campanella, in his *De sensu rerum et magia* of 1620, cites the case of a girl of twelve who was possessed by a devil when the planets reached a certain position, recovered after a year, and lived devoutly with a good husband until the age of thirty-five, when the planets, in another position, prompted her to fall into a trance, see visions, and become a notable authority on theology, without having studied a word of it. Similarly, Jacques Gaffarel, Richelieu's chaplain, asserted that astrological images could be used in magic (though they were not in themselves diabolical).

Lilly's interest in the occult, then, is not surprising; and from time to time led him into interesting situations. In 1634, for instance, the King's clock-maker, one Davy Ramsey, had come by the knowledge—or at least had heard the rumour—that a valuable treasure was to be found buried in the cloisters of Westminster Abbey. The Bishop of Lincoln (Dean of the Abbey) had given him permission to search for it (with the careful proviso that the Church should have a share, if any was found); and

Ramsey had enlisted the help of a certain John Scott, of Pudding Lane, who had been (Lilly says) 'a page, or such like', to Lord Norris, and professed some skill with the Mosaical rods—divining rods for discovering precious metals, or indeed any hidden objects.

Divining by rods was a science of immemorial antiquity, and Sebastian Munster in his *Cosmography*, published in the early part of the sixteenth century, gives a startlingly well-reasoned and interesting account of it. Dee had been an energetic and sometimes apparently successful diviner; in the seventeenth century, a certain Goody Faldo of Mortlake told Aubrey that Dee 'did most miraculously have the divining power to find things that be missing and with his rod did bring back to many persons silver and such objects which had been missing sometimes over years'. On one occasion, when Dee and some friends found a wedge of gold in a pool in Breconshire they were arrested as conjurers and suspected of worse—for their activities had been followed by such a severe storm at harvest time that 'the country people had not known the like'.

Scott and Ramsey invited Lilly to go along with them to the Abbey, together with a select gang of labourers and a sack to put the treasure in. They chose to enter the cloisters at night, for no very readily understandable reason—the 'magic' to be employed was, after all, minimal. 'We played the hazel-rod round about the cloisters,' Lilly records;

> upon the west side of the cloister the rods turned one over another, an argument that the treasure was there. The labourers digged at least six foot deep, and then we met with a coffin; but in regard it was not heavy, we did not open, which we afterward much repented. From the cloisters we went into the Abbey church, where upon a sudden (there being no wind when we began) so fierce, so high, so blustering and loud a wind did rise, that we verily believed the west-end of the church would have fallen upon us; our rods would not move at all; the candles, and torches, all but one, were extinguished, or burned very dimly.

Lilly pulled himself together, and 'gave directions and command to dismiss the demons; which when done, all was quiet again', and the men, too, dispersed quietly and uneasily to their beds. Lilly could never be persuaded to go in for similar midnight adventures in churches again. He argued later that the atmosphere was quite wrong for such investigations on hallowed ground: there were twenty or thirty people looking on, 'some laughing, others deriding us; so that if we had not dismissed the demons, I believe most part of the Abbey church had been blown down. Secrecy and intelligent operators, with a strong confidence and knowledge of what they are doing, are best for this work.'

Though his own ventures into the occult were restricted, Lilly certainly knew some dubious characters who were involved in attempts to raise devils or other spirits. He was particularly interested in the odd figure of the club-fisted John a Windsor, who despite his physical deformity, made a living as a scrivener or professional scribe, writing with a pen held between his two wrists. 'He was much given,' Lilly says, 'to debauchery, so that at some time the Demons would not appear ... he would then suffumigate: sometimes, to vex the spirits, he would curse them ...'

Then there was the Dutchman John Hegenius, a medical man who was also an astrologer, and with whom Lilly experimented in the use of divining rods; and the notorious Sarah Skelhorn, who was particularly good at crystal-gazing.

Lilly also knew people who knew people who had talked with fairies, and was quick with anecdotes of them. Perhaps the nearest he got to encountering the Queen of the Fairies herself was when 'a very sober, discreet person, of virtuous life and conversation ... went with a friend into my Hurst Wood'—the grounds of the house he bought at Hersham.

> The Queen of the Fairies was invocated, a gentle murmuring wind came first; after that, amongst the hedges, a smart whirlwind; by and by a strong blast of wind blew upon the face of the friend—and the Queen appearing in a most illustrious glory, 'No more, I beseech you!' (quoth the friend)

'My heart fails; I am not able to endure longer.' Nor was he: his black curling hair rose up, and I believe a bullrush would have beat him to the ground: he was soundly laughed at.

'It is not for everyone, or every person, that these angelical creatures will appear unto,' Lilly reminds us soberly; 'though they may say over the call, over and over; or indeed is it given to very many persons to endure their glorious aspects'. There were also certain men who had forfeited the right to fairy favours—a man called Gladwell, for instance, brought to Lilly by Sir Robert Holborn, had formerly had sight and conference with Uriel and Raphael, 'but lost them both by carelessness; so that neither of them both would but rarely appear, and then presently be gone, resolving nothing'. 'He would have given me two hundred pounds to have assisted him for their recovery,' wrote Lilly; 'but I am no such man.' He takes up rather an 'I could an' if I would' attitude to fairies and angels and the possibility of raising them. 'Neatness and cleanliness in apparel, a strict diet, and upright life, fervent prayers unto God, conduce much to the assistance of those who are curious these ways,' he assured his friend Ashmole. 'I may seem to some to write incredibilia; be it so, but knowing unto whom, and for whose only sake, I do write them, I am much comforted therewith, well knowing you are the most knowing man in these curiosities of any now living in England.'

Indeed Ashmole was always ready to listen, and always ready (as was Lilly himself) to preserve quaint occult stories, the paraphernalia of white witches, or cures for those bewitched. In *Christian Astrology*, for instance, Lilly gives a recipe for cleansing the body and house of someone who had been bewitched:

> Take two new horse-shoes, heat them red-hot, and naile one of them on the Threshold of the Door, but quench the other in Urine of the party so Bewitched; then set the Urine over the fire, and put the horseshoe in it, setting a Trevet over the Pipkin or the Pan wherein the Urine is; make the Urine boyle, with a little salt put into it, and three horse-nails in till it's almost consumed, viz. the Urine; what is not boyled

> fully away poure into the fire; keep your horseshooe and nailes in a clean cloth or paper, and use the same manner three severall times; the operation would be farre more effectuall, if you doe these things at the very change or full Moon, or at the very hour of the first or second quarter thereof ...

How much Lilly deluded himself in these matters is difficult to conjecture. The Westminster Abbey affair has the genuine ring of credulity about it. Otherwise, one suspects hearsay and an active and vivid creative imagination. It would be less than honest not to admit that Lilly's autobiography is full of incidents which are more or less in the category of 'incredibilia'. He claims, for instance, to have taught one John Humphrey the astrological means of discovering where on a client's body one might find moles or other distinguishing marks.

> As we were at supper, a client came to speak with him, and so up into his closet he went with his client; I called him before he set his figure, or resolved the question, and instantly acquainted him how he should discover the moles or marks of his client: he set his figure, and presently discovers four moles the querant had; and was so overjoyed therewith, that he came tumbling down the stairs, crying 'Four by God, four by God, I will not take one hundred pounds for this one rule!'

And indeed, it might have been worth it.

The technique of discovering 'secret marks of the body' by astrological means was fairly widely employed. But what is the explanation of a scene such as that one? Had Humphreys made a lucky hit? Was Lilly, remembering the incident in old age, embroidering? We cannot know.

For most of his life, Lilly seems both as an astrologer and as a friend to have been regularly caught up in the amorous adventures of others. There were, of course, the love affairs of his clients: well, that was only to be expected, and what with astrological knowledge, common sense, and a quick wit, he was able to perform what seemed wonders.

In 1635, for instance, a young lady of Greenwich ('who had tried all the known artists in London, but to no purpose') came to him in a fearful state: seduced by a nobleman, she had found that once he discovered she was pregnant, he no longer wanted to know her, and had ordered his servants to lock the doors against her. Now, he was in prison. Lilly did a few quick calculations, and told her to go to the King's Bench at a particular hour of a particular day. There, to her delight, she found the doors open, no warders about, and her lover alone in bed. 'So,' says Lilly, 'she was pleased.' We are not told what followed; but she had apparently prepared a draught of rat-bane to take if the matter had not been happily resolved.

Then there were the non-astrological escapades—as when, in 1639, a farmer's daughter attempted to foist a bastard child on Lilly's friend William Pennington. Lilly went out of his way to intervene, and arranged for the girl's arrest (she went to Newgate, then to the Assizes in Cumberland to be whipped and imprisoned for a year). Or when, again coming to the aid of Mr Pennington, he was able to discredit the Rev. Isaac Antrobus (accusing Pennington before the Committee for Plundered Ministers) by showing that 'he had knowledge of such a woman and of her daughter, *viz* of both their bodies, in as large a manner as ever of his own wife', and worse, that 'being drunk, a woman took a cord and tied it about his privy members unto a manger in a stable'.

Lilly's life during the 1630s might seem rather enviable. He was still young enough to enjoy living in London, he enjoyed his work, enjoyed experimenting with horoscopes, was fascinated by his subject and its allied arts; and he had no financial worries. As well as inheriting the Corner House, he had also come by a sum of money which must have represented something like £25,000 in the currency of the 1970s. Then he had inherited all the furniture he needed, too: plain and rather uncomfortable, no doubt, in the Jacobean style—bench or trestle tables, benches or stools for sitting, with perhaps one chair for the master or mistress of the house; the one really comfortable piece of furniture being the four-poster bed with its thick curtains and carved head-board and head-posts.

At first there was only one, or possibly two servants (Jane Rowley would not have approved!); but Lilly himself had plenty of time both for work and play. He took breakfast at six or seven in the morning, did most of his work before dinner, which was served at noon, and then generally went out and about to meet friends or enjoy himself at the bowling-alley or bowling-green. Then there was the ale-house (Lilly always had a taste for good ale), and more talk.

But life was in fact too mild, too easy, for a man with such a lively and contentious mind as his. There was little variation in his work, and the people who came to consult him seemed dull, uninteresting and unthankful (though they paid their fourpence or their half-crown, depending on their situation or their problem).

He soon became thoroughly bored with the kind of life he was leading, and had some sort of psychosomatic illness which took him out of town. He grew melancholy, burned a number of his books, lost his appetite and much weight, and became—in his own words—a hypochondriac. In the spring of 1636, he took a house at Hersham, near Esher, and moved there to live for five years almost as a hermit. He and his wife shared a house with a Captain Gibson and his wife and servant (the Gibsons contributing 30s. a week to the rent and housekeeping). 'Wyne we had little, wenching wee had none,' he later told Ashmole. 'Washing [Gibson's] own servant did—for him, his wife and her selfe.'

Lilly's health throughout all this time was indifferent: in his introduction to *A Prophesy of the White King* (1644) he remembers that he 'was afflicted with much sicknesse; and enforced to betake himself in the Country to avoid the multiplicity of my acquaintance more than the infirmenesse itself'; and in 1640 he had a bad fever, and was bled by Mr Evans of Kingston. It was during this time, he claimed, that he had the first of several visions of violence and disorder which he took for warnings of the Civil War violence to come.

Life at Hersham was healing: the difference between living in the Strand and living in the country was almost as great in the seventeenth century as it is today—the noise of a city street was different in character, but scarcely in pitch, with wooden wheels clattering over cobbles, street traders shrieking, horses striking sparks from the stones. In the country it was above all quiet, and there was fresh air rather than the constant smell of raw sewage running in the gutters, or the thick stink of the smoky air.

Here, there was a small herb-garden, sweet-smelling and neat; the larger kitchen garden, with carrots, beans, cabbages, peas, parsnips, onions and pumpkins, for good soups. Mrs Lilly and Mrs Gibson saw to the household business, the setting aside of fat for tallow candles or soap; the setting up of stores for the winter months; the supervision of the 'great wash' of dirty linen, once a month or so, in vast tubs. And Lilly was able to settle to his reading, considering his charts, only occasionally interrupted by a visitor so desperate that he had made the journey from London to consult him.

Though he does not admit it in his autobiography, there may have been more to Lilly's removal from London than he lets us know. By this time, the city must have been uncomfortable for anyone with puritan sympathies, even if he was ostensibly a King's man. Charles was ruling without a Parliament, and engaging in the art of making himself as detestable as might be to as great a number of his subjects as possible. The High Church was favoured, the Catholics tolerated, and the puritans persecuted. The Short Parliament, called to raise money for an army to fight the Scots, came and went; and in 1640 the Long Parliament forced the execution of Strafford. During this unsettled time, when, as Lucy Hutchinson was to write, 'before the flame of the warre broke out in top of the chimneys, the smoake ascended in every county', Lilly gradually revised his royalist opinions, and by the time he made up his mind to live again in London—and he moved back into the city in September 1641—he had decided that while monarchy might on the whole be a good form of government, Charles I was himself not an extraordinarily upright representative of the system ('Without a Parliament preserved in their just rights, [Monarchy] would vanish to nothing.').

In his autobiography, written under Charles II, he was naturally guarded, but stated frankly that 'before that time, I was more Cavalier than Roundhead, and so taken notice of; but after that I engaged body and soul in the cause of Parliament, but still with much affection to His Majesty's person and unto monarchy, which I ever loved and approved beyond any government whatsoever.'

It is easy enough to accuse Lilly of being a sort of astrological Vicar of Bray; he was, later, both to advise Roundhead troops of the infallibility of coming victory, and simultaneously take part in the plot to enable the King to escape from Carisbrooke Castle. But really, if one disengages aftersight, and thinks of Lilly (and thousands like him) trying to resolve his attitudes to a complex political and social situation, it becomes more difficult to condemn him. For one thing, he was too intelligent not to see that with all his political faults Charles was a noble and courageous man.

In 1651, Lilly was to publish his *Several Observations upon the Life and Death of Charles I late King of England*, in which he paid tribute to at least some of the King's personal qualities:

> To speak truly of him, he had many singular parts in nature; he was an excellent horseman, would shoot well at a mark, had singular skill in limning and pictures, a good mathematician, not unskilful in musick, well read in divinity, excellently in history, and no less in the laws and statutes of this nation; he had a quick and sharp conception, would write his mind singularly well, and in good language and stile, only he loved long Parenthesis ...

But in 1651 Cromwell had decisively beaten Charles II—recently crowned at Scone—and sent him packing to France; England was obviously safely republican for some time to come. So Lilly naturally listed the king's defects too, sometimes fairly, sometimes less so. He quotes Charles's nurse as saying that as a child 'he was beyond nature wilful, and unthankful'; he was a great—even an admirable—dissembler (which quality 'questionless he had partly from his father, and partly from the climate he was born in, *viz* Scotland'), and a great lover of the clergy, 'insomuch as under him they grew first insolent, and then saucy; and indeed, his indulgence unto them did in part procure unto himself the people's hate'.

It is an interesting essay, for peeping through the puritan protestations comes a sometimes uneasy, sometimes almost envying admiration for the King and his *style*:

> He was manly, and well fitted for venerious sports, yet rarely frequented illicit beds, I do not hear of above one or two natural children he had, or left behind him. He had exquisite judgement by the eye, and physiognomy, to discover the virtuous from the wanton. He honoured the virtuous, and was very shy and choice in wandring those ways, and when he did it, it was with much cautiousness and secrecy; nor did he prostitute his affection, but unto those of exquisite persons or parts; and this the Queen well knew, nor did she wink at it.
>
> He was observed in his diet to feed heartily, and would drink wines at meals freely, but not in excess. He was rather violent than moderate in exercises; when he walked on foot, he rather trotted than paced, he went so fast. He was nothing at all given to luxery, was extream and sober both in his food and apparel; in the latter whereof he might be rather said to go cleanly and neat, than gaudy or riotously ... In the general he was not vicious; and yet who ever shall say he was virtuous, extreamly errs ...

For the past four or five years, Lilly had watched the King drawing himself surely into conflict with Parliament, and could scarcely approve his methods. His puritan emotions were engaged on Cromwell's behalf, and while he may have been a supporter in theory of the monarchy, he saw perfectly clearly that a draught of independence was needed.

And apart from all this, there was the matter of contriving to remain alive and make a living. This was all right for those totally pledged to the King's or Commonwealth's cause to give up everything for conscience, but Lilly was not one of them. He would have sympathized with Dr Plumtre, caught in Nottingham during the seige, who when told that the considerable damage to his property which he suffered during the war was 'for the advantage of the more publick interest of the Cause, in great passion replied "What is the cause to me if my goods be lost?"'

No, if the way across the chasm of these difficult years was by tight-rope, Lilly was going to tread it; and was to be adept enough. And of course he had astrology to help him. If his astrological reasoning is to be dismissed by us, it must be remembered that *he* had confidence in the revelations of the planets regarding his future, and that while he may have sought for soothing news for whoever happened to be employing him at any one time, he must have tempered his own actions by what he believed would happen. No use, if you wished to survive, praising the King if the planets were on Cromwell's side. And there were now a number of real, quite non-astrological signs, that the King's domination of Parliament was coming to an end.

On January 4th, 1642 (he gets the date wrong in his autobiography, years later) Lilly happened to be dining in Whitehall,

> and in that very room where the Halberts, newly brought from the Tower, were lodged, for use of such as attended the King to the House of Commons. Sir Peter Wich, ere we had fully dined, came into the room I was in, and brake open the Chests where the Armes were, which frighted us all that were there; however, one of our Company got out of Doors, and presently informed some Members, That the King was preparing to come into the House, else I believe all those Members, or some of them, had been taken in the House ...

This was the day of Charles's attempt to arrest the five members of the House of Commons on charges of high treason. It was the final calamitous mistake of his reign; in August 1642 he raised his standard at Nottingham, and (as Aubrey notes)

> the first brush occurred between the Earl of Northampton and Lord Brooke, near Banbury, which was the latter end of

> July, or the beginning of August 1642. But now Bellona thundered, and as a cleare skie is sometimes suddenly overstretched with a dismall Cloud and thunder, so was this Serene Peace by the Civill Warres ...

Lilly, while by now quite clear in his own mind which side he was to support, had not lost all his sympathy for the royal family. He stood in the streets of London and

> beheld the Old Queen-Mother of France departing from London, in Company with Thomas Earl of Arundel; a sad Spectacle of Mortality it was, and produced Tears from mine Eyes, and many other Beholders, to see an Aged lean decrepid poor Queen, ready for her Grave, necessitated to depart hence, having no Place of Residence in this World left her, but where the Courtesy of her hard Fortune assigned it; She had been the only stately and magnificent Woman of Europe ...

While the war began to boil, Lilly returned to his study of the techniques of astrology, and to building up his astrological library and dealing with an ever-increasing number of clients. The technique of his craft always fascinated him—apart from his textbooks, his almanacs always contained rather more astrological detail than those of his contemporaries.

By this time, his library was quite large, containing not only the comparatively few textbooks printed in English, but some brought to him from overseas. Of the 228 titles he lists in the Bibliography to *Christian Astrology*, twenty-one were printed in England (seventeen in English, four in Latin), and the remaining 207 were Latin works printed on the continent. These certainly included Ptolemy's *Tetrabiblos*, the earliest and perhaps still the most seductive of all; the *Commentary on Alcabitius* by Valentine Naibod, an astronomer-astrologer of the previous century, who had contributed greatly to both sciences by calculating the mean motion of the Sun; the works of Guido Bonatus, the thirteenth-century astrologer who worked for the Count of Montefeltro, advising him in his military campaigns—Lilly was later to publish his 'considerations' in a translation by his assistant Henry Coley under the title *Anima Astrologiae*: a short extract from a very long textbook.

Then there was the *Liber Completus in Judiciis Astrorum* of Albohazin Haly, sometimes called Abenragel, more often just Haly. He had been an eleventh-century Arab whose book was the most comprehensive of all the Arabian astrological textbooks (something like five times the length of the *Tetrabiblos*) and covers the whole field, though Lilly evidently saw him as mainly informative about horary astrology—the specific answering of questions asked at a specific time.

All these works were 'easie to be had', Lilly says. He also had a number of books which were more difficult to procure, including one of the earliest almanacs in the Western world, produced by Regiomontanus (John Müller) the contemporary and friend of Copernicus, in 1475; the works of Hippocrates, the physician of the fourth century BC, who had made his students learn astrology in order to know the 'critical days' of illnesses; and the aphorisms of Girolamo Cardan, the sixteenth-century Italian physician and mathematician. There were more.

Towards the end of his life, Lilly was to find a useful source of income in the publication of translations of some of these little-known astrological books and manuscripts. The working translations were made by Coley, but Lilly kept an eye on them, and between them the two men produced at least one best-seller—the 1676 translation of the *Seven Segments* of Cardan, containing the aphorisms. It is a delightful work, with various astrological tips which seventeenth-century readers found irresistible:

> When Venus is with Saturn, and beholds the Lord of the Ascendant, the Native is inclinable to Sodomy, or at least shall love old hard-favoured Women, or poor dirty Wenches ... A Woman that has Mars with the Moon is *Right*, I'll warrant her ... Make no new Clothes, nor first put them on when the Moon is in Scorpio, especially if she be full of light and beheld of Mars, for they will be apt to be torn and quickly worn out

... If a Comet appear while a Woman goes with Child, if it be either in the fourth, fifth or eighth month, such Child will prove very prone to anger and quarrels, and if he be of quality, to Sedition.

The 1640s were to be important years for Lilly: to establish him as a well-known astrologer in London and the provinces, and to bring him in touch with some distinguished men who were subsequently to be of great help to his career, and indeed to him personally. In 1643, for instance, a Mrs Lisle, an extreme Parliamentarian (the wife of the regicide John Lisle, who at Charles's execution said that 'her blood leapt within her to see the tyrant fall', and who was later condemned by Judge Jeffreys for harbouring a rebel from Monmouth's army) brought Lilly a sample of urine for his opinion about the prospects for recovery of a sick friend. Lilly set up a 'figure' for the moment at which the urine was brought to him (or possibly, if Mrs Lisle had secured it, the time when it left the patient's body), and told her that her friend would recover, though there would be a relapse in a month's time.

The invalid recovered: but not until after a relapse caused by eating too much trout at a dinner-party. Lilly was sent for, and assured him that the planets would preside over a return to full health. He and the patient became friends; and the patient was Bulstrode Whitelocke, who was soon to become an influential man, and in five years' time to be made Keeper of the Great Seal. He, like Lilly, was to keep a shrewd balance between the extremes of republicanism and monarchism. He declined to take part in the King's trial, and opposed the abolition of the House of Lords. But he also tried to persuade Cromwell to accept the English crown. After the re-establishment of the monarchy he is said to have paid Charles II £50,000 for a pardon, though some contemporaries claim that he was so respected for his continual defence of the law against prejudice that his fine was never actually collected. He was certainly a sensible and well-balanced man, as his *Memorials of the English Affairs* (1682) eminently shows; and he was to be of considerable service to William Lilly.

His earliest service was the introduction of the astrologer into his own circle of friends—who included Denzil Holles (one of the five members), Sir Philip Stapleton (later a prominent Parliamentary leader), Robert Reynolds (who would speak up for Lilly at a Parliamentary Committee in a few years' time), Sir Robert Pye, and Sir Christopher Wray.

In 1644 Lilly published his first almanac, *Merlinus Anglicus Junior* (he was to publish an annual almanac from that date until his death). It was a good way of advertising himself and his services; valuable as a means of arguing with and (perhaps) putting down rival astrologers; and, for an honest astrologer, a means of warning or preparing the country for horrors and delights to come. Many other astrological almanacs were published at this time, but Lilly's were to become incomparably the most popular and sought-after—evidently from the first, for soon after his new friend Whitelocke appeared in the House of Commons carrying a copy, a number of members also bought it.

It is easy to see why Lilly should so quickly and easily have captured the market with his earliest almanacs: so many of the others then available were silly sooth—like the *Erra Pater*, which gave lists of lucky and unlucky days, and which was based on very tattered and elderly fortune-telling material. And the non-astrological fortune-telling books such as *The Sphere of Pythagoras*, to which a number of readers was addicted, were simple-minded and clumsily written. Lilly's almanacs had a different tone: no doubt often as superstitious, but more literate and more likely to appeal to the educated man—and literacy was by this time much more common than a generation ago.

From the earliest years of printing, the Government had shown considerable interest in controlling the sort of material published by printers: its fear of popular uprisings led it to read sedition into the most innocent publications—and it must be said that almanacs often had been, and were to be, far from innocent in a political sense.

The granting of a Charter to the Stationers' Company in 1557 seems to have been in the main an attempt to establish governmental control over the printers' publications, and while a printer who obtained the Company's permission to print a particular book or pamphlet passed on responsibility for it to the Company, it was often the case that (for this very reason) some months, and occasionally two or three years, passed by before the Company was sure enough of a book's innocence to license it for publication.

During the Civil War, the regulations were ignored by many printers, and in 1643 Parliament issued an ordinance authorizing the Stationers' Company to search for and seize unlicensed printing presses (it was this which led to Milton writing the *Areopagitica*, or *Speech ... for the Liberty of Unlicensed Printing*, published in 1644, which the author himself failed to have licensed). Lilly, in the same year, was not prepared to take the risk, and decided to apply for a licence.

The licenser of all 'mathematical' (i.e., astrological) books was one John Booker, former haberdasher's apprentice from Manchester, later writing-master at Hadley, and clerk to two City of London magistrates. He had become an astrologer by the time he was in his mid 'twenties (he was a year younger than Lilly), and had earned a considerable reputation by correctly predicting the deaths of Gustavus Adolphus and the Elector Palatine. Lilly himself admired him, and in 1640 thought him 'the greatest and most compleat astrologer in the world'.

But evidently Booker was of a jealous disposition; he himself published an annual almanac, and with some justice saw *Merlinus Anglicus* as a dangerous rival. Before he would license it, he 'made many impertinent obliterations', and even then only passed it after considerable niggling argument (he had suffered the same interference from another censor a few years earlier). Lilly had the same sort of trouble with the printer, but the result was happy all the same, for the first impression was sold out within a week, and its success with various Members of Parliament was such that Lilly was able to ask them to order Booker to license the complete, unexpurgated version; reluctantly, he did so, and 'the second time it came forth as I would have it'.

By the time *Merlinus Anglicus* came out, such pamphlets—or books, for some of them were of considerable dimensions—were rather less commonplace than they had been ten or twenty years before, for the political situation was such that astrologers were less happy to commit themselves to statements which might later be used against them. But before the outbreak of the Civil War they had been produced in considerable numbers for at least a century.

The term 'almanac' has two connotations, but connotations so closely linked as to be indistinguishable. In the one sense, all that is meant is a calendar which includes astronomical detail; in the other, the same detail is embroidered with astrological comment. From the earliest times, single records have combined the two purposes. During the last three centuries BC, manuscript texts were prepared which were based on a consistent theory of lunar and planetary motion. The astrologers of the period had to know, for instance, the precise moment of a particular conjunction or opposition, and their tables were devised to tell them.

Later, of course, such tables were of purely astronomical, then of navigational interest; what was important to the pure astronomer (though such an animal scarcely existed until after Newton) was the *ephemeris* only—the astronomical details alone, without an astrological gloss. But for our purpose, the word *almanac* implies a table of astrological, as well as astronomical significance.

Several texts of this sort exist from ancient Babylonian and Egyptian civilizations, while the Romans had their *Fasti Diurni*, or official yearbooks, with dates and directions for religious ceremonies; the origin of the Roman calendar. As astronomy became more sophisticated, more detailed almanacs were prepared and published, so that by 1551 Copernicus was publishing his own astronomical tables as a matter of course.

Astrologers appended their own interpretations of celestial events to simple ephemerides from a quite early date; in manuscript at first, and as soon as the possibility presented itself, in print. One of the earliest English almanacs was printed by Wynkyn de Worde, Caxton's assistant, who inherited his master's press at the latter's death in 1491. This was, on the face of it, purely astronomical:

> Here begynneth ye seycle or chaunge of ye mone, with ye coniuncyon/ and sheweth what day/ houre/ minute/ signe/ and degree ye mone chall chaunge. Also ye may know the eclypse of the sonne and mone from the date of our Lord M.CCCCC. and XXII. unto ye date of our Lord M.CCCCC. and XXXVII; and truely corrected by a true copye with great dylygence.

It was printed in 'the Feltstrete at the sygne of the Sonne'.

Eleven years later, we find a definitely astrological almanac composed by Master John Thybault, 'medycyner and astronomer of the Emperyall Majesty'. It contained records of 'the four parts of this yere and of the influence of the mone, of peas and warre, and of the sycknesses of this yere, with the constellacions of them that be under the seven planettes, and of the revolutoons of kings and princes and of the eclipses and comets'. It was the year in which Henry VIII was excommunicated; but no observation is made on his future.

Almanac publication throughout the sixteenth century was fairly constant, though the same difficulty attaches to tracing them as to children's books: by their very character, they were well used, and more often than not either fell to pieces or became so tattered that they were thrown away. But enough remains to show that purely astronomical, purely astrological, and mixed almanacs were regularly published. Indeed, they were so popular that to a publisher 'prognosticating almanacs' became 'readier money than ale or cakes'! Some of them were prepared by doctors, for astrology and medicine went hand in hand: so we get, in 1541, an almanac written 'by ye renowned Doctor in Astronomy and Physick, Peter Apianus'; and some were offered as a help to agriculture—such as the 1555 'perfyte pronostycacion perpetuall ... good for husbandmen of the countrey to know the years that shall be pleanteous and the yeres the whiche shall be grevous and in scasytie, &c.'.

Other almanacs provided advice for the sportsman, as did one printed in London, but intended for the use of the gentlemen of Yorkshire, in 1550. Anthony Askam provided 'A Prognossicacion and an Almanac fastened together, declaring the Dispocission of the People, and also of the Wether, with certaine Electyons and Tymes chosen both for Physicke and Surgerye, and for the Husbandman. And also for Hawkeing, Hunting, Fishynge, and Foulinge, according to the Science of Astronomy'.

Astrological weather forecasting, of course, had been practised from time immemorial, and many almanacs specialized in it. The most famous, and most amusing, was that of Leonard Dygges, published in London in 1555 by 'Thomas Gemini', a pseudonymous printer whose list of agricultural publications was very lengthy indeed.

Dygges's 'Prognostication ... contayning playne, briefe, pleasant, chosen rules, to judge the weather for ever, by the Sunne, Moone, Sterres, Cometes, Raynbowe, Thunder, Cloudes, with other Extraordinarie tokens, not omitting the Aspecces of Planetes, with a brefe Judgement for ever, of Plentie, Lacke, Sicknes, Death, Warres, &c.' bears re-reading for its curiosity and (often but not always) unconscious humour.

Many of Mr Dygges's rules are based on ancient lore: the Sun being red in the evening, 'the next daye fayre, but in the morning redde, wynde and rayne'; or if the stars 'appeare of muche light, in bignes great, more blasing than they are comonly, it betokeneth great wynde or moysture in that part where they shewe'. But then he goes on to consider the planets' aspects to each other, and their meteorological significance: 'The conjunction, quadrature, or opposition of Saturne with Mars in watry signes, declare in somer rayne, often shoures, with hayle, thunder and lightnyng'; or 'The conjunction, quadrature or opposition of Mars, with Mercurie in hot signes, great heate: in drye signes, drouth: in watrie, rayne: sometimes thunders, lightninges, with sodayn fierce wyndes'.

Later, he goes on to examine the causes of natural phenomena, such as earthquakes: 'Plentye of wyndes, entred into holes, cones or caves of the earth, whiche absent from above the earth, causeth quietness: the violent brusting oute of them (the earth closed agayne) is the earthquake: *Signus est futurorum bellorum.*'

As astrologers became more confident, so their almanacs became more expansive, and they claimed to be able to assist their readers in more and more spheres of everyday life, so that towards the end of the century they became veritable catalogues of good and bad effects: 'The varietie of the ayre, and also of the Windes throughout the whole yeare, with infortunate times to bie and sell, take medicine, sow, plant and journey, &c.'

Between 1557 and 1570, the number of almanacs on sale became comparatively huge. The list of names of their authors is a long one indeed—Robothum and Hackett, Master Wally and Thomas Marshe, Henry Rocheforthe and Jhon (*sic*: the name is printed almost twenty times in that form), Waley and Thomas Purfoote, and Master Doctour Low.

The Stationers' Register is the most reliable record of almanacs printed, entering them by title and author's name, and giving also some peripheral information, such as that in 1562 twenty printers were fined for selling the Prognostications of Michael Nostradamus (not then in good repute; indeed, never in good repute in Britain).

Incidentally, in the list appears a work more familiar to the general reader than most almanacs: '1591. *The Shepeard's Calender*. Containing twelve aeglogues proportionable to the twelve months. Entituled: To the noble and vertuous gentleman, most worthy of all titles, both of learning and chivalry, maister Philip Sidney. By Edmund Spenser.' Sidney was a great friend of Dr John Dee, and evidently showed some interest in astrology (his own birth chart survives); the poem has some astrological allusions.

There are other publications which are in part astrological but also serve other purposes. It is not surprising, when one remembers Dr Dee's interest in and contribution to the art of navigation, that one finds some astrological almanacs directed in part at the seaman: as in the 1571 'Almanack and Prognostication for Three yeares ... now newlye added unto my late Rules of Navigation that was printed iiii yeres past, practised at Gravesend, for the meridian of London, by William Bourne, Student of the Mathematical Sciences ...' And in 1574, Philip More provided in his almanac 'a Fly for young mariners to practise themselves in, verie easy to understand'.

While during the 1550s and 1560s there had been a superabundance of almanacs, there is a sudden dramatic falling-off of the number published after 1570; indeed, for the six years after 1570 there is an almost total blank in the records (though in the absence of any such great collection of ephemera as the seventeenth-century Thomason Tracts, it is very easy to overlook individual works). In 1570 Queen Elizabeth had granted a special licence to two men, Richard Watkins and James Roberts, to print 'all almanacs and prognostications'; she renewed the licence in 1588, for a period of twenty-one years. Apart from their publications, no almanacs seem to have been issued during the forty or so years after 1570, though it is difficult to believe that a total censorship or ban can have been imposed.

At the turn of the century, the number of almanacs increased again, greatly, and their tone became more varied and interesting. Later, of course, when the Civil War broke out, they were to be used as vehicles for propaganda — this, and Lilly's considerable involvement in it, will be discussed in Chapter IV. But the everyday almanac, generally quarto in size, continued to concentrate on providing, first, an almanac or calendar, and secondly a prognostication. Good or evil days were carefully recorded, and there were rules for bathing (dangerous when the planets were unpropitious) and for the taking of medicines and purges (the terms were often synonymous!).

There were, too, descriptions of the four seasons and rules for discovering the weather; and by the 1640s, when Lilly began publishing his almanacs, it had become a general rule that there should be an astrological prediction of events during the coming year—a 'scheme', as astrologers called it (though the word 'scheme' could refer to the calculations and the chart itself, or to the predictions made from it). Some astrologers, on the whole the less inventive ones (or possibly the less proficient), puffed out their almanacs by including such material as a list of country fairs, tables of interest, rules for making out bills, and so on.

During the sixteenth century, the almanac-makers described themselves most frequently as 'Physitians and Preests'; but in the seventeenth century one finds many other titles—'Student in

Astrology' (most often; it was almost invariably Lilly's description of himself), 'Philomath', 'Well Wisher to the Mathematics'. Sometimes the pseudonym concealed illustrious names: *An Almanacke for the yeere of our Lord God 1631*, for instance, was published under the name of William Beale, Philomathist, Gent. Mr Beale was in fact the servant of Henry Gellibrand, commoner of Trinity College, Oxford, and astronomy professor of Gresham College, whose work the book was.

Most of the almanacs were prepared by honest astrologers, though a few were published simply as an advertisement for their wares by quack doctors such as William Salmon and John Partridge. Some astrologers were uncommonly long-lived, it seems, until one realizes that the Stationers' Company often continued to publish almanacs under their authors' names long after they were dead. George Wharton, in the Epistle to the Reader of his 1655 *Ephemeris*, condemned as forgeries 'the almanacks yearly published under the names of Slade, Allestree, Pond, Gallen, Woodhouse and Vaux ... the men themselves being long since dead'.

The Stationers' Company had 'inherited' the monopoly of publication of almanacs after Elizabeth's lease to Watkins and Roberts had come to an end at the beginning of the reign of James I. So almanacs became uniform in size and appearance, and the name of the printer vanished from most of them: they were simply 'printed for the Company of Stationers', which makes investigation into them a more confusing matter. But of course the authors remained individuals, and individualists.

The first of Lilly's own almanacs, the *Merlinus Anglicus* of June 1644, was a relatively slender affair of only twenty-two pages and something like 10,000 words; later that year, his second publication was much more ambitious: *England's Prophetical Merline*, which came out in October, had 126 pages and over 60,000 words. The title-page advertised *Anglicus* as 'The English Merlin revived: or, His prediction upon the affaires of the ENGLISH Common-wealth, and of all or most Kingdomes of Christondome this present Yeare, 1644'.

In a Note to the Reader (written from 'The Three Flower de

Luces neere Somerset House', practically on his own doorstep) Lilly contends that the almanac had been printed because it had interested so many people in manuscript form, and had been so widely read and copied. And then, comes an interesting preface 'To Any or Every Man'—a classic astrologers' warning to over-credulous readers:

> It's far from my thoughts that there's any binding or inevitable necessity in what I predict by the radiation of heavenly bodies; the stars have no such unlimited lawes, they are bounded, and give light to us or some small glimpses of the great affaires God intends upon earth, but if we rely on our judgement, without relation to the immediate rule and direction of his eternall providence, alas, how soone of wise men we become errant fooles and Ideots ...

It has been suggested that the preface was placed at the front of the book at the instigation of the publisher; but it seems very unlikely. Apart from the fact that it adequately represents Lilly's own point of view, there is no evidence to show that any of Lilly's publishers were in the least interested in the matter of his almanacs or books—their sale was what mattered to them. George Wither, author of *The Schollers Purgatory*, sets us right about the stationers and publishers of the 1640s:

> What book soever he may have hope to gain by, he will divulge, though it contain matter against his prince, against the state, or blasphemy against God. All his excuse will be that he knew not it comprehended any such matter. For (give him his right) he scarcely reads over one page of a book in seven year ...
>
> He will fawn upon authors at his first acquaintance, and ring them to his hive by the promising sounds of some good advertisement; but as soon as they have prepared the honey to his hand, he drives the bees to seek another stall ... If his employment be in binding books, so they will hold together but till his workmaster hath sold them, he desireth not they

1. Lilly's birthplace, at Diseworth, Leicestershire

2. 'Dns Prickman if his Mrs would live.' Inside the chart, from one of his notebooks, Lilly writes: 'Shee died within a fortnight' (*Curators of the Bodleian Library*)

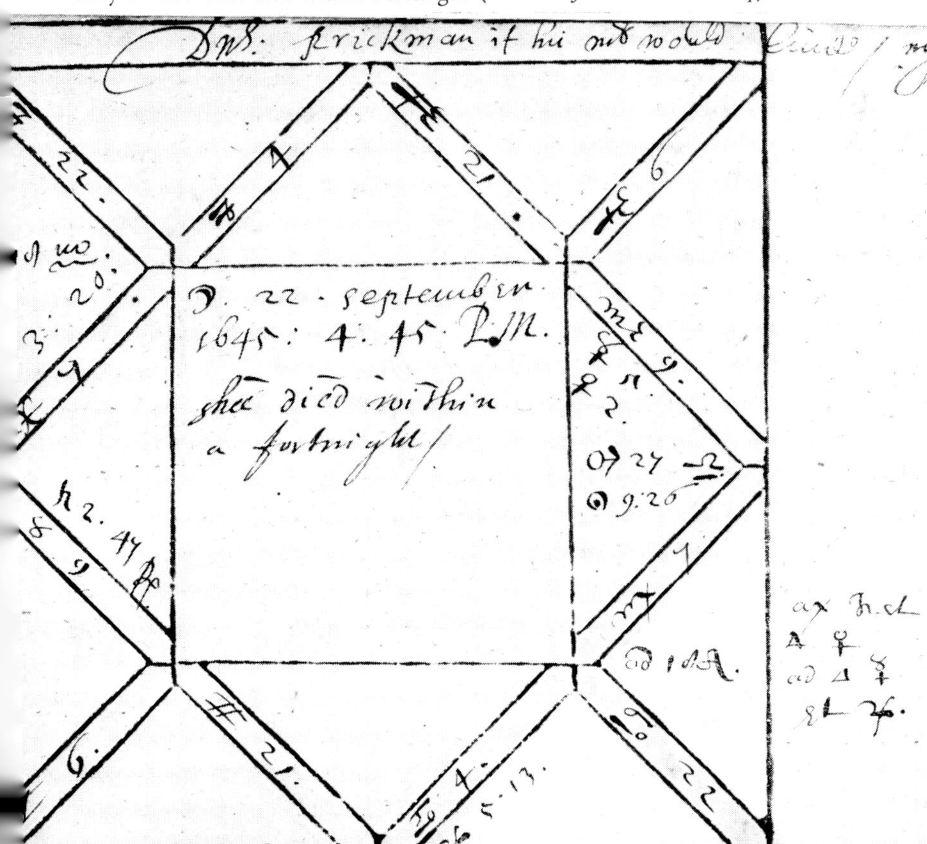

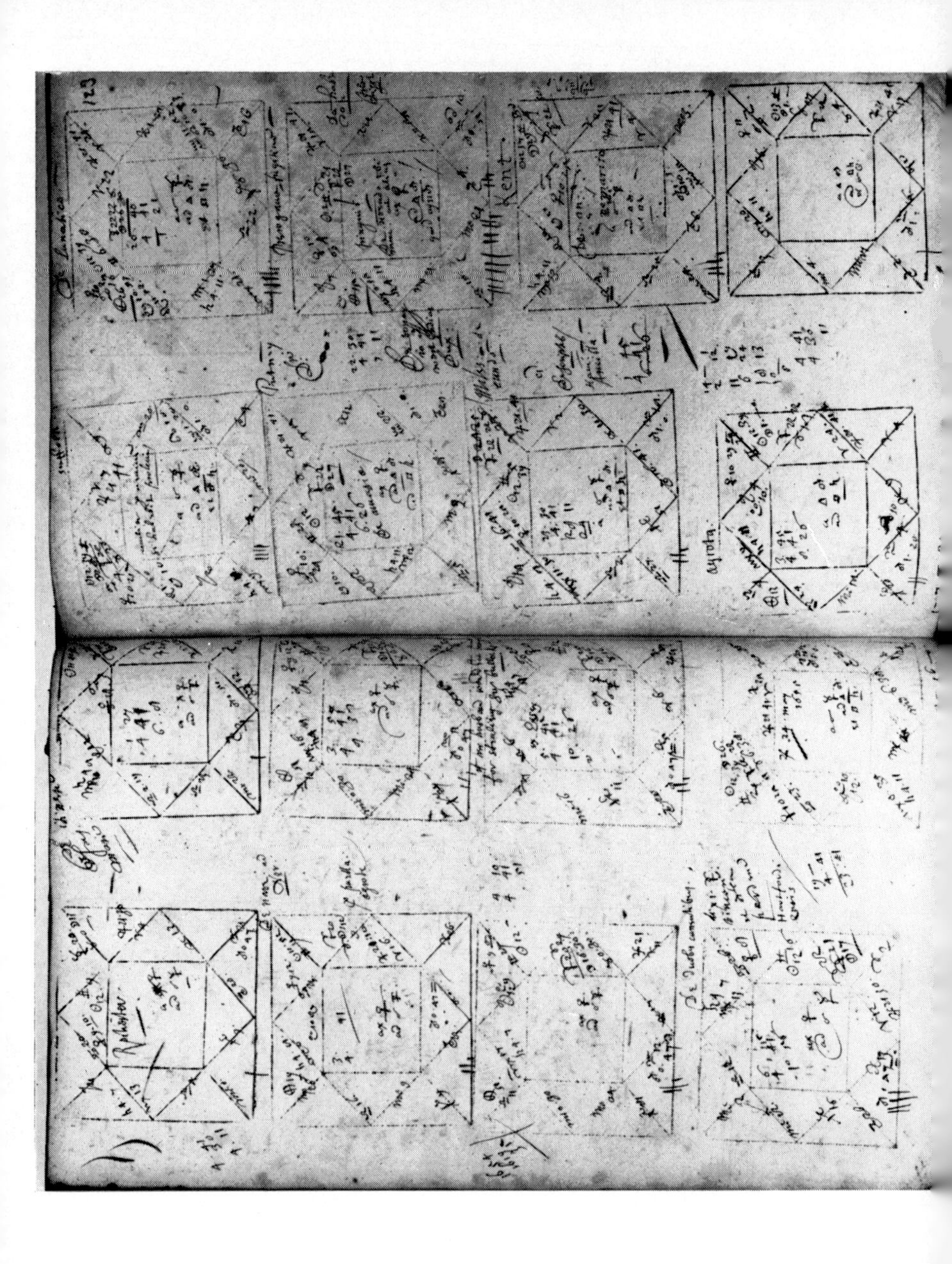

3. Charts cast for Lilly's clients, in one of his notebooks. The second chart in the second column was to determine 'if my husband would be hanged for stealing 30 bullocks' (*Curators of the Bodleian Library*)

should last a week longer; for by that means a book of a crown is marred in one month which would last a hundred years if it had twopence more workmanship.

Lilly's almanacs were certainly ill-bound, and got such usage from his readers that very few of them have survived outside the great libraries. But they remain more than ephemeral records of what the planets were promising in one year or the other: they reflect the history of astrology, too.

Evidently Lilly had already noticed the increasingly critical attitude taken by some people towards traditional astrology, for he goes on to protest:

this learning is ancient, and hath had society with Kings; it's now despicable, it hath few favourers, and as few to understand it. I desire to be judged by those that apprehend something in Astrology, and not by the censorious criticall Asse, that beleeves no influence, scarce [of] heaven: It was folly in me to judge of any science I was never acquainted with; hee's as much foole as Phormio that censures my labour, and knowes not what I write of, nor the principles of that Art from which I draw my judgement; I beleeve God rules all by his divine Providence, and that the Stars by his permission are instruments whereby many contingent events may be foreseene as well in the generall accidents of the world as in particular men's fates ...

Lilly then gives another warning to the credulous, not to expect too much of astrologers:

The Planets and Stars are ministers not masters: Expect not that all accidents* shall precisely happen to a day or a weeke. Do not we first fit the ground, then sow, and after some

* The word *accident* is used to mean 'an occurance, an incident, an event,' not necessarily bad; astrologers were particularly fond of it, perhaps because of its association with 'fortune' — with events happening 'accidentally'.

> expiration of time gather and crop? It's impossible for the weaknesse of man at all times to hit the certaine day, or weeke, of many accidents, sometimes we do, or very near, but not constantly ...

The predictions in the 1644 *Anglicus* are fairly vague; later, Lilly was to become more particular. He starts with a general picture of the year to come (giving, as he was always to do, the astrological reasons for his statements):

> If the rules of Astrology fail me not, or God Almighty cloud not my understanding, and so make me uncapable of judgement, some more than ordinary action and accidents shall this yeare happen in our Clymate, which is England; and in our neerest adjoyning neighbour countries, which are Scotland, Ireland, France, Denmark, the United (perhaps disjoynted) Provinces, as also in the dominions of his Majesty of Spaine, in Flanders, and Brabant: the Celestiall Scheame it selfe is very strange, all the Angles being fixed, the Moone and Mars in fixed signes, the Sunne, Saturn, Venus and Jupiter being all in the Equinoctiall and Cardinall sign Aries the ascendant of England, as if by this their position they pointed out wee should have action enough, and variety of it, &c., onely Mercury the father of lyes and untruths, and scandalous Pamphlets is in a Common Signe, as if he intended all this whole yeare to vex us with flying reports, continuall feares, false alarums, untoward speeches, contradictory newes, lying messengers, and cozening Accomptants, Receivers, Treasurers, and the like, &c.

There are a few more particular predictions: 'A proper goodly Noble-man of red or flaxen haire will vex or disturbe the North or North-west or West of *Scotland*, and perhaps some others the South,' he remarks, adding in the margin: 'I heare some such thing hath happened!'

Theft and violence were promised throughout the year; more aborted births than usual; and a conjunction of Saturn and Mars at the end of May which, though it need not mean outbreaks of plague (as some astrologers had promised), 'may produce great weaknesse in people's sights; the head-ach more than ordinary, and stoppings at the brest, and much slimy fleagme in the throat ...' There would be a general shortage of money, and 'the Nobility and Gentry shall not be so flush of money as to buy bables and trifles'. One would not have thought that there was much in that first *Anglicus* to dispel doubts about the efficacy of astrology as a means of prediction for the mass of the people, or the country at large. But nevertheless (and by comparison with the other almanacs available) it was an enormous success, and four months later the much more substantial *England's Prophetical Merline* was published.

In the preface Lilly asserted that, long though the book was, it would have been even more substantial 'had I not been as much, during its writing, oppressed with taxes and weekly assessments', and had he not omitted much that might be offensive to the Crown, 'for I love Monarchy, and would not easily displease my Soveraigne'. He also promised 'more misfortunes', for 'truth is truth, and a spade is a spade, if I might freely so call it'.

Before beginning the main body of his text, Lilly again emphasized (for the casual reader) what astrology could, and could not, do. It could not find lost or stolen goods, though many clients demanded that service (and privately got it, though illegally). It could warn a man if the woman he loved was unsuitable; it could advise in matters of health; on the success of voyages; on times when business projects might succeed; on physical danger; and to some extent could predict the results of unwise actions. Lilly could, he said, have warned Charles I that at such-and-such a time 'he should have some scuffling with his subjects'.

Throughout his life Lilly was always repeating these warnings, though in his private practice he often disregarded them. He never stopped attempting to teach the general reader something about his art—and his almanacs contain many more astrological technicalities than anything published since. This makes them somewhat tedious to a twentieth-century reader; but many seventeenth-century readers would have had the smattering of astrological knowledge necessary to understand them, and since Lilly used current astrological language rather than out-dated jargon, his almanacs were in fact textbooks as well as predictive pocket-books. The warnings he gave in his prefatory notes were a protection against the law: *he* believed he could find stolen articles, and that the law was an ass to say that he should not. The apparent inconsistencies are really quite consistent.

The *Prophetical Merline* proper begins with a long and technical essay on the conjunction of Jupiter and Saturn which took place on February 15th, 1643. Lilly notes the effects of nine previous conjunctions of that sort before proceeding to his conclusions, which are gloomy, and to the effect that he is not surprised that England is in her present unfortunate state. He promises a settlement in 1660, however, by which time all will be well again. (It is doubtful whether in the event he was to consider the Restoration quite the panacea he now had in mind.)

Then comes the ephemeris of a current comet, and reflections on it, listing many difficulties with which it is likely to visit Britain. Then a list of eclipses and lesser conjunctions, with short, snappy comments, some more helpful perhaps than others: January 31st, 1645: 'I fear the plague generally.' February 24th: 'Scarcity of bread and provision.' July 4th: 'Londoner, adventure not too much to sea.' December 26th: 'Arise, O Lord, and help'!

Then comes a didactic section in which Lilly prints, and analyses, several full birth charts. The first is that of 'a Gentleman', which Lilly dissects at length, with the comments of the anonymous subject as footnotes. These are usually favourable, but naturally do not extend to the astrologer's final comment that in 1657, when he would be 73, the subject 'at the fall of the leafe ... becomes ill, and is oppressed with the wind chollic, but striving to be rid of that, and his Medicines not operating to purpose, it puts the native into a fever, of which, about the 5 of December, according to natural causes, he ought to die.' 'I positively conclude not his death,' Lilly kindly mitigates, 'for that's onely in the hands of God.'

A chart drawn up for the moment at which Lilly received a

sample of the urine of John Pym, M.P., who was ill at the time and died shortly afterwards, precedes that for a lawsuit. 'I judged the Querant should overcome his enemy, and so he did,' writes Lilly. 'I said that the judge at the tryall would be angry, and so he was, for the adversaries witnesses knew not what to swear.'

Then there is a chart drawn up in an attempt to discover the characteristics of a thief who had stolen some goods from a client. Lilly did not like that kind of work, he explained, for apart from the fact that nobody seemed to believe that it could be properly done, there could be mistakes and wrongful accusations. In this case, having consulted the chart, he opines that the thief

> was such a one as is signified by Mars, *viz* A fellow of middle stature, strong and well set, broad shoulders, a wrangling swearing fellow, of some earthly sordid occupation, that did frequently do drudgeries in the house, of a darke flaxen curling haire, a sun-burnt Complexion, and some materiall cut or gash near the left eye ... I said further that the fellow had two sweethearts at that time.

The thief, when discovered, answered the description, though the client only recovered half of his stolen goods.

The examples given in the almanac all came from Lilly's private practice, which was obviously in a very healthy state. But his publications for the year were not complete: *A Prophesy of the White King* was still to come, and was to have the greatest success of the three, and to gain considerable fame (or notoriety) for its author. It was as much a political publication as an astrological one, however, and for tidiness' sake should be considered in the next chapter.

Early in January of each year (though occasionally publication was delayed) Lilly would publish his *Anglicus* with an ephemeris for the *following* year. The almanac for 1646 began, as usual, with a mildly political comment (mild because Lilly usually reserved his more splenetic attacks for special publications). His preface in the 1646 almanac begins with a plea for the uniting of the country—'for what's he, whose heart bleeds not to see a fruitfull kingdome depopulated and wallowing in its owne blood, only to plead the humour of a few?'

Then comes the ephemeris, showing the position of the planets at noon of each day, the Moon's aspects to each planet, astrological judgments on these positions, and the means to tell what planet 'governs' every hour of every day—an invaluable aid to living one's life, and especially for the gathering of herbs for medical use, which were much more effective if they had been gathered at the right time.

There are again special notes on the progress of the war: Charles will have bad news in May and October, and generally speaking things will go ill for him during the year. (Clarendon, without the aid of astrology, was able to make the same sort of prediction: 'The actions of the last year were attended with so many dismal accidents and events that there were no seeds of hope left to spring up in this ensuing ill year,' he wrote.)

Lilly is not entirely uncritical of Parliament: though he promises the cause general success, he suggests that in January 'our soldiers [will] cry out for money; sure I am that some officers will be removed,' and that there will be some 'crooked and clandestine Councils' in the Parliamentary leadership.

He was not so far out: indeed by January the soldiers were beginning to complain very bitterly about their arrears of pay, which by March amounted to over £300,000. He would have noticed hints of disaffection for that reason during the previous year: at York the troops had mutinied, holding Major-General Poyntz at pistol-point while they shouted 'Money, money, money!' in his face. But Lilly had after all been smart enough (assuming that the Army's predicament was not indeed to be read in the planets) to see that things would reach such a pitch that within the first three months of 1646 infantry regiments would be eighteen weeks in arrears, and cavalry regiments forty-three.

As for the 'crooked Councils' in Parliament, these showed up in the Commons debate of March 29th, when Lilly's enemies the Presbyterians showed their lack of sympathy for the soldiers, and even attempted to have the complainants dealt with as enemies of the State. Lilly of course knew perfectly well who would be most annoyed at his taking the soldiers' side; and that it would do him no harm with Cromwell (supposing the Protector had the time and the inclination to trouble himself about an astrological almanac), since he was extremely incensed by the Presbyterians' attitude. The Presbyterians might try to make trouble for Lilly, but not the kind of trouble which would do very much harm; indeed, the 'success' of this kind of prediction was very good publicity, and the chances of their being able to do him any real harm were small, for 'I had abundance of worthy men in the House of Commons, my assured friends, no lovers of Presbytery, which were then in great esteem and able to protect the art ... for should the Presbyterians' party have prevailed ... I knew well that they would have silenced my pen annually.'

For the first time, Lilly began including in the almanac what could be called 'pop astrology'; now, as well as medical aphorisms to assist in the curing of illness, he included profiles of physical types for each Zodiacal sign: Gemini, 'a straight, well-set body, good complecion and colour, and the haire browne, of good speech wit and discourse', for instance.

He was learning all the time from his private clients what they demanded of an almanac or an astrologer. It is clear that during this period Lilly's private practice was building up very satisfactorily. The evidence is rather sparse, but from time to time a note or an incident surfaces which shows that his work was gaining considerable reputation. The attacks made on him are one symptom of his increasing popularity. During 1647, for instance, there was a mild scandal when a clandestine royalist newspaper of which George Wharton (one of Lilly's rivals) was co-editor, published an attack on 'that Jugling Wizard William Lilly, the States Figure-Flinger Generall, a fellow made up of nothing but Mischiefe, Tautologies and Barbarism', who, it was alleged, had helped a Mr John Howe of Lincoln's Inn to gain the affection of Lady Annabella Scroope (daughter of the Earl of Sunderland, and worth at a conservative estimate £2,500 a year), and then marry her, by 'cheating tricks' and 'abhominable practices'. Howe was a fairly well-known politician, which made it important for Lilly to dispose of the accusation if he was to keep his reputation for honesty.

A reply to the allegations was given in a pamphlet published in February 1647, entitled *The Late Storie of Mr William Lillie*, by an anonymous 'Colonel Th.'. In June or July of 1646, the Colonel says, an unknown man had called on Lilly and paid him ten shillings to discover what sort of woman he would marry (including 'the private moles of her body', presumably so that he would readily—or eventually—recognize her). Lilly had drawn up a chart, and given him the necessary description. Five or six days later, a maid had come on behalf of an anonymous woman, who sent five shillings for a description of the man she should marry. The description was forthcoming and sent off with the maid, and a few days later the woman herself had come and paid a further ten shillings for confirmation.

'But,' writes Colonel Th., evidently answering the particular charge (which is no longer extant), 'as for wishing her to goe to the Spring garden, or appointing her to such or such a walke, and that there she should see the Gentleman should be her husband, or telling her his apparrell, &c ... these are all malicious and lying suggestions, untruths, and meere forgeries.'

Clearly it had been suggested that for a bribe, Lilly had told the heiress to walk in a particular place at a particular time, and she would see her future husband in such-and-such a dress; and had arranged the whole thing with Mr Howe. What Lilly claimed was that the unknown man had returned to him saying that he had seen the woman who answered Lilly's description of his wife-to-be, and asked if he should press his suit. Certainly, said Lilly, and charged for the advice. Twice more, the man had returned, and been given the same encouragement. Now, the astrologer was hurt and annoyed (having only received, he says, fifty shillings from the man and fifteen from the woman) at being accused of 'hindering' two noble lords who were also after the heiress, and of telling Lady Annabella that she should 'have none but Master H.'.

But in the event, Lady Annabella confirmed Lilly's version of the affair, and the scandal subsided. 'If Wharton,' the Colonel asserts, 'had smelt of anything but the dung hill, hee would have been ashamed to have related such notorious untruths.' It is not of course impossible that Lilly himself had his head in the Colonel's helmet; indeed, it is likely.

It was during this time that Lilly celebrated his increasing prosperity by having his portrait painted—the only likeness to survive, for all the existing engravings and woodcuts are modelled on it. Lilly stands in front of a piece of drapery, to the right of an open window through which can be seen a somewhat lurid sky, and a piece of anonymous and sickly creeper. But the figure itself is rather impressive: a keen look in the blue-grey eyes, a gingerish moustache and a small tuft below the lower lip; shoulder-length hair above a severely cut collar; and holding a blank birth-chart headed 'Aetatis 45', from which the picture can be dated.

There seems no way of discovering who the artist was; the style is respectably polished as to the portrait, but unremarkable. The picture was given by Lilly to his friend Elias Ashmole only five years or so after it was finished, and survived in his great collection.

One interesting feature of it is that the blank chart also bears the words 'non cogunt', underlining the astrologers' constant assertions that (as the ancient astrological saw has it) 'the stars incline, they do not compel'. No man was forced by planetary intervention to do, or omit to do, anything. He could always overcome 'his fortune'; the astrologer simply predicted possible trends in his life, and the client himself retained free will. (It is this aspect of astrology which makes it acceptable to the Church; the Roman Catholic view in the 1970s is that astrology is acceptable provided that astrologers do not claim to predict events.)

Apart from working for clients, during the 1640s Lilly was working on a book which was to place him as a serious astrological scholar: his *Christian Astrology modestly treated in Three Books*, which came out in 1647. This remains his major published work, and was the textbook from which he taught his pupils.

It is a remarkable work (in all, over 350,000 words long), and anyone requiring evidence that astrology in the seventeenth century was extremely complex and finely organized could do no better than look through it. One thing is abundantly clear: however fond Lilly may have been of turning an honest, or even dubiously honest, penny, he knew his subject well, and treated it with the utmost nicety and care. He also wrote with wit and enthusiasm, and sometimes with some nobility of style. The *Epistle to the Student In Astrology* which appeared as a prefatory note has been reprinted since in many specialist astrological textbooks, and remains the astrological equivalent, if you like, of the Hippocratic Oath. It is worth quoting at length:

> My friend, whoever thou art, that with so much ease shalt receive the benefit of my hard studies, and dost intend to proceed in this heavenly knowledge of the starres; In the first place, consider and admire thy Creator, be thankfull unto him, and be humble, and let no naturall knowledge, how profound or transcendant soever it be, elate thy mind to neglect that Divine Providence, by whose al-seeing order and appointment all things heavenly and earthly have their constant motion: the more thy knowledge is enlarged, the more doe thou magnify the power and wisdome of Almighty God: strive to preserve thyself in his favour; for the more holy thou art, and more neer to God, the purer judgement thou shalt give ...
>
> Having considered thy God, and what thyself art, during thy being God's servant, now receive instruction how in thy practice I would have thee carry thyself. As thou daily conversest with the heavens, so instruct and form thy mind according to the image of Divinity: learn all the ornaments of virtue, be sufficiently instructed therein: be humane, curtius, familiar to all, easie of accesse: afflict not the miserable with terrour of a harsh judgement; direct such to call on God to divert his judgements impending over them: be civil, sober, covet not an estate; give freely to the poor, both money and judgement: let no worldly worth procure an erronious judgement from thee, or such as may dishonour

the art. Be sparing in delivering judgement against the commonwealth thou livest in; avoyd law and controversie: in thy study be *totus in illus*, that thou mayest be *singular in arte*. Be not extravagant, or desirous to learn every science; be not *aliquid in omnibus*; be faithfull, tenacious, betray no ones secrets. Instruct all men to live well: be a good example thyselfe; love thy own native country; be not dismaid if ill spoken of, *conscientia mille testes*. God suffers no sin unpunished, no lye unrevenged. Pray for the nobility, honour the gentry and yeomanry of England; stand firme to the commands of this parliament; have a reverand opinion of our worthy lawyers, for without their learned paines, and the mutual assistance of some true spirited gentlemen, we might yet be made slaves, but we will not; we now see light as well as many of the clergy. Pray, if it stands with God's will, that monarchy in this kingdom may continue, his Majesty and posterity reigne: forget not the Scottish nation, their mutual assistance in our necessity, their honourable departure. God preserve the illustrious *Fairfax*, and his whole armye, and let the famous city of London be ever blessed, and all her worthy citizens.

Setting aside the contemporary political cant, it is not an ignoble address. It became well known in the nineteenth century, when 'Zadkiel' reprinted it as the preface to a book which he called *An Introduction to Astrology, by William Lilly*. Published in 1835, it has often been spoken of as a book written entirely by Lilly—an error supported by Lilly's habit of writing, in his autobiography and elsewhere, of 'my *Introduction*.' The first Book of *Christian Astrology* is titled *An Introduction to Astrology*, and this was in fact what Lilly meant. It is ironical that in the nineteenth and even the twentieth century, Lilly has probably been best known for a book he did not write—a much abbreviated and revised edition of *Christian Astrology*.

'Zadkiel' must have done well out of his abridgement of Lilly: it was reprinted in 1852, together with a work wholly by 'Zadkiel', and was reproduced again and again from stereotype plates.

He put together Books One and Two of *Christian Astrology*, often altering, often omitting, sometimes adding material of his own, so that it is difficult to judge, when reading Zadkiel's edition, what is Lilly and what is not.

'Zadkiel' himself was an interesting character;* his real name was Richard James Morrison, and he was for many years a naval officer. His *Almanac* became extremely popular in the 1830s. An educated man, he was rather careful to disguise his astrological interests when in polite society, and after his real name was revealed during a libel action in 1863, moved from London to Cheltenham where 'the minds of several people ... [were] rendered unhappy by astrological predictions'. But his main achievement, as far as we are concerned, was to make Lilly's name once more familiar to English readers—even if under a largely false assumption.

*Christian Astrology* is the work we must turn to as representative of Lilly's astrological theory at its most comprehensively argued and explained. It is one of the most ambitious textbooks of astrology ever printed in English, the subject 'modestly treated of in three books' (which calls into question Lilly's definition of the word 'modesty').

In Book One, he describes the use of an ephemeris, and the drawing-up of an astrological chart; the 'nature' of the twelve Zodiacal signs, and of the planets. Book Two tells the student how to deal with the questions he may wish to resolve by the use of astrology; and Book Three how to interpret a birth-chart and rectify it by the use of 'Annual Accidents'.

Lilly dedicated his book to his friend Bulstrode Whitelocke, 'to acquaint the present and future times, of your ardent and continuall promoting me and my poore Labours,' and paid generous tribute to Whitelock's constancy not only to the cause of astrology, but the cause of Parliamentary democracy.

Ptolemy, publishing one of the earliest comprehensive astrological textbooks in the second century BC, had pointed out in his

* There is a full account of him in Ellic Howe's *Urania's Children* (William Kimber, London, 1967).

prefatory notes that he had presented to the reader nothing new, but simply a compendium of the astrological knowledge passed down in MSS and by word of mouth over the preceding centuries. Similarly, Lilly explains in a Note to the reader that he has consulted a great number of earlier astrological writers (a bibliography at the end of the book lists them), but 'though it was no small trouble unto me, to see the discrepancy of judgement amongst them and the more ancient printed Authors, yet I have with some trouble reconciled their disagreements, and reformed and corrected what might have led the Reader into an errour'.

He excuses the more foolish statements in the ancient authors by simply blaming the translators. And he claims that where he differs from the acknowledged authorities, he does so for the best of reasons: that his own researches have led him to believe otherwise!

Lilly's technical explanations are full and straightforward. A general readability adds to the distinction of *Christian Astrology*. Lilly must have been a good teacher: with his customary confidence, he claims that he 'never undertook the instruction of any, whom I have not abundantly satisfied, and made very capable of the Art, in lesse time than any could expect'.

The calculation and erection of an astrological chart is not the simplest of matters, and there are several points at which it is extremely easy to allow a reader to take a wrong turning. Lilly's book is no exception; but he takes pains to write in the very simplest terms: in discussing the drawing-up of a birth-chart, for instance (and he refers to the square charts such as are illustrated between pp. 96 and 97), he writes:

> In the first place you are to draw the figure thus; and to know that those twelve empty spaces are by us called the twelve Houses of Heaven, that square in the middle is to write the day, year, and hour of the day when we set a figure: the first house begins ever upon that line where you see the figure 1 placed, the second house where you see the figure of 2 stand, the third house where you see the figure 3 ...

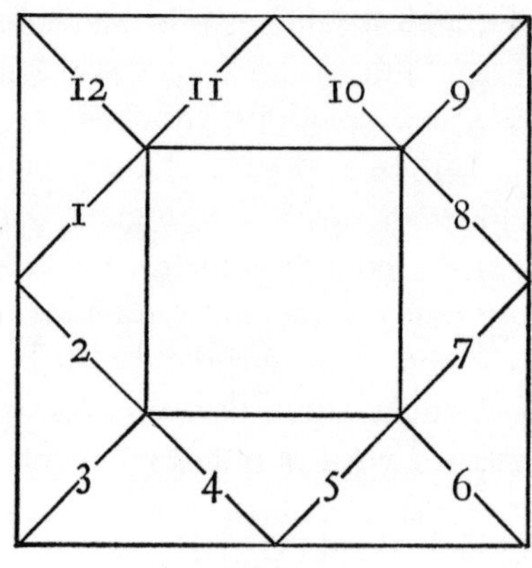


Fig. 1

and so on through the twelve houses. Not much room for misunderstanding.

Lilly then takes the reader through the calculation and setting-up of a chart for a particular time and place, in the clearest detail.

Then comes a discussion of the houses: an astrologer associates each house with a particular aspect of a client's life, or with particular characteristics and events: these are traditional, and some of them were indicated as long ago as 2000 BC. Lilly again lists them very fully and carefully:

> The Sixth House. It concerneth Men and Maid-servants, Gallislaves, Hogges, Sheep, Goats, Hares, Connies, all manner of lesser Cattle, and profit or losse got thereby; Sicknesse, its quality and cause, principal humor offending, curable or not curable, whether the disease be short or long; Day-labourers, Tenants, Farmers, Shepherds, Hogheards, Neatherds, Warriners; and it signifieth Uncles, or the Fathers Brothers and Sisters. It ruleth the inferiour part of the Belly, and intestines even to the Arse ...

Lilly then deals with the planets separately and at very considerable length. Each planet's astronomical characteristics are summarized, then its astrological significance—the physical and psychological traits it contributes to a man at whose birth it was well (or ill) placed in the sky; the occupations such a man might best try; the sicknesses from which he might suffer; the colours he would like, herbs which would do him good, places he would be happy in; and some characteristics not associated with human beings at all—the planet's effects on the weather and on plants.

Lilly's writing is, as always, extremely readable, witty, and of considerable charm. He has the gift of continually interesting the reader, either by an unexpected epithet, a piece of surprising information, or a casual, almost 'flip' style. One might look at his pages on Venus, for instance, which open as usual with astronomical notes:

> After the *Sunne* succeedeth *Venus*; who is sometimes called *Cytherea, Aphrodite, Phosphoros, Despurgo, Ericina.* She is of a bright, shining colour, and is well known amongst the vulgar by the name of the evening Starre or Hesperus; and that is when she appeares after the Sunne is set: common people call her the morning Starre, and the learned Lucifer, when she is seen long before the rising of the Sunne: her meane Motion is 59 min. and 8 seconds: her diurnall motion is sometimes 62 min. a day 64. 65. 66. or 70. 74. 76. minutes; but 82. min. shee never exceedeth; her greatest North or South latitude is nine degr. and two min. in February 1643. she had eight degr. and 36 min. for her North latitude ...

But then come the astrological details: the qualities the planet can contribute to a horoscope when 'well' or 'ill' 'dignified'—that is, according to its position in the birth chart. Venus 'well dignified' tends to make a man or woman

> quiet, not given to Law, Quarrel or Wrangling; not Vitious, Pleasant, Neat and Spruce, loving Mirth in his words and actions, cleanly in Apparel, rather Drinking much than Gluttonous, prone to Venery, oft entangled in Love matters,

> Zealous in their affections, Musicall, delighting in Baths, and all honest merry Meetings, or Maskes and Stage-Plays, easie of Beliefe, and not given to Labour, or take any Pains ...

With Venus 'ill dignified', a man becomes

> Riotous, Expensive, wholly given to Loosenesse and Lewd companies of Women, nothing regarding his Reputation, coveting unlawful Beds, Incestuous, an Adulterer, Fantastical, a meer Skip-Jack, of no Faith, no Repute, no Credit; spending his Meanes in Ale-houses, Taverns, and among Scandalous, Loose people; a meer Lazy companion, nothing careful of the things of this life, or any thing Religious; a meer Atheist and natural man.

Physically, Venus could give one 'a lovely Mouth and cherry Lips, the Face pretty fleshy, a rolling wandering Eye, a Body very delightfull, lovely and exceeding well shaped, one desirous of Trimming and making himself neat and compleat both in Cloaths and Body, a love Dimple in his Cheeks, a stedfast Eye, and full of amarous enticements'.

Lilly goes on to suggest suitable employments for people with Venus strong in their charts:

> Musicians, Gamesters, Silk-Men, Mercers, Linnen-Drapers, Painters, Jewellers, Players, Lapidaries, Embroiderers, Women-tailors, Wives, Mothers, Virgins, Choristers, Fidlers, Pipers, when joyned with the Moon Ballad-singers, Perfumers ... all such as sell those Commodities which adorne Women, either in Body (as Cloaths) or in Face (as Complexion-wafers).

Then there are the sicknesses which might be likely to attack such a person: 'principally in the Matrix and members of Generation; in the reines, belly, backe, navill and those parts; the

Gonorrea or running of the Reines; French or Spanish Pox; any disease arising by inordinate lust. Prihpism,* impotency in generation, Hernias &c. the Diabetes or pissing disease ...'

Similar details are given for every planet; then Lilly passes on to short descriptions of the Zodiacal signs. It is interesting that these get only about one-sixth of the space devoted to the planets: a reminder of the inordinate attention given to the signs as opposed to the planets in modern popular astrology; in a book of this kind published in the 1970s, the opposite proportion would be allowed.

Lilly is technical only when he has to be. His technical expositions are of course couched in what has been called 'astrologers' jargon', and it is perhaps fair to point out that astrologers used the language available to them; any lack of clarity is the result of the modern reader not having the basic knowledge many sixteenth- and seventeenth-century readers possessed.

When Lilly says (discussing how to discover 'Whether a Damsel be Virtuous or not') 'Behold the lord of the 7th, the cusp of the 7th, and the Sun; and if they be in fixed signs and well aspected, you may judge that she is correct', he is making a simple astrological statement. A modern reader, even one who reads his daily horoscope with meticulous attention, will not know what 'the lord of the 7th' is, what 'the 7th' is, what a 'fixed' sign is, or when they are well or ill aspected.

For the astrologer, Book II is perhaps the most fascinating, providing an insight into Lilly's methods of work; to the lay reader it is of negligible interest, however—except inasmuch as it provides insight into Lilly's professional life, the sort of questions his clients brought him, and in some cases into his private life (for he did not hesitate to use personal examples if they were illuminating).

The book consists of a list of questions an astrologer might wish to ask, or might be asked, and Lilly's means of solving them; all in technical astrological language and in great detail. One example will perhaps suffice: 'Whether one absent will returne or

* priapism.

not, and when?' Lilly's guide to the discovery of the answer to that question occupies over a thousand words, starting with a consideration of the astrological houses involved:

> Consider by what house the absent party is signified, and what Planet is his significator;* then see if his significator be in the first house (let his Journey be whither it will), yet if it be a long Journey, and beyond seas, then see if it be in the ninth, or if in the twelfth, if a very long Journey was undertaken; or if he be in the fifth, if a moderate Journey was intended, or in the third, if a short Journey: If he be in any of these houses, or do commit his disposition to any Planet in any of these houses, it signifies the absent will not dye in that Voyage, but returne: if he be in the seventh, he will returne, but not in hast; nay, he will tarry long; and he is at the time of the Question in that country unto which he first went, nor hath he hitherto had any thoughts of returning; howsoever, now he hath: If he be in the fourth, he will stay and abide longer than if he were in the seventh: if his significator be in the third or ninth, and in any aspect with any Planet in the ascendant, the absent is preparing to come home, and is fully resolved thereof; or if he be in the second, in aspect with a Planet in the ninth, he is endeavouring to provide moneys for his Voyage homewards, nor will it be long ere he be at home; but if he be in a Cadent† house, and not behold his own ascendant, he neither cares for his returne, or hath any thoughts thereof, nor can he come if so be he would ...

And so on. When it is considered that Lilly goes into this sort of detail for no less than 200 questions, the size and comprehensiveness of *Christian Astrology* can be judged. And then, in Book III, he goes on to deal with other technical matters, to give alternative

* Significator: in this case, the planet which rules the Zodiacal sign rising over the eastern horizon at the time the chart was drawn.

† Cadent: the third, sixth, ninth or twelfth houses.

methods of house erection, to print various tables, to consider the houses once more, together with certain questions the answers to which are particularly geared to them ('The Sixth House: of the Infirmities of Bodies, Kinds and Qualities of Diseases, how discoverable from the Planets and Signs ... of the Tooth-ach, Of the Falling Sicknesse ... Of violent Falls ... Of servants and small cattle ...'

Then (and only then: it is the lay public that has always placed greatest emphasis on 'foretelling the future' in a literal sense) he turns to the possibility of discovering certain trends in the future lives of his clients.

It can hardly be denied that even if Lilly's enormous success as a consultant astrologer depended to a great extent on his own quick wit and the gullibility of his clients, his *Christian Astrology* is a remarkable book, gathering together and rationalizing the extant astrological lore, broadening it by adding his own observations, and presenting it as a scientific body of knowledge.

If one looks at the astronomical and scientific, medical or chemical textbooks of the period, one can only admire Lilly's industry; and his comprehensive knowledge of his subject.

The laudatory verses printed at the front of the book (as the custom was) are negligible: the one friend of Lilly's who at his best was an entertaining amateur poet was Elias Ashmole, and he was ill when the author was collecting the verses from his other acquaintances—from John Booker, so recently his enemy, and the rest. But when Ashmole recovered, and read the book, he sent Lilly a set of verses celebrating it. Too late for printing, even at the end of the book, it conveyed his sincere congratulations:

> I have read your Booke, & though I crawle
> (As th' Sick must doe) behind the press, and all
> That sung your praise in Front; yet in ye rear
> (Rather than not be seen) let me appear;
> And tell the World, it owes much to your Pen
> That has unlockt these cloyster'd secrets, when
> None else would do't; teaching us how to read
> The Minde of Heaven in English, and not dread

It to be Conjuring; so that by your paines
No room for that black scandall now remaines ...

Though that was an over-optimistic view, *Christian Astrology* was certainly the major and the most complete astrological text-book to be written in English during the seventeenth century.

# 4

# Astrologer at Work

*Behold Urania with a Lilly deckt,*
*Presents her selfe to England's gracious view.*
*Let Envie's square, or opposite aspect*
*Nor dare at her a frowning looke to shew;*
*Lest it be said, for such ungratefull scornes,*
*A Lilly late hath sprung among the thornes.*

WILL ROE, introductory
verse to *Christian Astrology*

The publication of *Christian Astrology* brought Lilly much congratulation and admiration, and many clients; it also brought him a considerable number of more or less lunatic correspondents. A few letters survive: three awful poems from 'F.T.', addressed to 'my woorthy freind Mr William Lilly on his incomparable Arte of Astrology', and two or three other sets of verses not much better.

Then there were reports of strange lights seen in the sky, and requests for Lilly's interpretation of them; reports of several parhelia, or 'mock suns', carefully illustrated; a number of requests from one Jeremiah Shakerley for help with his calculations (he was trying to teach himself astrology); and two reports of earthquakes in Norwich, from Thomas Dey, who reported that one of them—on December 9th, 1654—was 'suche an earthquake as many did plainly feele the bed shake under them', and what did Mr Lilly intend to do about it?

Several letters survive, too, from readers wanting Lilly to cast their horoscopes: Robert Sterrell, for instance, wrote from the

Parsonage of Little Wigborow, in Essex, giving his birth date, and detailing 'the markes of my body ... a red, little wart on the left side of my nose, betwist the nostrill and the nose end', and several others. 'My mayne query,' he said, 'is whether I shall attaine any Competent Skill in Astrologie, which I have ever loved, and honoured, in despite of malicious Ignorance ...'

And there were letters such as the famous one written from Greenham near Newbury on September 8th, 1649, 'at halfe an houre after 4 in the afternoone', and 'left with the postmaster of Speenhamland to be conveighed unto' Lilly. One Roger Knight had been in touch with the astrologer some time ago. Now, he wrote again:

> Sir. I was born three weeks before my time, near Newbury, on the 16th August, 1619; but what houre I cannot learne, I am very tall of stature, goeing stoopinge a little at the shoulders, I am leane, havinge thinne flaxen haire, of a longish visage & a pale complexion, gray-eyed, havinge some impediment in my upper lippe, which hath a small mole on the right side thereof: I have also on the right side of my forehead an other little mole, I am of a mellancholly disposition, havinge been all the course of my life in an unsettled condition. When I was last with you, I was very desirous to know your judgement about what time you did thinke I might be settled, and I did then acquaint you that there was a match propounded unto my father for me unto a gentlewoman who lived south from the place of my usuall residence: she was borne near Worcester, in May, 1613, but for the most part of her life she had lived south or south west from me. She is an Aynesse* of a reasonable tall stature, of a brownish haire, of an ovall visage, and a saturnine complexion, very discreete, and excellent well spoken, all which when I was with you, you described unto me, and told me that possibly I might succeed in the businesse if she was not

* Aynesse: firstborn, eldest child.

preengaged which I should know before the 10th of Maye then following, and in case it did come to anything, it should notwithstandinge goe but slowely on at the first, and that I should have many rubbs and delays, during the time of Mercury his beinge retrograde, but at his coming to be direct all thinges should goe fairly on.

Things, however, had not gone fairly on, and Mr Knight, enclosing eleven shillings for favour of reply, wished to know when he might again approach the lady, and if she did not receive him, whether he had better not go abroad immediately. Lilly's reply, alas, is lost.

For the best view of Lilly at work in his consulting-room, we must go to his notebooks and records, some of which survive in his friend Ashmole's collection, now at the Bodleian Library. The names of his clients are often omitted from the charts he drew up to answer their queries: often these are headed by an obvious pseudonym, or left blank except for the often-repeated words *Quid agendum*—what to do?

Still, it is possible to get a very good idea of the range of his clientele: from servant-maids, members of the armed forces, tradesmen, to professional men and aristocrats like Lady Wildgoose, Lady Kensington, Lady Slingsby, Lady Abergavenny and Lady Diana Porter; then there were Lord Galloway, Lord Gerard, the fourth Earl of Pembroke, and the first Earl of Shaftesbury. Lilly was not alone in being consulted by the nobility: many other astrologers—notably John Booker, who was to become the second best-known astrologer in England—had equally notable clients; and Ashmole was to be consulted by the King himself, during the 1670s.

Lilly's caution about writing full details of his cases in his notebooks, irritating though it is for us, was natural; apart from laying him open to the accusation of taking the part of one person or party against another, full notes could have proved more than interesting to any potential blackmailer.

The casebooks contain file on file of astrological charts (over 4,000 between June 1654 and September 1656). The square, blank 'figures' were stamped into the book with a home-made die, and the positions of the planets entered in them after the calculations had been done (sometimes in the margin of the notebooks). Occasionally the question asked would be jotted in the margin too. In March 1644, for instance, appears a chart drawn up for 'Mr Whitby, if good for his son to go to war, and if returne safely.' And underneath, the comment that 'The young man is fixed and resolved to go to ye warre ...' and the conclusion that he would return safely.

Then there were questions of health (a young man of twenty-one 'had been a souldier, but without health or fitness ... subject to the stone, gravell in the kidneys ...'), of career ('if good to stay out his apprenticeship, yea or no?'), of trade ('if good to take a shoppe'); other questions of stolen property (he was asked about £20 stolen from 'a fat woman in Southwark', about £150 missing from a Spanish ship, about plate lost in Gray's Inn); success in this undertaking or in that; good or ill fortune in love ('Of two propounded, which to accept?' as one girl asked); then marriage, pregnancy; and matters of life and death ('If my husband would be hanged for stealing 30 bullocks?').

Most of Lilly's clients came to see him; of the relatively few that wrote, he did not keep many letters. There is one, undated, from an Anne Veisey, of Oxfordshire:

> Be pleas to doe me the favor ... as to set doune in righting the nature and quallity of those men you conceave broke up my house as allso what accidents are like to happen this yeare to us, either by theeves quartering* or payments or what else you please to insert.

Then there are the miscellaneous enquiries, some of them throwing interesting light on common problems of everyday life at the time—such as a letter from one Richard Robinson, who in 1672 wrote to both Lilly and Ashmole asking them to find him, by astrological or other means, a job. He had learned mathematics, but

* Presumably the billeting of soldiers.

trowly, I dare not publickly to profess ye mathematicks for feare of being prest to sea (for ye Press is very hot), & they say they would be glad of mathematicians if they could find them; but I hate ye Sea, and should make but a pittyful souldier: for Venus is Lady of my Ascendant and Mars Lord of my geniture I thinke, so that I was not cut out for a Souldier ...

Alas, we do not know what became of Mr Robinson. Nor have we any information about the future of one Matthew Andrews, who approached Lilly in 1670 to ask whether it was an apt time for him to enter into an arrangement with Lord St Albans to procure a Register's place in Chancery, and a Commissioner's place in the navy. Then there was 'W.B.', who on May 4th, 1651, found himself, like many similar men, in prison. He wrote:

I have allwaies in faithfulnesse and integritie ingaged in the publique Cause of my country, against all warres, Invasions & Insurrections, & have not in the least blemished the truth or steyned my owne honour by being perfidious to that righteous cause, by adheringe either in principles or action to the profest enemies of peace, and my country; and for my zeale, and faithfullnesse unto those thinges, and those many righteous declarations, and desires of those that are now in present power, I am reduced into dangers and streights by havinge incurred the hatred of their interests ... And yet now I have been this twoe yeares, and above in greate affliction by the present power, and my conscience testifies unto me that I am truely innocent and have been the greatly wronged partie ...

And would he be released in the near future? No trace of his name is to be found after 1651.

The case brought to Lilly's attention by Vincent Wing was less serious. He wrote to Lilly on July 28th, 1650:

Honoured Mr Lilly, a worthy gentlewoman of this town hath requested me to write a line unto you, concerning a great number of fine linens that was stolen in the night time, the last week, out of a private garden close under her house. And because she much fancies astrology, I would desire you to give her your advice therein, and to write a line or two back, whether you think they may be recoverable or not. Her husband is a Member of Parliament, and one (I suppose) well known to you, and is a man that highly esteems of your singular parts. Your very real friend and servant, Vincent Wing.

That letter is an example of the respect in which Lilly was held by his peers: Wing was himself a well-known astrologer—by profession a land surveyor, but a man who had issued his own ephemerides for over twenty years ('the best to be had', according to the astronomer Flamsteed); he was himself often consulted on astrological as well as astronomical matters, and was to fulfil one of his own prophecies by dying on the day and prompt to the hour he had foretold. But in this case, Lilly probably declined to be of assistance, on legal grounds.

He had to be extremely wary. It would be quite illegal (as will be seen) for him to attempt to tell anyone where stolen goods were, by astrology or any other means. And there were other embarrassments lying in wait for the incautious astrologer: only a decade or so earlier, a man who had been robbed at a Huntingdon inn had been given a description of the thief by an astrologer, and as a result had had the landlord's son arrested. Unfortunately, he had failed to look his suspect in the mouth: the astrologer had claimed that the thief had discoloured teeth. The boy's full set was white and sparkling. His accuser was in turn accused of wrongful arrest, and the astrologer presumably suffered in consequence. Lilly himself received at least one anonymous threat of a beating if he continued to accuse a particular man of theft. In *Christian Astrology*, however, he did not flinch from giving several rules for discovering as much about stolen property as anyone could possibly want to know. (After all, if the consultation was a failure, it was always possible that a mistake had been made in the timing of events—crucial to the setting-up of a proper chart;

or perhaps, even, there had been an error in the astronomical calculations.)

One could discover, provided the time had been correctly observed, and the 'figure' was accurate, 'whether the thing missing be stolne, or fled of itselfe,' and having fixed that it had been stolen, one could find out the age of the thief, whether man or woman, the colour and kind of his clothing ('you must know the colour of the cloathing by the Planets, Signs and degrees, and the House the Significator is in; and after the mixture the one with the other, accordingly judge the colour of their Cloathes'). Then one could discover whether the thief's names were long or short, and with luck the letters they began with, though further than that Lilly himself would not go:

> They who are conversant in judging many thefts, might much perfect the judgment; I have known it hold true very many times; my greatest imployment keeps me from further observations ... Some modern Professors have endeavoured to give a probable conjecture what Christian name the Thief is of ... for my part I never use this way,nor yet have much credited it.

But he would certainly claim to be able to discover whether the thief was at home, in town or country, with or without the stolen goods about him; in what direction his house was, and perhaps some distinguishing marks which would reveal it:

> If the Moon be square, conjunction or opposition to Mars, the door is burned with iron, fire or candle, or hath been cut with some iron instrument; if the Moon be in trine or sextile to Mars, say the door of the Thief's house is mended with iron; if the Moon be but newly encreased in light, his gate or door is part under the earth, or under a Bankside, or they goe down by a step, Moon in a fixed or moveable Signe, he hath but one door outwardly, in common Signe more than one ...

Another area of the chart would show where in his house the thief had hidden the stolen goods: 'in a dark place or part of the house, or in a desolate or stinking place and deep, be it a siege-house or jakes, where people seldome come'; in a kitchen, hall or shop, a cistern or library; 'the place or the seat of a Woman, or Bed, or Cloathes, or where women are most conversant.'

*Christian Astrology* reveals, like the notebooks, the range of questions Lilly's clients asked him. He was often, of course, asked about the possible time of someone's death, and was (like all astrologers) extremely cautious: 'You must carefully avoid pronouncing Death rashly ... concerning the absolute time of death of any party, I have found it best to be wary, and have as much as I could refrained this manner of judgment.' If this disappointed the clients, Lilly might perhaps rely on a little retrospective astrology, just to show how well the system worked—much as a modern scientist might demonstrate the efficiency of a lie-detector by working with questions the answers to which were confirmable. He notes that when a client approached him, who had been born on March 14th, 1632, and appeared sceptical, he told him his wife was a virago, and that he had recently had a dispute with her regarding the disposition of her property; true, said the man. And, Lilly went on, 'some great lord or courtier' had been engaged by her to act on her behalf. The client was convinced. At other times the astrologer relied on his old trick of being able to tell a man 'what marke, mole or scarre he hath in any Member of his Body', which he apparently did with continuing accuracy.

The questions, once put, revealed the sort of worries one might expect during a period when no quick means of communication existed: 'a woman being at my house in the country, demanded if her son were with his Master, or at her own house'—no telephone, of course, to reveal the answer. A long passage in *Christian Astrology* deals with the resolution of a very common question indeed: 'of a ship, and whatever are in her, her safety or destruction'. And of course during the war there were many enquiries about the safety of a loved one.

In November, 1646, a Citizen of London being gone into the West of England, and no newes for many weeks had where

> he was, his owne Brother with great importunity moved me to give my judgment concerning these particulars: 1 if living or dead? If dead, whether killed by souldiers? for at this time our miserable Kingdome was full of souldiery. 2 If living, when he should heare of him? and where he was? 3 when he would come home.

A visit to an astrologer was about the only hope of discovering what had happened when, for instance, someone was absent from home for a prolonged period. Wives and mothers left behind when their men marched off to join the King or Cromwell often came to Lilly for his advice: in 1649, one woman asked whether her husband was alive or dead, to be told that he had died soon after leaving for the war six years before.

There are many enquiries on record about missing ships and mariners: he was asked whether a ship was likely to have been in danger, whether particular members of the crew—the carpenter, the surgeon, the commander—were safe; when a return to port was likely, and whether it would be safely effected. If a ship was missing, and eventually presumed lost, he would be asked how it had been sunk, and when—often by the insurers (who sometimes checked up in advance, by asking his opinion of the chances of a safe voyage, before the ship had left port).

Particularly in the last two years of the civil war, there were many questions about troop movements and coming battles:

> In the year His Majesty's Army being then Rampant, severall Reports were given out, that his Majesty had taken Cambridge, &c., a wel-affected person enquires of me, if the Newes were true or false? Whereupon I erected a Figure, and Gave Judgment All that he heard was untruth, and that the Towne neither was, or should be taken by Him or his Forces.

The notebooks still in the Ashmolean collection are incomplete, but there is sufficient evidence to show that Lilly was drawing up at least 2,000 charts a year at his peak; Booker would have been doing as well. The regime they followed was a strict one. There was no question of guessing where, say, a lost article was to be found—all was set out by rule:

> If the Significators be strong, and in watry signes, it's in the Buttery, Dairy or Wash-house, or neare Water ... if in a fiery Signe, it's near the Chimney, or where Iron is, or in, or near, the Walls of the house. If in earthy signes, the thing hid in the ground or earth, under or neer some Pavement or Floor, and if you find the thing to be mislaid out of the house in any ground, it lies near the Bridge or Stile where people come into the ground.

Many of the domestic problems Lilly had to deal with were, of course, amatory; and again, he was extremely careful in giving advice. 'I must charge all sonnes of Art,' he warns, 'to be sparing in delivering judgment upon these queries, rather to be silent; for as men we may erre, and so by delivering an unluckie judgement, be authors of much mischiefe.'

However, he did not hesitate to claim that he could advise a man whether or not to marry, how many husbands a woman would have, who would be master of the two, whether a woman was rich or not, how the couple would agree after marriage, 'whether she be a Maid, or Chaste, of whom the querie is ... of a woman whether she be corrupt, or hath a Lover besides her Husband, or sweetheart ... whether a woman trades with any but her Husband.' (Not, if may be noted, whether a husband traded with any but his wife.) But again, he emphasizes that 'these judgements must be carefully observed and well delivered before judgement be propounded in the negative, *viz* that she is not honest.'

Concrete examples of these questions appear in the note-books: a weaver asks 'if her friend loved her as he should love her,' and Joan Jones, who lived in the Strand, asked if John Fuller would indeed marry her. (She was no maid, Lilly noted, and answered in the negative.) Against another chart, he scribbles: 'One got with child—if the man would marry her?' and elsewhere there are other questions about the honesty of men making proposals of marriage. These questions are often the seventeenth-century counterpart of letters to the women's magazines of today: should the writer marry 'the little man'? No, came the answer.

The astrologer's interest in a family need not end with marriage: he could go on to say whether one would have children, and when; whether a woman were pregnant or not; whether the child would be male or female; when the birth would occur; and later could explore and advise on the relationship between parents and children, or, in the case of necessity, 'whether the child is the Sonne of him who is reputed to be his Father'.

While modern astrologers would join Samuel Butler in making fun of Lilly's notes for discovering the whereabouts of a stolen object, many of the questions he was concerned with are still being asked today. But the answers are now given on a different basis, for Lilly's astrology was still largely horary astrology—that is, based on the moment when a question was asked, rather than on a birth-time. The reason was simple: few ordinary people in Stuart England—outside royalty or the nobility—would have known accurately the time of their birth. Ordinary people, even if they felt inclined to note the time of a birth, almost always lacked the means to do so.

Horary astrology is now generally discredited. But Lilly's clients accepted it. They had to; there was, generally speaking, nothing else available to them. And it did not occur to Lilly to doubt the proposition that it was a proper way of going about things. He discussed the questions put to him with high seriousness, and there is no indication that he doubted the efficacy of the astrological arguments involved.

The notebooks contain, as I have said, only a few written queries, other than those Lilly noted for some reason or other in the margin (perhaps because he wanted to quote them in his books). When he does make a note, it is generally very terse: as when in 1645 Dennis Prickman came to ask 'if his Mrs would live', and inside the centre of the chart the astrologer noted 'shee died within a fortnight'.

But there is one example of his work which shows a full astrological judgment such as a modern astrologer might write for an interested client: a character delineation for William Pennington, a Royalist client whom Lilly rescued some years previously from a designing woman, and who had become a friend and supporter. Beautifully penned, the judgment consists of twelve pages of characterization and ten pages of 'progressions', or notes on the future. It is technically written—indeed, I have found not one example of a judgment written in lay terms, which confirms that Lilly more often than not talked to those of his clients without a working knowledge of astrology, and only wrote when he was questioned by his peers, by someone like Pennington, or Ashmole, who could understand the astrological allusions.

The headings in the first section of the Pennington judgment show the thoroughness with which Lilly worked: first comes 'a generall astrological judgement', then 'Temperament; of Riches; of Kindred; *De Matrimonia*' (written in a strange mixture of Latin and English), 'Children; Honour and Preferment; of Travell; *De parentibus*; Of freinds and freindshipp; Life and death, number of years, and quality of death.'

Lilly's reputation was growing: his clients were becoming more distinguished, and he was gradually becoming well known to the man in the street. But the extent to which he was to take part in the astrologers' war of the 1640s was to make him even better known.

I have something more to write of Charles the ~~second~~ First
his misfortunes, wherein I was concerned, the matter
happened in 1648 but I thought good to insert it hear,
having after this no more occasion to mention him,
his Maty being in Carsbrook Castle in the Isle of Wight
the Kentish men in great numbers rose in Armes and
joyned with the Lord Goring, a considerable number
of the best shipps revolted from the Parlament,
the Citizens of London wear forward to rise against
the Parlament, his Maty layd his designe to escape
out of prison, by sawing the Iron Barrs of his chamber
window, a small shipp, was provided and anchored
not farr from the Castle to bring him into Sussex, horses
wear provided ready to carry him through Sussex into Kent,
that so hee might bee in the head of the Army in Kent,
and from thence to march imediatly to London, where
thousands then would have armed for him; the Lady W Horwood
came to mee, acquaints mee hearwith, I gott G: ffarmer +
to make a Saw, to cutt the Iron barrs in sunder, I meane
to saw them, and Aqua fortis besides, his Maty in a small
tyme did his work, the barrs gave liberty for him to go
out, hee was out with his body till hee came to his breast,
but, then his hart failing, hee proceeded no further, when
this was discovered, as soon after it was, hee was narrowly looked
after, and no opportunity after that could bee devised to
inlarge him; About September the Parlament sent
their Commissioners with propositions unto him into the Isle
of Wight, the Lord William Sea being one; the Lady
W. came again unto mee from him or by his consent, to
bee directed; after perusall of my figure, I told her the
Commissioners would bee ther such a day, I elected a day and
hour when to receive the Commissioners and Propositions, and
so soon as the propositions wear read, to sign them, and
make hast with all speed to come up with the Commissioners
to London, the Army being then farr distant from London
and the Citty inraged stoutly against them, hee promised
hee would so do; that night the Commissioners came, and old
Sea and his Maty had private Conference till one in the
morning, the King acquaints Sea with his intention, who
clearly disswaded him from signing the Propositions, telling
him they wear not fitt for him to signe, that hee had

William Lilly

+ He was a most ingenious Lock-Smith, and dwelt in Bow-Lane.

4. The fair copy of Lilly's autobiography: he describes his involvement in the escape attempt of Charles I
(*Curators of the Bodleian Library*)

5. 'Hieroglyphic' forecasting the Plague (1665), printed in *Monarchy or No Monarchy* (1651)
(*Curators of the Bodleian Library*)

# 5

# Astrologer at War

*Do not our great Reformers use*
*This Sidrophel to forebode News;*
*To write of Victories next Year,*
*And Castles taken yet i' th' Air?*
*Of Battles fought at Sea, and Ships*
*Sunk two Years hence, the last Eclipse?*
*A total Overthrow giv'n the King*
*In Cornwall, Horse and Foot, next Spring?*

*Hudibras* (II,III:171)

One tends to forget, when reading about the Civil War, that to a large number of Englishmen it was in the main simply a nuisance. Historians chronicle the adventures of the heroes—of those men who felt passionately on either side of the question. But thousands of Englishmen simply tried to go on living their lives as though nothing were happening; though as the war went on, this became gradually more and more difficult. They stayed at home and faced the problems the war brought without too much complaint (dangerous to complain, whichever side one's auditors were on); their horses were confiscated or simply stolen by the army; soldiers were quartered on them, broke their furniture and offered no payment.

Lilly was not among the most passionate adherents of Parliament. At first, he was dragged into the war to the extent that other people were: he bore with ill-humour the weekly assessment imposed for the support of the armies (he was fond of money, and his support for Parliament fell a good deal short of paying such taxes cheerfully). He had by now a sufficient fortune not to be seriously inconvenienced by the demands of the tax-collectors. Some of his neighbours fared much worse: many villagers and cottagers were ruined by the war, or at least seriously impoverished by it.

All the same, his income diminished like everyone else's. The Excise, or purchase tax, put up prices, and there was a rapid rate of inflation—one London diarist, a barrister called Green, wrote in his journal that 'we begin now to see that a Kingdome according to human discourse is not so easily ruinated and will commonly hold by stronger roots than we imagined; we may hold out, if God has not determined otherwise, two or three years longer at this rate—only grow poorer and poorer'.

That was in 1642, and the war was to go on for another three-and-a-half years. For the first eighteen months, the King looked very much like winning, or at least holding his own. London was a Parliamentary citadel, and on his visits from Hersham to the city to see important clients, or to keep an eye on the house in the Strand, Lilly found it in a sorry state: the Royalist army menaced the capital, the people were panicky and disturbed, and the Common Council very properly set up defences. Some streets were bricked up (St James's, Holborn, St John Street), there were turnpikes where one was challenged and had to provide evidence of identity. It was all highly unpleasant, even if the situation did persuade a large number of people to go to Lilly for diagnosis of the situation and of their personal prospects.

Lilly had a shrewd political sense, and while the Royalist forces had the advantage (by the end of 1643 Charles was master of all England west of a line from the Wash to Southampton) he kept fairly quiet. But gradually it became obvious that as Parliament got its forces properly organized, the King's chance of victory waned. Heavier taxes supported the development of a strong parliamentary cavalry to match the Cavaliers' splendid horse; in 1643 Cromwell persuaded the Scots to support him. Marston Moor, in July 1644, marked the turning-point.

Now, out at Hersham, Lilly began to think it time to contribute to an aspect of the story of the Civil War which historians have neglected: the battle of the astrologers.

It is not easy to gauge the extent to which astrology was used as propaganda during the war, or the extent to which such propaganda was 'official'. Naturally, astrologers supporting one side or the other emphasized those planetary trends which favoured the combatants they supported. This kind of activity, while acceptable to the respective armies, was scarcely official. On the other hand, there is no reason to disbelieve Lilly's account of the visit he and John Booker made to Colchester in 1648 to encourage the Parliamentary troops then laying siege to the town; and the pension of £100 a year awarded to him that year was certainly partly in recognition of those services.

Most English astrologers of the seventeenth century published their opinions on the war; in fact considering the gamble involved in coming out strongly in favour of either side, the number of astrological pamphlets with a definite political bias one way or the other is suprising. But Lilly and the royalist astrologer George Wharton were by far the two most active.

Wharton was an enthusiastic supporter of the King, and not only astrologically. A blacksmith's son, he had been publishing almanacs since 1641, calling himself 'Naworth'—a pseudonym which provided his enemies with many opportunities for cheap gibes. In 1642, he sold all his estates at Kirby Kendal, in Yorkshire, and raised a troop of horse which was totally routed in a fight at Stow, near Gloucester, in 1643. Whereupon Wharton took himself to Oxford, and the King, and concentrated on paper skirmishes, at which he was rather more accomplished.

Life in Oxford was, at first, not at all unpleasant: fashionable women (always interested in astrology) danced in the rooms of the colleges; plays were written and acted; fashions in dress were discussed; there were wooings and undoings, and Wharton—a personable man of some wit and education—was in his element.

His first literary and astrological opponent was none other than John Booker, the licenser of astrological books with whom Lilly had already been arguing. Booker, in a paper called *Mercurius Coelius*, attacked Wharton's 1644 almanac, written 'with

His Majesty's command'. Wharton scurried to his desk and replied in *Mercurio-Coelico-Mastix*, 'an Anti-caveat to all such, as have (heretofore) had the misfortune to be cheated and Deluded by that Grand and Traiterous Imposter of this Rebellious Age, John Booker'. Then came Booker's rejoinder (neglecting, for once, the demi-semi-Latin beloved of the quasi-scholars of the time), *A Rope for a Parret, or, a Cure for a Rebell Past Cure*. Wharton sought, he wrote, 'to wound the Parliament, and in it the whole Kingdom, Religion, Law, Libertie &c.' The pamphlet is full of splendid, typical polemic:

> As for the word *Rebell*, I tell thee *Rogue* (it is thy own name) I can give thee no other Title: and I meant thee, and all thy Adherants, that have thus rent (almost in peeces) the most flourishing Kingdom of the Christian World: Rent, said I? you have divided the King from his Parliament; the Head from the Body; of which Body, you are a rotton Member ... and many more such like as yourself; all of you must be cut off, or else there will be a grievous pain in the Head ... I heartily and hourly pray God that the King would return to His Parliament at Westminster ... where the true Physitians and Chirurgians of the Kingdom are in daily Consultation.

Lilly had so far escaped Wharton's notice. But then came the publication, on August 8th, 1644, of *A Prophesy of the White King*. Lilly made his future political stance quite clear: 'You see what stormes, what miseries, what cruell warres our Nation is once like to suffer by the meanes and procurement of a King called a *White King* [who] brings over strangers to destroy us, and God gives us command to provide sepulchers and graves for him and them ...'

The White King was immediately recognizable as Charles, for, Lilly says, the ancient prophecy which he translates and interprets refers to a king who 'either by his oft and frequent wearing of a white apparell, or extremely delighting in that colour, or ... by some action or actions of his should give his subjects occasion to repute him the White King.' And had not Charles insisted in wearing at his Coronation white clothing rather than the more usual purple? Though Lilly carefully accused of knavery those who might claim that anyone living could fit such a description, the inference was obvious.

The prophecy itself is given in Latin, but was translated from the Welsh of about 677 AD (Lilly claims). Among other things, it foretells that after a battle at 'an ancient seate near a running River ... assaulted before and behind, or on all sides ... the White & noble King shall dye;' after which 'the chicken of the Eagle' should eventually pacify the Kingdom.

Lilly himself, via the prophecy, foretold

> a serious consultation or debate of the States of the Kingdome, whether they shall againe admit of Monarchy, by reason of the generall hatred the people had to the White King (so that here appeares an extreme unwillingnesse to accept of any Kingly title) the unnaturall deportment of the White King having so much enraged the British spirits.

And he encourages Parliament to hope for victory, despite setbacks:

> I observe by the best and truest relations, we have not had on the Parliament's side one victory of any consequence, but in our hearts we first despaired of the successe: Let us still call on this mercifull God in all our wayes: cherish and countenance our Generals and the respective Officers of our Armies of each Nation: extend compassion to the maimed souldier: and really pay the fighting souldier his wages, but specially be at unity amongst ourselves.

A Royalist defeat had come while the *Prophesy* was still at the printer's: on July 2nd, Prince Rupert's 11,000 foot soldiers and 7,000 cavalry had faced the Roundheads' 20,000 foot and 7,000 horse at Marston Moor (the battle after which Rupert for the first time gave Cromwell the nickname 'Ironsides'). Though 6,000 Royalist horse escaped, 3,000 Royalists were killed, York surrendered, and the north was lost to the King.

Even the fiasco at Lostwithiel, when Essex had to sail out of Fowey, his tail between his legs, while his men were captured at Castle Dore, and marched through towns and villages populated by mocking Royalist supporters to captivity or (most of them) death, could not upset the new balance in favour of Cromwell. Wharton, like other Cavalier supporters, was disconsolate and accordingly short-tempered. In his 1645 almanac he attacked Lilly by name.

The latter (rather unreasonably, on the whole) was 'highly incensed' and

> to vindicate my reputation, and to cry quittance with Naworth ... to work again I went for *Anglicus* 1645; which as soon as finished I got to the press, thinking every day one month till it was public: I therein made use of the King's nativity, and finding that his ascendant was approaching to the quadrature of Mars, about June, 1645, I have this unlucky judgment; 'If now we fight, a victory stealeth upon us;' and so it did in June, 1645, at Naseby, the most fatal overthrow he ever had.

It was a lucky stroke for Lilly, despite the fact that the almanac also contained various prognostications that were not fulfilled. Prince Rupert, for instance, would probably die in his twenty-eighth year, Lilly asserted. He lived to be sixty-three—despite the fact that Lilly sought to prove the truth of his prediction by the old trick of asserting that 'on his right arme he will find some eminant Mark or Scarre, and on his right legge another not farre from his navell, and on the reines of his backe two more.').

By now, Lilly's almanacs had a large circulation—his name familiar through the success of *A Prophesy of the White King*, which sold out its first printing (of 1,800 copies) in three days, and had been often reprinted.

Though the size of editions of books registered with the Stationers' Company was limited by regulation, almanac-printers were exempt; carefully restricting the impressions of most books to 1,250 or 1,500 copies, the regulation excepts grammars, prayer-books and catechisms (of which there might be four impressions a year, each of 2,500 or 3,000), and excepts also 'the *statutes* and *proclamacons* with all other bookes belonginge to ye office of her majesties printer which by reason of her majesties affayres are to be limited to no numbers. And except all *Calenders* printed Red and Black and also except all *Almanackes* and *prognostigations*.'

The *Merlinus Anglicus* of 1646 sold 13,500 copies; of the following year, 17,000; of 1648, 18,500. By 1649, Lilly could count on a scale of somewhere near 30,000—and of course there were many more readers, for most almanacs were passed from hand to hand. When Thomas Gataker, the Puritan, tried to buy a copy of Lilly's 1653 prognostication, on which he was preparing an attack, he was at first unable to do so—it was sold out.

This does not mean that Lilly made an enormous income from his almanac sales: most small almanacs sold for 2d each, the larger ones for 6d, which barely covered printing costs. But the value of such a circulation as advertisement was enormous.

Despite the increased cost of living, Lilly was living very comfortably in his rented house at Hersham. Many of his clients were local, and were only too happy to pay him in kind: fresh eggs, wildfowl snared down by the Thames, a duck or a chicken ... it all had to be eaten fresh, of course, for the price of salt was prohibitive; but there was no hardship in that.

By this time their fellow-lodgers had left, and Lilly and his grumpy wife had the house to themselves—not a particularly happy arrangement. Later in his life, friends would come to stay; at this period, people disliked travelling any distance unless on absolutely necessary journeys, and Lilly anyway had few intimate friends. He still occasionally went into London over the rough London–Southampton road, miry in winter and hard and dusty in summer. On the way, signs of the war (even in a part of England undevastated by actual battle) could be seen: a house burned down because its owner did not take kindly to housing soldiers billeted there; another house empty because of eviction for non-payment of taxes.

From time to time, he rode his horse into a spinney or behind a hedge, as a clatter of hooves announced the approach of a band of soldiers. They might be friendly to a passing stranger; they might not. High-spirited young men bored by inaction, they often captured and stripped a passer-by merely for amusement.

They might not have touched Lilly, of course, for he was beginning to be extremely well known: his almanacs were read by literate to illiterate, and in fact he had done a great deal to help create a feeling of corporate loyalty in a Parliamentary army which consisted largely of an uneasy mixture of pressed men and enthusiastic volunteers.

Lilly's success cannot have pleased Wharton (it probably infuriated him more than the rather quiet *Modest Reply* to his criticisms which Lilly appended to the 1645 almanac). In *An Astrological Judgement upon hs Majesties Present Martch: Begun from Oxford, May 7, 1645*, Wharton attacked both Booker and Lilly on the grounds that their

> sole endeavour hath hitherto been by most disloyall and ambiguous Phrases to animate and hasten on the *Rebels* and other *Conspirators* to plot and attempt *Mischiefe* against His *Majesty* ... whereas an honest and discreet Artist ought not to divulge any thing (especially of *Princes*) that may any way tend to endanger their Persons, but either not to meddle at all, or else to deale privately with the Prince himselfe.

Wharton's main purpose in this pamphlet was to encourage the King and his forces on their march from Oxford; and he did so in no uncertain terms:

> It is most apparent to every impartiall and ingenuous Judgement; That (although His *Majesty* cannot expect to be secured from every triviall disaster that may befall his Army, either by the too much presumption, ignorance, or negligence of some particular persons, which is frequently incident and unavoydable in the best of Armies) yet the severall Positions of the Heavens duly considered and compared among themselves ... doe generally render His *Majesty* and his whole Army unexpectedly victorious and successfull in

> all his Designes: Beleeve it (*London*) thy miseries approach, they are like to be many, great and grievous, and not to be diverted, unlesse thou seasonably crave pardon of *God* for being *Nurse* to this present *Rebellion*, and speedily submit to thy Princes Mercy.

Wharton, and the King, had some reason for optimism: there had been good news from Wales and from Scotland, and spies told him that there was considerable dissention in Cromwell's New Model Army—Lilly might print comforting messages in his almanacs, but deserters, mutineers and thieves were being hanged every day (the King learned); a blasphemer had had his tongue bored through with hot iron; Fairfax was having trouble with discipline even in his own regiment. Wharton could afford to put a cheerful face on things.

It would be a mistake, incidentally, to assume that Lilly or Wharton had to rely entirely on rumour, or to wait for special messengers to bring them intelligence of the latest moves in the war, or the national state of things. The popular interest in developments day-to-day had by now led to a great increase in the number of news-sheets being published: in fact for the first time they begin to bear a positive resemblance to our own newspapers.

For some years, in London, before the war, Lilly had been familiar with *The Weekly Newes from Italy, Germany, etc.*, published by Nathaniel Butter in regular monthly or sometimes fortnightly issues. In 1641 the first newspaper to contain a full report of proceedings in Parliament came out; and by 1643, interest in the War encouraged stationers to print a great number of different papers.

Lilly mainly took in the Parliamentary papers, of course (of which there were over twenty a week): *Mercurius Britannicus, Mercurius Veridicus, The Kingdom's Weekly Intelligencer, The Weekly Post.* He cannot have read them all; but a small selection gave him ammunition for his own writings, for every paper had its own lurid version of new Cavalier outrages. Then he will have taken care to see one or two Royalist papers too, for accurate knowledge of how things were going was important to him. Marchmont Needham, for some time editor of *Mercurius Britannicus*, in 1647 changed his coat and began to publish *Mercurius Pragmaticus*, a Cavalier paper; then two years later was producing *Mercurius Politicus*, 'in defence of the Commonwealth, and for Information of the People'—another reversal.

It was not a question of 'subscribing': one of the reasons for Lilly's periodical and tiresome (not to say dangerous) journeys over seventeen miles of rough roads into London, was to see what new papers were about, and to carry off copies. There was often an embarrassment of choice: at least 170 weekly papers are said to have been started in the city between 1642 and 1649. The fact that relatively few copies have survived to our own times may account for the fact that we can find no announcements by Lilly in the advertisement columns; or perhaps he did not bother with them, considering himself sufficiently well known for his almanacs.

Among the information to be found in the papers, there was usually 'evidence' to support one's own side in the war, however fortunes were in fact tending. Lilly looked into his ephemerides for indications which were provoking Parliamentary victories; down at Oxford, Wharton found in the same tables clear indications of the success of the King's latest venture.

Given that the planetary positions did appear to support Wharton's optimistic view, it cannot be said that he failed to make the best of them (he was to be rewarded for his work by Charles II, with the post of Treasurer and Paymaster to the Office of the Royal Ordnance, with an official residence in the Tower; and by a Baronetcy, in 1677). But he also took the opportunity to attack Lilly again, this time as 'an impudent and senseless fellow'.

Lilly counter-attacked in *The Starry Messenger*, published on June 14th, 1645. An acquaintance, Sir Samuel Luke, had come across a copy of Wharton's attack at Newport Pagnell, and sent it to Lilly. The Parliamentarians evidently had no difficulty in getting hold of Royalist material, even from beseiged cities. No doubt Wharton's pamphlet was purposely sent out to worry the opposing party; but in any event, as Lilly says, there were several well-wishers unto the Parliament at Oxford, where each left his letter, putting it in at the hole of a glass-window as he made water in the street. What was put in at the window in any of those houses, was the same day conveyed two miles off by some in the habit of town-gardeners, to the side of a ditch, where one or more were ever ready to give the intelligence to the next Parliamentary garrison.

However *An Astrological Judgement* reached Lilly, he was not long in replying to it. Within twelve hours he had written a rejoinder, 'and the printer printed both the *March* and my answer unto it, and produced it to sight, with my *Starry Messenger*, which came forth and was made public the very day of the Parliament's great victory obtained against his Majesty in person at Naseby, under the conduct of the Lord Thomas Fairfax.'

In *The Starry Messenger* Lilly showed himself an even more determined supporter of Parliament, and opened indeed with a gratuitous non-astrological tribute to a Cheshire man, Sir George Booth, who had promised a free lease to the bereaved families of any of his employees killed in the service of the Parliament. Lilly did not want, he said, to terrify the King with the present pamphlet, but wished that His Majesty would take notice, nevertheless, of such obvious signs of personal disaster as the three suns seen in London on his birthday (November 19th, 1644) at 9.45 a.m. This promised 'a generall Infelicity' to 'a Family, and that no mean one ... a storm, and that also a furious one, is ready to rush down upon their heads.'

An 8,000-word interpretation of the eclipse of the Sun which was to come on August 11th, 1645, clinched the unhappy monarch's future, and that of his supporters:

Oh what sculking, sneaking, running into corners, mouse holes, sawpits, Cunny berries,* tossing and tumbling the ungodly out of one County into another, doe I foresee: 'Face about, Gentlemen,' says one, 'for our honour, as you did at

* Rabbit-holes.

> Newberry, that is with a good pair of heeles, or alls lost say I.' Oh the way to *Bristol*, from there to *Exeter*, then into *Cornwall*, thence into a safe harbour, if any can be found for Malignants ...

Naworth spoke falsely, his astrological judgment 'set forth purposely ... to advance their declining condition, to impedite the Parliament, and dishearten the City and Citizens of LONDON.' But all in vain: 'God is on our side; the Constellations of Heaven after a while will totally appeare for the Parliament, and cast terrour, horrour, amazement, and frights on all those Dammee-Blades now in Armes against us.'

As *The Starry Messenger* was being read in the streets of London, news came of the King's calamitous defeat at Naseby—of the 150 officers and gentlemen killed; of the Parliamentarians' slaughter (according to Clarendon) of over a hundred women, many of them officers' wives; and of the King's and Prince Rupert's escape to Ashby-de-la-Zouch, then to Lichfield, then to Bewdley.

Lilly's prediction of the victory was not only made in his almanac, but confirmed in conversation. Bulstrode Whitelocke recorded that on June 9th he

> met with my kind friend Mr William Lilly accidentally in the street, who asked me the news of the two armies being near one another; I told him it was true, and that they were very likely to engage: he then replied, 'If they do not engage before the 11th day of this month, the parliament will have the greatest victory they ever yet had.'

Lilly's career, from the moment of the publication of *The Starry Messenger*, was assured—at least with the general public. His success as a prophet and Cavalier-baiter had its drawbacks, however, for his almanacs were more widely read, and reached the hands of some—even some Parliamentarians—who did not care for them. Miles Corbet, chairman of the Committee of Examinations, was among them. He took exception to the *Messenger*, probably because Lilly spoke in it of possible disaffection among some Parliamentary officers, and renewed his pleas for prompt payment of the Parliamentary army, notoriously slow and inadequate. This was a sore point with many members of the Long Parliament, who could not see that it would have been immeasurably to their advantage to pay the ordinary men of the New Model Army, even if they had to use rougher measures against the more violent Independents in it.

Corbet was a man of strong, irascible opinions—as was seen in his pugnacious prosecution of Archbishop Laud. The Committee of Examinations, under his chairmanship, had become notorious for his arbitrary and inquisitional procedure—'a continual horse-fair', Denzil Holles (that noble, courageous man) called it. For whatever reason, Corbet (who Lilly describes as 'my mortal enemy') instructed the Sergeant-at-Arms to seize the astrologer. Fortunately, as he was being escorted to Westminster, he met a group of friends—Sir Philip Stapleton, Sir Christopher Wray, Robert Reynolds and Denzil Holles—all readers of his almanacs, and supporters of his. They promised to hasten to Westminster to defend him.

When Corbet arrived, he found it necessary actually to produce evidence against Lilly. He read one passage from the 1645 *Almanac*, which the committee pronounced harmless. He then turned to the *Starry Messenger*, and to Lilly's plea for payment for the Army. 'In the name of the Father, Son and Holy Ghost,' Lilly had written, 'will not the Excise pay the souldiers?' Corbet read: 'Will not the eclipse pay the soldiers?' The committee laughed, and Corbet's case subsided.

By this time, the news having got about that Lilly was before the Committee, a few people perhaps with old scores to pay (Lilly does not discuss their motives) set up a clamour. The Solicitor for the Excise claimed that his house had been burned down as a result of Lilly's slander. But Reynolds pointed out that the *Messenger* had not appeared until after the fire which destroyed the property, which disposed of that complaint. A Mr Bassell, a Presbyterian, complained that it was high time the astrologer's books were publicly burned. But the Committee had had enough. After a short discussion, Lilly was released.

A few days later there was another mild rumpus, when a number of Leicester citizens complained of him to the House of Commons (through Sir Arthur Hazelrigg, 'a furious person'). But once again, his friends rallied round, and the Committee of Examinations once more found the complaints frivolous. Baron Rigby, the chairman, made it quite plain that he would not be prepared to listen to any more arguments about the propriety or impropriety of Lilly's almanacs.

So he was free to continue his work; and within a month had produced a collection of *Ancient and Modern Prophesies* (by a variety of people, including a fifteenth-century Italian monk, and Old Mother Shipton; and from a variety of sources, including Old English). The pamphlet was loyally dedicated to Charles I, with a preface reminding him that if Pharoah had listened to Moses, and Zedekiah to Jeremiah, their subsequent careers would have been happier. The pamphlet included a printing of the speech which, it was alleged, Strafford had intended to make at his execution, and an examination of his chart ('When Mars is in configuration, either with the Sun or Moon, he that is then born perishes by some famous kinde of death, or else by command of his Prince in displeasure ...').

The attacks made on Lilly by the Committee of Examinations had brought him some new friends, among whom the most valuable, for the time, was undoubtedly John Booker. In *A Bloody Irish Almanac*, published in 1646, Booker took time off from warning that the English should stop squabbling among themselves and unite to defeat the common enemies, 'the blood-thirsty Irish, Papists, Jesuits and their confederates', to congratulate Lilly on his work.

The congratulations were not unanimous, however. Wharton returned to the attack in *Merlini Anglici Errate, or, The Errors, Mistakes and Misapplications of Master Lilly's New Ephemeris for the yeare 1647. Discovered, Refuted and Corrected.* Wharton had clearly been nettled by the continual jokes about his pseudonym, and devotes some space to explaining that the anagrammatic name had been assumed in order to preclude silly questions by foolish people. But then he devotes even more space to attempting to prove that Lilly's calculations were wrong, and launches into his real attack:

> All the ambition & aime of this trifling fellow is to be thought a Necromancer, a Conjurer, another Lullius, Trithemius, or the Ghost of Agrippa, or what ever you will have him to be, so he may but obtaine a popular esteeme, and by that meanes more easily cozen and cheate the poore people of their money, for otherwise why should he monstre* such a confused heape of ridling trash ...?

And he descends in the end to vulgar abuse: 'You were but a Taylours Boy in Saint Clements Parish, and ... the summity of all your honour was to be afterwards a Scriviner's Man, and he dying your Mrs taught you first to write Secretary,† in which respect I account you not worthy of the just revenge of my Pen.'

Lilly's astrological success no less than his continued enthusiastic support of Parliament had really got under Wharton's skin (and under that of a great number of other people, too). By now, he had abandoned all pretence of being independent, at least as far as the main arguments of the war were concerned. In the very publication Wharton had attacked, he had rejoiced in the recent Parliamentary victories:

> God be thanked, and blessed be his name, that this Parliament hath overthrown those Catterpillars, Locusts, devouring Wolves, the lazie Humble-bee Bishops, lubbardly Canons, slovenly Prebends, the sucking Venerian Doctors and Officials of Spiritual Courts; these shoare poor silly sheep, but never fed any ...

One cannot but be suspicious that Lilly had followed instructions in making this attack on alleged ecclesiastical villainy;

* demonstrate.

† A style of handwriting used chiefly in legal documents from the fifteenth to the seventeenth centuries.

there is now some reason to suppose that from time to time he was inserting one or two paragraphs in his almanacs at the direct suggestion of his Parliamentary friends (though it is doubtful whether he would have allowed them to dictate what he would actually say; and he would certainly not have allowed any tampering with the purely astrological pages of the almanacs).

Scarcely allowing Lilly time to draw breath (the volubility of these seventeenth-century astrologers is astonishing), Wharton returned to the attack in *Bellum Hybernicale* (1647), once more bracketing Lilly and Booker together, and accusing them of such incompetence that neither of them could even draw up a 'figure'. Lilly, Wharton claimed, not only had all his charts drawn up for him by someone else, but had plagiarized most of his material from Sir Christopher Heydon, an astrologer of the previous generation (some of whose manuscripts were certainly in Lilly's possession).

*Bellus Hybernicale* is in fact a rather moving document. The King was imprisoned, and his cause seemed certainly lost. Though he struck out at Lilly and Booker, Wharton was much more concerned—heart-breakingly so—for his King and the ruin in which the country stood. His passion for his cause was as genuine as Lilly's was opportunist:

> Oh good God! Where is the world become? Saints are turned to Serpents, and Doves into Devils: the English nation which hath been accounted fierce only against their Foes, and always faithful to their Friends, are now become both fierce and faithless against their Lawful and Loving Prince, and have most Barbarously betrayed him. Who would ever have thought that Christians, that Civil People, that any Men would thus have violated all Religion, all Laws, and all Honest and Civil demeanor? And although the Heavens blush at the view ... yet they neither feel the horror nor shrink at the shame, nor fear the revenge; but stand upon terms, some of Defence for the Lawfulness of their dealing, and some of Excuse for the Necessity. Well, let them be able to blind the World ... yet shall they never be able to escape

> either the sight or vengeance of Almighty God, which we daily expect, and earnestly desire to be poured upon them.

And the pamphlet closes with a lament for the King which cuts right through the astrological content of the work, and expresses what every Royalist must have been feeling at that moment:

> Alas, good King Charles, thy Nature was too gentle and thy Government too mild for so stiff and stubborn a People: What King will ever repose any trust in such unnatural Subjects, but fetter them with Laws as thieves are with Irons? What time will be sufficient to blot out this blemish? What other Action could they have done more joyfull to their Enemies, more woful to their Friends, and shameful to themselves? *O Corruption of Times! O Conditions of Men!*

Lilly, of course, took the opposite view, concentrating on displaying to his readers planetary promises of increasing stability under Parliamentary rule. Wharton was even further infuriated, and rose to new heights of vituperation. He took Lilly's almanac page by page, almost line by line, demonstrating 'errors' here, sneering there, slipping in additional paragraphs of personal attack and propaganda. Simple enough, of course, to discuss Lilly's mistakes, since most astrological arguments are in the strict sense of the word arguable; there were often two or three possible interpretations of a particular planetary aspect or progression, especially in judicial astrology. And Wharton was (like Lilly, it is fair to say) at this stage an outright propagandist. When he claims that Lilly's almanac is 'no better than a meer Scarecrow purposely devised to deter His Majesties Friends from any longer adhering to him' he is doubtless speaking the truth; equally, he was himself busy scaring other crows.

By this time it was unthinkable that the Parliamentary cause should not triumph. Any chance of reconciliation with the King was extremely slender. In June 1646 the capture of Oxford had sent Charles scurrying for safety into Scotland, and within seven months the Scots had handed him over for £400,000 and the promise of the establishment of Presbyterianism.

Now the Levellers set out to lay down their own requirements for a perfect society: franchise was the birthright of 'the poorest he', and not the privilege even of men like Cromwell. They demanded religious toleration, freedom from impressment, and equality before the law. The political situation fragmented as independent sects flourished. The astrologers continued internecine arguments.

Late in 1647, Wharton began publishing a series of weekly pamphlets called *Mercurius Elenchicus*, printed in London, and satirizing Parliament (a dangerous occupation, later to serve Wharton ill, as he must have expected). *The Late Storie of Mr William Lilly* was published to refute various slanders Wharton slipped into *Mercurius*. It was written by a certain Colonel Th. (as we have seen), and pointed out that while Lilly's politics were perhaps to be deplored, it was obvious that that Roundhead was an honest astrologer who simply reported his accurate interpretations of the planets' prognostications, and that Wharton was on the contrary 'a despicable Astrologer, whom we hissed out of Oxford for his vanities, [and] who is reduced to such necessity that were it not for his penning that Elenchicus and such trash, must starve'.

Another defence of Lilly appeared as a postscript (*A Whip for Wharton*) to *The World's Catastrophe* (1647), written 'by a learned Gentleman out of the Country', who claimed that Wharton was a buzzard, a publican, a renegade, and an ignoramus, content to smooth the King's path to destruction by promising a by now impossible victory; while Lilly could be said to be more faithful to His Majesty in pointing out his inevitable defeat!

Lilly himself contributed a prefatory note, alluding to Wharton ('who lives like an obscure scurrilous traitor to his country now at present in this City, and hath the curse that God bestowed upon Caine hanging upon him'), defending Booker ('who for so many years maintained the reputation of the Art, almost then utterly decayed, by his own vertue and abilities'), declaring that he was perfectly capable of setting up a chart, and challenging

Wharton to mention even one prediction of his own that had been fulfilled.

The Gentleman then takes over, defends Lilly and Booker as 'those famous Ptolemies of their Nation,' and turning on 'Corporall Wharton', who 'like a bleezing traveller, that by his buzardly clumsiness tumbles into a quick-sand, and there sticking, raileth and rageth against those that hit the right way by the same, better than he, calling them all to pieces because they were not as very buzzards as himself, to plunge into the same puddle for company.' Surely that is Lilly's own voice?

Wharton seems to have been rather overcome, for the best he could manage by way of reply was *No Merline, Nor Mercurie*, with an essay entitled *Lilly lasht with his own Rod*, claiming again that Lilly's calculations were all out (they were not).

During all this time, Lilly was also giving aid and comfort to Charles I (and one wonders what advice he gave the client who asked him 'whether best to adhere to King or Parliament'). The truth of the matter is that he was continuing his Vicar of Bray performance (the Cavaliers might manage to arrange a compromise with the Parliament, after all), and ensuring the success of his career as a consultant astrologer—many of his private clients were Royalists. With his voice raised so loudly against the Cavaliers in his almanacs, it is surprising that any Royalist should have thought it advisable to come to him for advice on the King's behalf: but that is what happened.

The first occasion was in 1647, when the King was holding court at Hampton Court during a sort of amnesty. While Cromwell was often present, and there were guards in attendance, this was for the King's protection as much as for his imprisonment. In any event, he had given his parole not to escape.

But what with Cromwell being under constant pressure by some of his supporters, and with the importuning of the Levellers, who were preparing to make a bid for the control of the Army with a view to killing the King and subverting constitutional government, the position soon became difficult. Charles withdrew his parole from Cromwell's cousin, Col. Edward Whalley, who was guarding him, and began plotting escape with John

Ashburnham, his friend, and one or two others. It was at this stage that Lilly was consulted.

The plotters got in touch with Jane Whorewood, one of the most remarkable of all women Royalists: a red-haired, tall, graceful woman somewhat scarred by smallpox, but all the same extremely handsome at thirty-three. Her father and stepfather had both been at court, and she had known the King from the time when they were both children. She had been married at nineteen, but became the mistress of Sir Thomas Bendish, whom she persuaded Charles to send as Ambassador to Constantinople.

She had been with Charles at Oxford, where her influence on him had been noted; he had left his jewels with her when he fled to Scotland, and trusted her as much as he trusted anyone. Indeed, he was right to do so, for as Henry Firebrace—the King's page—wrote later, 'Had the rest done their parts as carefully as Whorewood, the King had been at large.'

So Jane Whorewood went to London, and called at the Corner House in the Strand late one night. Lilly was working on his *Christian Astrology* at the time, harrassed not only by that work, but by the fact that his maidservant had just died of the plague, and he was worried that he or his wife might be infected. (They escaped, though a second maid died shortly afterwards.)

At first, he declined to allow Mrs Whorewood into the house; but she joked him out of that. 'I fear not the plague, but the pox,' she said. Once in private, she explained that the King intended to escape, and she came, instructed by him, to ask Lilly to cast a chart and advise 'in what quarter of this nation he might be most safe, and not to be discovered until himself pleased.'

Did she indeed come directly from the King? It is difficult to believe that she would have made the journey simply of her own volition. She might have been instructed by Ashburnham or some other friend who was a believer in astrology, and had decided that Lilly was honest enough to give a sound opinion despite his ragings against the Royalists in his almanacs.

In any event, Lilly drew up a chart, and told Mrs Whorewood that the King should stay in Essex, about twenty miles from

London. 'She liked my judgment very well,' he writes, 'and being herself of a sharp judgment, remembered a place in Essex about that distance, where was an excellent house and all conveniences for his reception.'

On November 11th, the King made his attempt. A relay of horses waited at Bishop's Sutton, and in the early dark, at four in the afternoon, he left Hampton Court. For a while, he was not missed (though Whalley came two or three times and looked through the keyhole of his room, where he was allegedly writing a long letter to his daughter Mary, Princess of Orange).

Eventually his absence was discovered. But he was not making for Essex, but for Southampton, where he hoped to take ship either for Jersey or France. There was no ship available, and instead he crossed to the Isle of Wight: Ashburnham had persuaded him to surrender himself to the newly appointed Governor, Robert Hammond, who he thought would be sympathetic. And so he was; but he was also honourable, and the King found himself once more detained at Parliament's pleasure. When he heard that Ashburnham had revealed his whereabouts to Hammond, he burst out: 'Oh, Jack! thou hast undone me.' And so it was. Whether he had ever seriously considered travelling to Mrs Whorewood's secret hiding-place in Essex—whether he even heard of that scheme—we do not know. Lilly believed that he was 'either guided by his own approaching hard fate, or misguided by Ashburnham.' Events might certainly have been different if he had followed Lilly's advice.

Lilly received twenty pieces of gold for his consultation, of the five hundred the King gave Mrs Whorewood to arrange for his safety. An added mystery: why should the King have given half of his readily available cash to her, and then declined to take advantage of the arrangements she had made? Perhaps indeed he did hear of Lilly's plan, but had read Lilly's almanacs and decided not to trust him?

During 1648, Lilly was again approached by Mrs Whorewood. Ironically, it was during that very year that he was awarded £50 by the Council of State—Cromwell's Council—and a pension of £100 a year, which he received for two years, as thanks for his general services to Parliament, and also as token for some information he had received from France, passed to him by one John Shelly, confessor to one of the Secretaries of Cardinal Mazarin, successor to Richelieu.

Mrs Whorewood had managed this time to gain entry to Carisbrooke Castle, and had arranged a code with the King's valet, who waited at table. If he told his master that some asparagus had arrived from London, or some artichokes, His Majesty would understand something quite unconnected with vegetables.

The King had nothing to do except plan escape; and it was his first attempt, in March, with which Lilly was concerned. 'Honest Harry' Firebrace, now as much a friend as a servant, had laid a plan. On a moonless night, Charles was to climb through the window of his bedroom (the bars of which were to have been eaten through by nitric acid) and let himself down by rope. Outside the castle, a fast horse would be waiting to take him to a creek between Cowes and Ryde, where he would be rowed to the mainland, where Ashburnham would be waiting.

The centre upright bar of the bedroom window was removed, having proved loose; and though Firebrace believed that the others would have to be severed, Charles declined to wait for the means to cut them (the nitric acid having been spilt in transit). Where his head could go, the King decided, his body could follow. Not so. 'Too late,' Firebrace recalled, '[he] found himself mistaken; he sticking fast between his breast and shoulders, and not able to get forwards or backwards.'

The servant managed to pull his master back into the bedroom, and a light was placed in the window to disguise the loose bar. Meanwhile, Mrs Whorewood again set out for London and the Strand. This time, Lilly's help was severely practical. 'I got G. Farmer (who was a most ingenious locksmith, and dwelt in Bow-lane) to make a saw to cut the iron bars in sunder, I mean to saw them.'

Unfortunately, Hammond had a spy at the King's elbow: Lady Carlisle, whom Charles trusted sufficiently to tell her all his escape plans. So Hammond knew about the saw, the acid, the very window through which the King planned to escape. Half an hour before the time arranged for the attempt, Hammond came to Charles's room.

'How now, Hammond,' said the King, uncomfortably aware of the missing bars. 'What is the matter? What do you want?'

'I am come to take leave of your Majesty,' said Hammond sardonically; 'for I hear you are going away.' It was the end of the plan.

Mrs Whorewood came once more to Lilly—and again there is some mystery about who sent her. This was in September, when the Parliamentary Commissioners visited the King at Carisbrooke, to re-open negotiations in an attempt to persuade him to agree to the proposals already put to him at Hampton Court, and which might have led to a settlement avoiding a military dictatorship.

Lilly set up his chart, and advised Mrs Whorewood of a day and an hour when it would be propitious for the King to receive the Commissioners, to sign the proposals, and to accompany the Commissioners to London. But again the King either never heard the advice, or ignored it. Lilly's final anecdote about him suggests that he may have regarded Mrs Whorewood's reliance on this particular astrologer as misguided.

> Whilst the King was at Windsor Castle [at the end of 1648] walking upon the leads there, he looked upon Captain Wharton's Almanac. 'My book,' saith he, 'speaks well as to the weather.' One William Allen, standing by, 'What,' saith he, 'saith his antagonist, Mr Lilly?' 'I do not care for Lilly,' said His Majesty, 'he hath been always against me,' and became a little bitter in his expressions. 'Sir,' said Allen, 'the man is an honest man, and writes but what his art informs him.' 'I believe it,' said His Majesty, 'and that Lilly understands astrology as well as any man in Europe.' *Exit Rex Carolus.*

The King's interest in astrology seems to have been extremely limited—though when he was Prince of Wales, he had met, in France, Sir Kenelm Digby (later a founder of the Royal Society), who was an amateur astrologer, drew up the Prince's horoscope, and discussed it with him. But in any case, he was given to calling a spade a spade. When Henry Isaacson, the theologian and chronologer, presented to the King his *Tabula Historico-Chronologica* (which was partly compiled for astrological purposes), Charles, according to Aubrey,

> turned to his own Birth; sayd the King, *And here's one Lye to begin with* ... Poor Mr Isaacson was so ashamed at this unlucky rencounter, that he immediately sneak'd away and stayed not for prayse or reward, both which perhaps he might have had, for his Majestie was well pleased with it. 'Twas presented in an ill Hower. An Astrologer would give something to know that day and hower.

The King's final exit was yet to come. But meanwhile his mistrust of Lilly, though it may not have been based on any real knowledge of his actions, was justified. During 1648 Lilly and Booker were invited by Parliament to travel to Colchester, which Sir Charles Lucas and four thousand Royalists were defending in a protracted seige. There, they encouraged the attackers, 'assuring them the town would very shortly be surrendered, as indeed it was'. Meanwhile, inside the town, another astrologer, John Humphrey (one of Lilly's pupils) was daily reassuring Lucas that relief was on the way.

Lilly seems to have enjoyed the expedition, and describes with some relish his one adventure under fire:

> During my being there, the steeple of St Mary's Church was much battered by two cannons purposely placed. I was there one day about three of the clock in the afternoon, talking with the cannoneer, when presently he desired us to look to ourselves, for he perceived by his perspective glass there was a piece charged in the castle against his work, and ready to be discharged. I ran for haste under an old ash-tree, and immediately the cannon-bullet came hissing quite over us.
>
> 'No danger now,' saith the gunner, 'but begone, for there

are five more charging,' which was true, for two hours after those cannons were discharged, and unluckily killed our cannoneer ... I came the next morning and saw the blood of the two poor men lie upon the planks.

It need not surprise anyone that the Parliamentarian Army should think it worth bringing two astrologers from London to Colchester simply to cheer up the troops. As recently as 1943 British astrologers were helping to fake predictions which, printed in German in imitation of current astrological almanacs, were distributed inside the Reich in an attempt at demoralization. During the Civil War it was said (and by an enemy) that Lilly was at one time offered £50 a year to stop writing his almanacs, or at least to stop puffing the Parliamentarian cause in them; but that 'he wished us to give it to some maimed Colonels, for he would eate bread and water with the Parliament rather than roast meat with the Cavaliers'. Whereupon the Cavaliers made a plot to kidnap the astrologer, but arrived in Hersham in his absence, and the scheme fell through. If the King could have obtained Lilly's services, it was claimed they would outweigh in value the force of a dozen regiments!

Lilly himself had a high opinion of his influence on the troops: 'All the soldiery [were] my friends,' he wrote; 'for when [Cromwell] was in Scotland, the day of one of their fights, a soldier stood with *Anglicus* in his hand, and as the several troops passed by him, "Lo, hear what Lilly saith; you are in this month promised victory; fight it out, brave boys, and then read that month's prediction!"'

This was probably a typical reaction: it must be remembered that more than half of the infantry were pressed men, usually of little intelligence or education, and likely to accept the vaguest astrological encouragement quite uncritically. The cavalry were perhaps a different matter: they were in all ways superior, and it is doubtful whether the almanacs had much effect upon them—though many of them would not hesitate to consult an astrologer on a personal matter.

Some Parliamentary officers had doubts about the wisdom of

using astrologers for propaganda (or any other) purposes. General Fairfax seems to have been one. A civilized man, he was a strictly orthodox Christian, and evidently became concerned about the almanac war Lilly was still conducting with Wharton. He sent to London to command Lilly and Booker to attend him at Windsor.

For the first time, and wisely, considering the state of the country, with deserters pillaging and making a living as amateur highwaymen, the two astrologers decided to travel by coach. This meant commissioning one privately, for it was not until 1658 that one finds the first indication of public coaches leaving London regularly for, say, Salisbury, York or Exeter. It would have cost the two men at least £50 to reach Windsor and their appointment with Fairfax.

His reception of them was somewhat equivocal: he gave them a good meal, and a talk about the inevitable victory of the Parliamentary cause (of which Lilly was in little doubt). 'As for the art we studied,' Lilly wrote, 'he hoped it was lawful and agreeable to God's word; he understood it not, but doubted not but we both feared God, and therefore had a good opinion of us both.' Lilly assured him that they both expected a Roundhead victory, and that 'we do not study any art but what is lawful and consonant to the scriptures, and antiquity'.

While they were at Windsor, Lilly called on the impassioned evangelical Hugh Peter, finding him reading 'an idle pamphlet' come from London with a verse in it about him:

> From th'oracles of the Sibyls so silly,
> The curst predictions of William Lilly ...
> Good Lord, deliver me.

What Lilly and Peter talked about, we can never know; perhaps Peter, too, was suffering from an attack of nerves at the thought that he might be associated with an astrologer who, like Dr Dee before him, had occasionally been described as a sorcerer. Whatever the reason for their talk, it seems to have been amiable—as were most talks with the jovial padre whose own way of encouraging the troops was to ride in among them with a Bible in one hand and a pistol in the other, exhorting them to do their duty.

Apart from these excursions to the front line, Lilly was continually at this time reassuring and advising his private clients in matters to do with the war: telling mothers how their sons would fare, assuring Captain Willoughby that he would prosper, advising Mr Robinson how he should choose between the Army and a civilian career. And there were more particular questions than these: Lady Holborn, a Royalist, asked whether her husband, Sir Robert, should make his peace with Parliament. And an enquiry came too from Richard Overton, one of the most prominent leaders of the Levellers—that troublesome group which was always demanding of Cromwell that he should make the country a true republic, with universal suffrage and religious toleration.

Overton's visit to Lilly is another mark of the all-embracing influence of astrology: here was a man devoted to the most radical ideals, coming to an astrologer (in April 1648) to ask whether he would be successful in his efforts to engage the Army in the cause of 'the redemption of common right and freedom to the land, and removal of oppressions from the people'.

Lilly continued to show his devotion to Parliament in his literary output. In September 1648, by which time Cromwell had routed the Scots at Preston and the army was supreme, his *Astrological Prediction* for three years to come was published, and in his usual Epistle to the Reader he enjoined his readers to love the Parliament, and pointed out that 'His Majesty was not ordained to be fortunate in War; it's not a gift given to every Prince'. He called on the people to unite against the

> barbarous and perjured Scots that are entered already our Kingdom, and those who are also approaching, not to re-estate the King (as themselves cunningly pretend) but purposely to steal our Goods, ravish our Wives, enslave our Persons, inherit our Possessions and Birthrights, remain here in England, and everlastingly to inhabit among us ...

He made a point of drawing his readers' attention to the 'unjust scandals and affronts' he had suffered from other astrologers, taking his usual high tone ('I account it my greatest glory ... to be in enmity with, and hatred of them.') He always protested too much: but it was simply a facet of his character: he was never so happy as when he was attacked and attacking—completely confident of the support of his readers and clients, of his own powers as an astrologer, and of his rivals' insignificance.

He went on to give his usual judgments: of the conjunction of Mars and Saturn on July 28th 1648, for instance, which promised to place London in danger, and offered great calamities, dearth and famine, 'the city poysened with Malignants'; but 'the whole Kingdom would be happy in the Parliament and Army'. Then followed the weather forecast.

The following month, one Hugh Johnsen fired off a counter-blast 'clearly proveing [Lilly's] predictions to be groundlesse, absolutely void of Art, full of contradictions, Treason, falsehood, and such a ridiculous piece of foolery as an Artist would blush to owne ...' Johnsen dedicated his pamphlet, *Anti-Merlinus*, to the Prince of Wales, assuring him that astrology was a valid art, but promising to prove Lilly a false prophet (he pointed out that the Devil, 'the subtilest Astrologian in the world', had misled Lilly).

Incidentally, Johnsen pays some tribute to Lilly as a propagandist:

> Doubtlesse Fairfax and Cromwell could hardly have led the Kingdome by the nose thus long, had not Merlinus Anglicus, that welchified London incubus, entered the sceane, and prevailed as much upon the minds of giddy-headed men, with his screech-owles quill, as they upon their bodies with all their Armies, Engines, Weapons and subtile machinations. For people are, and were ever too apt to be seduced by any who but pretend to astrologie ...

Johnsen got in one or two shrewd hits. Had Lilly not predicted 'peace this year', and absolutely affirmed

> that this would be a year of joy, and merryment, not of Martiall exploits, in this our Kingdome ...? Did not Mr Lilly affirme, yea confidently also, that the Scots would not assist the King this year against the Parliament? no nor any kingdom else? he saith, Behold the Scots are honourable, and have no invasive design against us: nay, he saith further, that they, who are of this opinion, that the Scots will invade us, have no eyes. I shall willingly leave it to the Reader's judgement, who deserves most to ride blind Bayard. He adds afterwards, that he can speak no evil of the Scottish nation, sith the Heavens give him no information; but after he heard that they were come, contrary to his prediction, he could scarce invent any Oyster-whore language bad enough to revile them with.

Despite his enthusiasm for the Parliamentary cause, Lilly was not immune from the traumatic shock of the King's trial and execution, which indeed shocked a great number of people whose support of Parliament had never been in doubt. On the afternoon of January 20th, 1649, Lilly was walking in Whitehall when he met Hugh Peter.

'Come, Lilly,' said Peter, 'wilt thou go hear the King tried?'

Lilly, like many Londoners, had not so much as heard that a trial was imminent. 'When?' he asked in amazement.

'Now,' said Peter, 'just now; go with me.'

They walked down to Westminster Hall, and the well-known figure of Peter was allowed in instantly, with his companion, past the guards commanded by Daniel Axtell to keep members of the public to the north end of the Hall. At the south end, at the foot of the stairs, a bar was set; before it, a crimson velvet chair for the King, facing the judges.

Lilly, in his rather old-fashioned hose, and his doublet flared out over his breeches, fixed now by buttons rather than the pins he had used when he was a poor apprentice, wearing a waistcoat under the doublet for additional warmth in the cold of winter (he tended to feel the cold), was a rather drab member of a fashionable gathering—it was almost as though the Hall had become a theatre for the period of the trial; above Lilly and Peter, at the northern corners, were galleries in which ladies sat with fashionable gentlemen, some of them openly sympathetic to the King, like Lady Fairfax.

'Within one quarter of an hour,' Lilly recalled, 'came the Judges, presently His Majesty, who spoke excellently well, and majestically, without impediment in the least when he spoke. I saw the silver top of his staff unexpectedly fall to the ground; which was took up by Mr Rushworth ...'

It was one of the touches of drama which were to make the occasion even more like a play. Bradshaw, in a bullet-proof hat, called on the King to answer the charge that he had attempted to subvert the ancient and fundamental laws and liberties of the nation, introducing an arbitrary and tyrannical government, and in pursuit of his aims maintaining a cruel war in the land against the Parliament and the kingdom. Charles laughed aloud when he heard the word 'traitor' addressed to him; and when Bradshaw called on him to answer the charge, Lady Fairfax shouted from the gallery that it was Cromwell who was the traitor. Axtell ordered his soldiers to fire on the gallery, and the crowd in which Lilly and Peter were crushed surged backwards to the door; but the men ignored the order, and Lady Fairfax was hustled from the Hall by her friends.

Charles challenged the legality of the Court. Lilly, in his autobiography, recalls:

> When I heard Bradshaw the judge say to His Majesty, 'Sir, instead of answering this Court, you interrogate their powers, which becomes not one in your condition,' these words pierced my heart and soul, to hear a subject thus audaciously to reprehend his Sovereign, who ever and anon replied with great magnanimity and prudence.

As the King left the Hall, Axtell commanded his troops to shout 'Justice!' A cry of 'God Save the King!' came from the crowd behind them. Lilly's sympathies for the King were not so wholehearted that he complained in public about the trial, at the time;

nor did he believe that it was possible that Charles would escape death. The Presbyterians were hot in the King's favour, and several prominent supporters of Cromwell were against the trial; but Cromwell and Ireton were too strong for them, and Charles was condemned as 'a tyrant, traitor, murderer and public enemy to the good people of this nation', to be executed 'by the severing of his head by his body'.

Lilly never seems to have doubted the conclusion. Though he did not prophesy the execution, on January 6th he had published 'A peculiar Prognostication astrologically predicted according to art, whether or no His Majesty shall suffer Death this present year 1649: the Possibility thereof discussed and divulged.' It cannot be claimed that he was particular in answering the question; he promised 'the exile, vanishment, imprisonment or death of some great Prince or King, shedding of blood amongst the common people, and greater persons.' Well, rather like the headlines of popular newspapers today, that could be interpreted in a sufficient number of ways both to sell the almanac and enable Lilly to claim to be right however things turned out. He also promised, incidentally, 'discorde, mutual dissimulations, the motions of a great Army, wars, murthers, firing of houses, theeves, plundering, depopulations, miscarriages of women with child, sharp fevers and universal sickness amongst men, by reason there will be a pestilent air ...'

The King was executed. Lilly was not there. The whole episode genuinely horrified him, for he had a very real reverence for the monarchy, however strangely he may have seemed to show it in his almanacs. A fortnight after the beheading, he dined with Robert Spavin, Cromwell's secretary, and various other people. Not unnaturally, the talk turned to the execution, and who the executioner had been. It was a well-kept secret, though the general belief was that Brandon, the common hangman, had done the work, disguised in false beard and wig beneath his mask. Lilly writes:

> As soon as dinner was come, Robert Spavin took me by the hand, and carried me to the fourth window: saith he, 'These

are all mistaken, they have not named the man that did the fact; it was Lieut.-Colonel Joyce; I was in the room when he fitted himself for the work, stood behind him when he did it; when done, went in again with him. There is no man knows this but my master, Commissary Ireton, and myself.

Lilly is the only man in history to offer such evidence. Whether it is to be credited is another matter. There seems no reason why he should have invented his conversation with Spavin; he did not need the publicity, and as a means of ingratiating himself with the restored monarchy, it does not seem particularly diplomatic. Then, how much dependence can one place on Spavin's word? Barely six months later he was to be dismissed by Cromwell for his involvement in a profitable scheme for making money by selling forged passes in his master's name and under his seal. He was forced to ride from Westminster to Whitehall seated backwards on a horse, and wearing a notice around his neck announcing his crime. Not all racketeers are liars, but the incident does not inspire confidence; he sounds rather the type of man to make himself important by inventing 'inside knowledge'.

The mystery is never likely to be solved. Lilly may have had the truth of it. George Joyce had a career which certainly suggests he would have been an enthusiastic executioner: he had seized the King at Holmby Hall, Oxford, in 1647, apparently exceeding his instructions by doing so (he had a considerable disagreement with Cromwell about the nature of these instructions). When the King asked for his commission from his commander (Joyce was at the time a cornet in Fairfax's horse regiment), the young officer airily said 'Here is my commission'. 'Where?' asked the King. Joyce replied 'Behind me'— where indeed stood about five hundred troopers.

Though the escapade embarrassed Fairfax and Cromwell, it marked Joyce out as a dependable, ruthless, rather extreme young man who could be trusted with any anti-Royalist enterprise. He was one of the most enthusiastic prompters of the King's trial; was later awarded 'lands to the value of £100 per annum' by a grateful Parliament; and on the Restoration fled from England to

6. 'Hieroglyphic' supposed to forecast the Great Fire of 1666, printed in *Monarchy or No Monarchy* (1651)
(*Curators of the Bodleian Library*)

Honorande Patrone

117

having obtained the Laurell by golding, I may misse dicta
Ad rem: yr many benignitys and they considerable, yr
more than ordinary reception of my wife, cum multis aliis
make mee willing to beleave you had ☉ in ♓ in the
Ascend: viz: a princely hart. and a large soule —
Pro omnibus, ther can bee no more expected from mee
then an acknowledgment of all favors, and my cordiall thanks
And Ruth shee sayd — Esq: and his Lady would have given
mee cloth for shirts for thee — I sayd, you were a fool
you took them not: no fool sayd Ruth. their kindness
were so great I was ashamed, not knowing how to gratifie
them — I thank you for yr kindness therein, I am sure
to fare the worse for my wives modesty; but shee I
verily beleeve shee did it out of pure noblenesse of
spirit — shee and the 2 young Ladys are in opera
for my Gallant: you love no reiteration of words
Ergo, I conclude with my harty affection to yr selfe
and my brave noble Gallant. and say, that I am

Hersham 25o Aprill
1670

yr old loving friend
William Lilly

I am a better man than I was, my wife perusing
the letter, tells mee the cloth is come / happy man am
I that speed so well — and blessed bee my noble Gallant
that so loves mee, and long live Dr. Elias, that takes
such care of his very old friends: Ago rursus et rursus
gratias.

7. 'Happy man am I that speed so well ...' A letter from Lilly to Ashmole
(*British Library Board*)

settle in Rotterdam, whence he vanished when Parliament (mainly, it seems, on Lilly's evidence) issued an order for his arrest as a regicide. He vanished so effectively that even the date of his death, much less its whereabouts, is unknown.

As for Charles I: 'For my part,' Lilly wrote later, 'I do believe he was not the worst, but the most unfortunate of Kings.'

# 6

# Astrologer at Politics

*Some calculate the hidden fates*
*Of monkeys, puppy-dogs, and cats,*
*Some running-nags, and fighting-cocks;*
*Some love, trade, law-suits, and the pox;*
*Some take a measure of the lives*
*Of Fathers, Mothers, Husbands, Wives,*
*Make opposition, trine and quartile,*
*Tell who is barren, and who fertile,*
*As if the Planet's first aspect*
*The tender infant did infect*
*In soul and body, and instill*
*All future good, and future ill ...*

*Hudibras* II:III (933)

It was in 1646 that Lilly met the man who was to become perhaps his closest friend. He and Elias Ashmole were introduced by Jonas Moore, mathematical tutor to the Duke of York, who years later was to persuade Charles II to build the Royal Observatory for John Flamsteed, and to establish the mathematical school at Christ's Hospital.

Ashmole had one of the most interesting and lively minds of his time. Born at Lichfield in 1617, he was the son of a saddler; Simon Ashmole was as improvident as Lilly's father, preferring soldiering to saddlery. His mother tried desperately to persuade Ashmole to run his father's business, as soon as he was old enough; but the young man escaped to London with a kindly step-cousin in 1633, where he studied law and married a wife fourteen years older than himself, with whom he was extremely happy. Her sudden death only three years after their marriage had a profound effect on Ashmole, despite the kindliness of his in-laws, with whom he lived for some years. He slowly built up a legal practice, was admitted to Clement's Inn and sworn an attorney in the Court of Common Pleas, but tragically disappointed in romantic love, now gave much energy to the pursuit of a second wife—and a rich one; a quite cold-blooded pursuit, as his diary reveals.

The main object of his attentions was a certain Lady Manwaring, the rich widow of a Recorder of Reading (and of two previous husbands). She was a grandmother, twenty years older than Ashmole, and suspected of having the pox. But she was rich. One of the lady's sons evidently saw Ashmole's motives quite clearly, for only a few months after he first declared himself to her, the son 'broke into my chamber, and had like to have killed me'. But Ashmole wore the lady down, married her, and found himself at last 'in that condition I had always desired, which was that I might be enabled to live to myself and studies without being forced to take pains for a livelihood in the world'.

Ashmole was still assiduously courting Lady Manwaring when he met Lilly (the marriage was to take place in 1649), and was unable to devote as much time as he wished to astrology, which had increasingly claimed his attention during the past year, ever since while in Oxford quietly studying, and paying as little attention as possible to civil disorders, he had met George Wharton. Wharton's enthusiasm about astrology immediately won Ashmole's interest, and from that time onwards he never took any serious decision without first consulting the planets.

The day before Moore introduced him to Lilly, Ashmole had agreed to join Wharton in the publication of yet another of the latter's attacks on Lilly; but Ashmole had liked this second astrologer on sight, and withdrew from partnership with Wharton in that particular matter. Lilly introduced him to Booker, and two months later 'the Mathematical Feast was at the White heart in the old Baily, where [he] dyned,' and met many other astrologers.

The Astrological Feasts organized by the Society of Astrologers were held for many years in succession, and continued during the interregnum. Over forty astrologers who were normally at daggers drawn appear to have met convivially, suspending hostilities to enjoy a good meal and some technical gossip: Lilly, Booker, Wharton, John and Arise Evans, John Gadbury and his student John Partridge, Vincent Wing, John Mallet, Geoffrey Le Neve, James Blackwell, John Sabye and John Heydon, Sir Kenelm Digby, George Parker, Culpeper (the herbalist), and a great number of other astrologers, and guests who had a non-technical interest in the subject. On one occasion, for instance, John Booker brought Samuel Pepys.

The variety of personalities, political opinions and astrological attitudes represented makes it amazing that every Feast did not break up in violence and disorder: but Royalists sat next to Republicans (the discussion of politics being banned), psychic and cabbalistic astrologers next to scientists and astronomers, and drowned their differences in claret. The menu of one Feast still exists, perhaps because of the importance of the occasion: the Town Clerk of London had agreed to become Steward of the Feast, and the company dined on venison.

Lilly and Ashmole were on opposite sides, politically; Ashmole was a determined Royalist (and was to be of use to Lilly when the Restoration came). But they evidently struck up a friendship very rapidly, for when Lilly published in the summer of 1647 his *The World's Catastrophe, or, Europe's many Mutations untill 1666*, Ashmole contributed two translations from the Latin; and Lilly paid him a generous tribute in his Epistle to the Reader:

> In astrologie he is well versed, and in Antiquities no mean student; for who shall read Merlin in the Latin Copy, shall wonder at the dexterity and sharp apprehension of this gentleman, that being in years so young [Ashmole was still under thirty] should understand and distinguish terms and names, so obsolete, and not infrequently vulgar; and yet hath rendred them in our mother-tongue in so compliant and decent Phrase, as might well have become an Antiquary of double his years.

As yet, however, the friendship was still guarded, for the very day after Lilly had written that tribute, we find in Ashmole's diary the note: '6.30 after noon/ whether it will be good for me to discover myself to Mr Lilly or not.' Evidently he had set up an astrological chart for the moment at which he began to consider whether he should be frank with Lilly about their political differences. Interestingly enough, only ten days later Ashmole noted a dream he had had, in which Lilly had invited him to sit in the best place in a theatre where he was presenting a play; but Ashmole refused the honour.

For some months he reported to that other Cavalier, Wharton, everything Lilly told him, whether in confidence or not, which was against the Royalist interest. Wharton found the information extremely useful. But Lilly, no fool, soon began to suspect that Ashmole was betraying his confidences. In his diary for November 16th, 1647, Ashmole notes: 'This morning Lilly told me of my discovering his secrets to Wharton'; and three days later came Wharton's attack on Lilly for organizing the marriage of Lady Arabella Scroope.*

It says something for Lilly's generosity of spirit, and also perhaps for his admiration for Ashmole as a scholar, that he had forgiven his friend within a very short time—two months, in fact; and Ashmole's admiration for Lilly, too, overcame political ill-feeling, so that when *Christian Astrology* was published in October 1647, he wrote the poem in praise of it.† But in a short time a major row upset the relationship: an anonymous pamphlet was published, written 'in vindication of that arch Roundhead Lilly, lately scandalized by the sawcy Pen of Mercurius Elencticus (alias) Wharton'. In it, the author claims that Wharton had told him that his attack on Lilly had been inspired by 'one Ashinole [*sic*] an Atturney'. *The Late storie of Mr William Lilly* reached Ashmole's hands at noon on February 19th; he had read it through by two o'clock, and set up a chart to determine 'whether that book was of Lilly's contriving and whether he be not a secret enemy or public enemy of mine.' He felt that

* See p. 103–4. † p. 115.

'scandal threatens to fall upon me', and broke off relations with Lilly.

When, in 1648, Wharton was arrested (after the House of Commons had demanded that the Committee of the Militia should discover the author of *No Merlin nor Mercury: but a New Almanack*, in which Wharton attacked the Parliament even more rabidly than usual), Ashmole obviously suspected that Lilly had something to do with it, for he wrote a poem on his friend's predicament in which he treated 'the English Merlin' far from kindly. The two men had no personal contact for the next eighteen months or more—though they probably both attended the 1649 Astrologers' Feast at the Painter-Stainers' Hall.

Wharton was only in custody for five months; he escaped from Newgate in August 1649, but was recaptured in November and sent to the notorious Gatehouse in Westminster. He managed to produce his almanac for 1650, nevertheless, smuggling the text out somehow; and his anti-Parliamentarian feelings, exacerbated by the execution of the King, erupted in a poem:

> Touch me not, *Traytor*! For I have a Sting
> For all, but such as love and serve the *King*.
> I am no *Temporist*: Nor can I brook
> The Pocket of a *Bradshaw*, *Steel*, or *Cook*;
> Or any *Regicide* that liveth: I
> Disdain all Harbours of *Disloyalty*.
> URANIA is Divine! and (to be clear)
> I serve no mortal, but the CAVALIER.
> If then thou be'st not one, pray let me lie,
> Until thou canst affect as well as buy.

And there was a Postscript:

> *Gentlemen* I cannot call you, since you drench'd your Hands in His Blood, who was the Fountain of all our Earthly Honour and Happiness, the Life and Light of the Land ... Nor Countrymen, who have (so Nero-like) inhumanely ripp'd the Bowels of your natural Mother, and exposed her

> Nakedness to the view of the pitiless World ... For certainly none of you are of the right English race, in that all of you degenerate so far from the true English Nature ... Or if you be; the most Prodigious Monsters that ever the Earth groaned under: In whose proditorious breasts, the Spirits of all expired Traytors, by a kind of Pythagatorical Transmigration, are inclosed. —Let after-ages impose a Name suitable to your Merits, for surely this cannot. In the interim, it shall suffice: You know whom I speak to; and that I speak what I know.

As it happened, the Council of State had been extremely worried by the increasing number of 'seditious and scandalous pamphlets' which had been coming out recently, and 'tending to the disturbance of the Commonwealth'. John Bradshaw, Milton's friend and President of the Court that tried the King, whose signature headed his death-warrant, was particularly annoyed by Wharton's outburst. Soon, Ashmole heard from an authoritative source that Wharton was almost certain to be hanged.

He went to see Lilly, who 'professed himself very sorry'—despite the enmity with which he and Wharton had been publicly squabbling for the past several years. Whether it was simply a case of astrologers closing ranks against the world, or of Lilly carefully building up a store of friends who might be of help to him in the still politically unsound future, can only be guessed. But anyway, he promised Ashmole that he would approach his patron Bulstrode Whitelocke (the dedicatee of *Christian Astrology*, and now Keeper of the Great Seal and President-elect of the Council) to see what could be done.

Whitelocke advised that Wharton should follow his own example, and take the line of least resistance; should in fact 'lye quiet, without making the least Complaint, and after Christmas, when his being a Prisoner was almost forgotten, Bradshaw out of the way', he, Whitelocke, would be President of the Council, and might possibly arrange his release.

And so it was. Lilly visited Wharton, and persuaded him to this course. And the latter was indeed released in February 1650, on condition that in future he would write nothing against the

Parliament or the State. Wharton acknowledged Lilly's help in his almanac for 1651—referring to him as his 'Oaken-friend,' his 'approved friend'—but does not seem otherwise to have shown any special gratitude. The episode did Lilly no sort of good with Bradshaw, who, learning of Wharton's release, remarked: 'I will be an enemy to Lilly if ever he come before me.' But his generosity to an enemy commended Lilly to Ashmole, and the friendship between them was henceforth to be firm and unshakeable. And it did his general reputation no harm, for the episode became well known: a correspondent, Abraham Wheelock, writing to him a year later to congratulate him 'whom God hath raised up to be so happie a raiser & prompter of these admired studies [of astrology] in the Universities', pointed out that

> if there be anie that dare adventure to whisper against you in private, your charitie towards them in readiness to help them, is publicklie knowne; witnes your not onlie pardonninge of a ... traducer of some bodies, whom to require, or rather to teach him better manners, & to rule his tonge, you were pleased to fetch him out of prison ...

Astrologers as a body showed themselves properly grateful to Whitelocke; in the Ashmolean collection there is a letter in Wharton's beautiful writing thanking him for the 'good affection and great encouragement' he had given to astrology—and in particular for his help to Lilly, 'who not only held him by the hand when first he stept abroad, but [had] ever since afforded him [his] Countenance and Assistance in the whole Course of Conduct for his Studies'. The letter is signed not by Wharton, but by the Society of Astrologers of London; a tactful touch.

From 1650 until the end of Lilly's life, Ashmole and he were to meet regularly. Ashmole, in that year, was elected Steward of the Society of Astrologers; he sent Lilly clients, and submitted to him any astrological questions which were in dispute. They went together to call on other astrologers, apparently in an attempt to pull the profession together now that civil disturbances were stilling somewhat. (In June, for instance, according to Ashmole's diary, 'Mr Lilly & my selfe went to visit Dr Ardee at his house in the Minories.')

Ashmole remained cautious for a while, occasionally asking himself 'whether Mr Lilly will prove a real friend to me,' and setting up an horary chart to discover 'whether Mr Lilly told me true last night, when he said he had Pisces ascending and the part of fortune in Scorpio in his nativity.' (An astrologer seeking to mislead a friend about his true nature would naturally present him with inaccurate birth-data.)

But gradually confidence grew between the two men; and more strongly as Lilly became, in the years after 1650, more and more dissatisfied with the rule of Parliament. In 1651, though on the one hand he published *Monarchy or No Monarchy in England*, discussing whether '*England* shall no more be Governed by KINGS, or that this PARLIAMENT shall be subdued by any of the Issue or Race of the late KING,' on the other he also published in his 1652 *Merlinus Anglicus* the prediction that the soldiery, dissatisfied at conditions of service, would combine with the commonalty to overthrow Parliament.

No doubt this was astrologically revealed to him; but he can scarcely be acquitted of trying to stir up trouble, for (as he wrote later, in his autobiography)

> The Parliament now grows odious unto all good men, the members whereof become insufferable in their pride, covetousness, self-ends, laziness, minding nothing but how to enrich themselves. Much heart-burning now arose betwixt the Presbyterian and Independent, the latter siding with the Army, betwixt whose two judgments there was no medium.
>
> Now came up, or first appeared, that monstrous people called Ranters: and many other novel opinions, in themselves heretical and scandalous, were countenanced by Members of Parliament, many whereof were of the same judgement. Justice was neglected, vice countenanced, and all care of the common good laid aside. Every judgement almost groaned under the heavy burden they then suffered; the army neglected; the city of London scorned; the ministry,

> especially those who were orthodox and serious, honest or virtuous, had no countenance; my soul began to loathe the very name of a Parliament, or Parliament-man.

It must be admitted that Lilly was also becoming somewhat right-wing in his late middle-age, and he found the increasing egalitarianism of the 'lower orders' distressing. The common people were less respectful than they used to be: the children threw dirt at gentlemen as they passed through the London streets, and it was not safe even to travel in a coach there, for (as Evelyn put it) car-men 'domineer in the streets, overthrow the hell-carts (for so they name the coaches), cursing and reviling at the nobles'.

Lilly had by now become something of a dandy—not, certainly, Cavalier in his dress, but in neat, clean clothes; and he disliked it intensely when men shouted 'French Dog!' at him in the streets because he was not untidily dressed, or threw sand at him. Things were not what they used to be, and he was beginning to think that that was all to the bad.

Naturally, Lilly made the most of his sudden about-turn in his autobiography, written after the Restoration; but that he did suffer a revulsion against Parliament is clear. And it was certainly not the case that he had in this instance, as so often, his eye on the main chance; for, as Aubrey put it, 'as to human foresight, there was not possibility of the King's returne'—nor does it seem that Lilly had astrological precognition of the Restoration.

He was by no means alone in his disillusionment. The Rump had outlived its usefulness, and was generally in disrepute. Censorship, heavy taxation, the confiscation of property, had all rebounded on the Parliamentarians' heads, as had the puritanical suppression of much popular entertainment, and the attempts to enforce a strict moral code. England was feeling the strain. Wenceslas Hollar, the engraver, told Aubrey that 'when he first came into England (which was a serene time of peace) the people, both poore and rich, did look cheerfully, but at his return, he found the Countenances of the people all changed, melancholy, spightful, as if bewitched.'

And elsewhere, Aubrey warms to the theme of the depressing state of England under the Rump:

> The greatest part of the Parliament-men ... were cursed Tyrants, and in love with their power ... Pride of Senators-for-Life is insufferable; and they were able to grind any one they owed ill will to powder; they were hated by the armie and the countrey they represented, and their name and memory stinkes—'twas worse than Tyrrany.

Indeed, the Rump seemed even in the early 1650s to be composed of men determined to be Senators-for-Life; and three years later was to introduce a Bill to perpetuate the existence of Parliament and the almost unlimited power of its members—even to provide that they should choose future M.P.s. This finally forced Cromwell to dissolve the disreputable House. But in 1651, there seemed no end to it; many people thought desperately of emigrating: Ashmole set up an horary chart to answer the question whether he 'had best to leave the kingdom in these troublesome times or stay'. Lilly's *Anglicus* for 1652 was among the earliest publications to reflect the revulsion of popular feeling against Parliament; moreover, it was 'so bold as to averr ... that the Parlamant stood uppon a tottering foundation, and that the Commonalty & Soldiery would join togather against them.' Parliament duly took notice of that passage:

'My *Anglicus*,' Lilly remembered, 'was for a whole week every day in the Parliament House, peeped into by the Presbyterians, one disliking this sentence, another finds another fault, others misliked the whole; so in the end a motion was made, that *Anglicus* should be inspected by the Committee for Plundered Ministers.' The Motion, passed by the House on October 26,

> *Ordered*, That the printed Book, entituled '*Merlini Anglici Ephemeris*, or Astrological Predictions for the Year 1652, by *William Lilly*, Student in Astrology' be referred to the Committee for Plundered Ministers to consider thereof: With Power to send for the Author, and secure him, if they see Cause ...

Fortunately for Lilly, William Lenthall, Speaker of the House ('ever my friend'), let him see a copy of the *Anglicus* with the offensive passages marked. Lilly immediately saw a way out of his predicament. He went to his printer, Warren, and had six new copies of the almanac printed with the objectionable passages either deleted or altered. (The printer was a Royalist, and when Lilly warned him that he might be examined by the Committee, remarked: 'Hang them! They are all rogues. I'll swear myself to the devil ere they shall have an advantage against you by my oath.')

Next day, Lilly appeared before the Committee, which showed great interest in the case—thirty-six members turned up, as against the usual five or six. The marked *Anglicus* was produced and handed to Lilly. He looked it over carefully, then looked the Speaker straight in the eye, and replied: 'This is none of my book. Some malicious Presbyterian hath wrote it, who are my mortal enemies. I disown it.'

The Committee seems to have been staggered. 'They looked upon one another like distracted men.' Lilly produced the half-dozen newly-printed almanacs, and distributed them. 'These I own,' he said; 'the others are counterfeits, published purposely to ruin me.'

Not unsurprisingly, the Committee was somewhat confused. There was a dumbfounded silence for some time, but perhaps equally unsurprisingly most members seem to have seen through the ruse (though they could prove nothing), and clamoured for the astrologer's imprisonment. 'Some were for Newgate,' Lilly writes, 'others for the Gate-House.' But eventually, one or two friends did speak up on his behalf—Walter Strickland, for instance, Parliament's former Ambassador to Holland.

> I came purposely into the Committee this day to see the man who is so famous in those parts where I have so long continued. I assure you his name is famous all over Europe. I come to do him justice. A book is produced by us, and said to be his: he denies it. We have not proved it, yet will commit him? Truly this is great injustice. It is likely he will write

next year, and acquaint the whole world with our injustice, and so well he may! It is my opinion, first to prove the book to be his, ere he be committed.

Another committee-man, Robert Reynolds, reminded his colleagues of Lilly's services to Parliament:

You do not know ... how many times, in our greatest distresses, we applying unto him, he hath refreshed our languishing expectations; he never failed us of comfort in our most unhappy distresses. I assure you, his writings have kept up the spirits both of our soldiery, the honest people of this nation, and many of us Parliament men. And now at last, for a slip of his pen (if it *were* his) to be thus violent against him: I must tell you, I fear the consequence ... It is my counsel, to admonish him hereafter to be more wary, and for the present, to dismiss him.

That plea, at all events, was justified: Lilly had given a great deal of encouragement to the Parliamentarian cause, not only in his almanacs, but in his private practice, when he was constantly replying to queries (some semi-official) about the war: Had the King taken Cambridge? Would Basing-hall fall? Would the King bring new troops from Ireland? When could the surrender of Pontefract be expected? How long would the Presbyterians continue to trouble Parliament? (a query from Sir Thomas Myddleton of Chirk). What would be the result of the elections? Would Cromwell continue to dominate the Council?

But it was no use: in the end, as Ashmole noted in his diary, Lilly was committed, and ordered to be taken in charge by the Sergeant-at-Arms. But as they were leaving the Court, a message came ordering their return. Lilly writes:

Oliver Cromwell, Lieutenant-General of the army, having never seen me, caused me to be produced again, where he steadfastly beheld me for a good space, and then I went with the messenger; but instantly a young clerk of that Committee asks the messenger what he did with me, "Where's the warrant? until that is signed you cannot seize Mr Lilly, or shall. Will you have an action of false imprisonment against you?" So I escaped that night, but next day obeyed the warrant.

That night Oliver Cromwell went to Mr R.* my friend, and said 'What, never a man to take Lilly's cause in hand but yourself? None to take his part but you? He shall not be long there.'

In fact, Lilly was in prison for thirteen days. Not a very long time—but any time spent in a seventeenth-century prison was too long. In 1648, one William Kith, prisoner in Newgate, petitioned the King: 'Having been preserved through your Majesty's sovereign mercy, from death, prays that you will extend the same mercy to his enlargement, and not let him remain here, the place being more full of horror than death.'

With Lilly in Newgate was Captain James Hind, who despite his reputation as a highwayman was really imprisoned for high treason (he had been a valiant fighter for Charles): he was hanged, drawn and quartered in 1652, and the journey from Newgate to the gallows at Tyburn was made sufficiently frequently to keep an erring astrologer fully in mind of the destination to which his lax tongue (or pen) might lead him. He was no doubt somewhat comforted by the visits of John Rushworth, Secretary of the Army; and after a petition had been supported by Sir Arthur Hazelrig, Richard Salway, Hugh Peter, and allegedly Cromwell himself, he was eventually released.

Apart from Lilly's autobiography, there is no evidence to prove the Protector's interest in the case. Reynolds left no memoirs. Lilly may have invented the story of his meeting with Cromwell, and the latter's intervention; though remembering the odium in which the Protector's name was held at the time when the astrologer wrote his memoirs, there seems to be no particular point in claiming him as friend or admirer. There is no temperamental

* Robert Reynolds.

reason why Cromwell should have taken the view that astrology was dangerous rubbish; in fact there are grounds for thinking that he may have looked upon the subject with sympathy, for while he was no great reader, and was unlikely to have read much about the astrological theory itself, he was certainly preoccupied with seeking out on earth visible signs of God's will, and there is no special reason to suppose that, in the prevailing atmosphere of the time, he might not have accepted planetary indications as godly ones. However, speculation is vain.

The whole uncomfortable episode revived Lilly's antipathy to the Presbyterians: not that it ever needed much encouragement. Though they had been officially removed from public office in 1648, he suspected (probably with justice) that various M.P.s were concealing Presbyterian sympathies, and that they had been responsible for his arrest. In *Annus Tenebrosus, or The Dark Year* (1652), dedicated to 'the commonwealth of England', he attacked them forthrightly:

> There is a people yet in being, and they pretending unto Godlinesse or Religion, which men we in our plain English doe call Divines, Ministers, Preachers, Ecclesiastical Men, or men conversant in holy things; in foraigne parts they are called Bishops, Cardonals, Abbots, Munks, Friers, &c. Men that step up sometimes into Pulpits, and pretend to instruct our Soules with the Doctrine of Christianity, but obedience to their own Constitutions; I say ... That there are yet left a generation of such Men, who are now privately designing some future trouble unto our State and Commonwealthes where otherwise they reside, which againe occasion the drawing of blood unto our State and other Nations, and destruction unto themselves ... I erre not, and there I hope the World will cleer me, that I doe not abuse or so much as once name or mention the *Presbyterians* or their *Proselytes*.

Again, this was a well-timed piece of rabble-rousing. Lilly was not alone in his dislike of the Presbyterians. Gadbury referred to 'the supercilious man in black', and Anthony Wood noticed that they 'would not goe to ale-houses or taverns, but send for their liquors to their respective chambers and tiple it there. Some would goe in publick; but then if over-taken, they were so cunning as to dissemble it in their way home by a lame leg or that some suddaine paine there had taken them.'

But Lilly, and astrologers in general, had special reasons to dislike the Presbyterians, and indeed all Puritans (not all Parliamentarians were Puritans, it is too infrequently remembered). The fact is that the Presbyterians led the barrage of attacks on astrology, with Thomas Gataker, John Vicars, and other laymen and clergy in the van. Indeed, in 1652, a group of Independent clergy actually petitioned Parliament to make judicial astrology illegal. They got nowhere.

The Presbyterian revulsion from astrology was temperamental: a successful astrologer was obviously an evil man (as opposed to an unsuccessful astrologer, who was simply a fool). It was also the case that many religious opponents of Presbyterianism – Archbishop Laud, for instance—took astrology seriously, and would certainly have been against any attempt to equate it with witchcraft.

Finally, the idea that it was possible to stare past the veil of time into the future, however vaguely, was anathema to a Presbyterian, to a Calvinist. Calvin himself had written:

> Let it ... be our first principle that to desire any other knowledge of pre-destination than that which is expounded by the word of God, is no less infatuated than to walk where there is no path, or to seek light in darkness. Let us not be ashamed to be ignorant in a matter in which ignorance is learning. Rather let us abstain from the search after knowledge, to which it is both foolish as well as perilous and even fatal to aspire.

That was the knowledge allegedly possessed by the astrologer. It was to be shunned, and those who attempted to practise it were to be despised and attacked.

There was always to be a section of political or social or religious life against which a polemicist like Lilly could sharpen his tongue. But in fact *Annus Tenebrosus* was to be almost his last piece of political invective. He had been perhaps the most political of all astrologers—partly, no doubt, because it was a satisfactory way of selling almanacs; but partly too, I believe, because he was naturally a political animal, with a mercurial mind delighting in argument—any argument—only partly because he really believed in it; chiefly for the fun of the battle.

This may have been a main reason for his much-abused political balancing-act. Self-preservation played its part; but so did a sheer delight in taking up one side of an argument simply because someone else (often someone he disliked) took up the other side. But this had made him enemies, and during the next fifteen years—indeed, virtually for the rest of his life—he was to be attacked by almost every other astrologer in England; to be showered with abuse, printed and spoken. Especially at the time of the Restoration, this was to give him some uneasy moments. But on the whole, he seems to have revelled in it ('William Wranglicus', he used to sign some of his letters to Ashmole). And during the 1650s he was to have every opportunity to do so.

# 7

# Fame and Disrepute

*Quoth Hudibras, the Stars determine*
*You are my Prisoners, base Vermine;*
*Could they not tell you so, as well*
*As what I came to know, foretell?*
*By this what cheats you are we find*
*That in your own Concerns are blind;*
*Your Lives are now at my Dispose,*
*To be redeem'd by Fine or Blows.*

*Hudibras* II:III (1072)

In 1652, Lilly bought Hurst Wood, a house in its own grounds, at Hersham, in the parish of Walton-upon-Thames, in Surrey—an area he knew well. It was a large house, of thirteen hearths, the hearth-tax records reveal, and stood in eighteen acres of parkland, some of which was rather roughly farmed. It cost him £950. It is difficult to equate seventeenth-century values with those of the 1970s; but in today's terms, the purchase price might have been between £23,000 and £28,000.

The house probably stood on the south side of Thrupps Lane (formerly Coniers Lane, and then Hatch Lane), two hundred yards from the River Mole, and about a mile from the Portsmouth Road, now the A3. A house called Le Hurst was demolished on that site as recently as 1963, and may have been the original.

It was Lilly's second decision to move out of London, and it was permanent—though for the time being he kept his house in the Strand, returning there from time to time to keep his hand in as a consultant astrologer. He seems to have stayed at Hurst Wood for a time before actually buying the house, for he told Ashmole some years later that 'in 1652 I and *uxor** and servants gave the Master of the house I now live in, 30s per weeke, for Diett onely, I found wyne ... our servant washed all our wearing linnen ...'

In his autobiography, he gives a pious reason for moving: 'I found it convenient to retire into the country, there to end my days in peace and tranquillity; for in London my practice was such, I had none or very little time afforded me to serve God, who had been so gracious to me.'

There is no reason to suspect that he was being unduly sanctimonious: he had always been a naturally religious man, and was later to behave with great generosity to the parish of Walton. He could, of course, afford to be generous, as far as money was concerned: by this time he was extremely comfortably off. In 1651 he had been able to invest £1,030 in fee-farm rents, to bring him an annual income of £110 (say £2,200–£3,300); and he still made a considerable income from his clients, and by teaching. In *Christian Astrology* he claims to have taught more students than any other astrologer, and among his papers can be found notes of students in Lancashire, Northamptonshire, Rutland, Norwich, Wiltshire, Cambridge and the West country, as well as inquiries from Madrid, Naples and Barbados.

His pupils paid him well. In 1640, John Humphrey's fee had been £40 (say £850), and he said he would have paid more. Lilly's financial position was always secure: it is unlikely that he was ever in serious difficulties after his first marriage. He did not earn a great deal from his almanacs—perhaps the equivalent of £1,500 a year. But he charged the equivalent of £3.75 (half-a-crown in his time) for a consultation, so that an average of 2,000 consultations a year would have brought him at least £7,500 in today's terms—and noble clients would have paid him considerably more than maidservants coming to the door, or the tradesmen who wrote him pathetic illiterate notes. One of his contemporaries claimed that in 1662 Lilly was making £500 a year, which one might estimate at about £15,000 in today's values.

* Mrs Lilly.

Such equations are arguable: but when one looks at average incomes during the seventeenth century, one gets a glimpse of just how well-off Lilly was. Gregory King, in 1688, made some computations of average incomes: he suggested that at that time (twenty years later than the time we are considering) the average income of the Temporal Lords of England (of which there were only 160) was £3,200 a year. But Baronets had an income of only £880, Esquires of £450, and 'Persons in greater offices and places' a mere £240 a year.

At the lower end of the scale, incomes were pathetically poor (to our eyes, and perhaps also to those receiving them): a common soldier would receive £14 a year, a 'labouring person' £15, a military officer £60 and a naval officer £80 a year. A cottager could exist on £6 10s a year—and 400,000 of them did. A man-servant could be employed for 8d a day, a woman for 4d. Lilly had no difficulty in keeping a comfortable house on his substantial income.

The 1650s were to be both happy and disturbing years for him; perhaps, naïvely, he did not realize how many people had been upset by his political polemics. Very few knew of his attempted help to Charles I (which was in any event fairly limited), and many of his contemporaries viewed him as either a fool or a villain. On the back of an almanac of his for 1651, a Victorian reader found and recorded a satirical squib written in a seventeenth-century hand:

> Here lyeth hee, that lyed in ev'ry page;
> The scorne of men, dishonour of his age;
> Parliament's pandar, and ye nation's cheat;
> Ye kingdom's juglar, impudency's seat;
> The armye's spanyill, and ye gen'rall's witch;
> Ye devill's godson, grandchild of a bitch;
> Clergy's blasphemer, enemy to ye king;
> Under this dunghill lyes that filthy thing;
> Lilly ye wise man's hate, foole's adoration,
> Lilly ye $\frac{\text{excrement}}{\text{infamy}}$ of ye English nation.

The choice of vituperative noun in the last line seems significant. At the same time, another squib was circulating:

To Lillie now all men may well say Phy
Because your name saith twice to you ye lie.
But if you say you have an L in more
Then add ye fiftie lies to two before.
Thus lies for weekes make up a good new yeere
O brave what Almanacker have we here.

Occasionally, private disputes brought private attacks. On December 7th, 1650, an anonymous letter was left for Lilly with a porter near his house (the caller at the same time made off with six of the astrologer's table-men and an andiron knob!). The writer seems to have been particularly upset by a private judgment in which Lilly had pronounced 'elder brothers childless, and younger brothers certayn heirs of their estates'. He accused him of going out of his way to 'foole women out of their money, and disturb the peace of families and private relaxation by ... false and dangerous predictions'. For good measure, the astrologer was also accused of raising the devil by 'Superstitions, Ceremonies and Consecrations by Popish priests (prohibited by law) and when nothing was wanted but humane sacrifice (at which horrid mention all others trembled) your help was offered with all alacrity.'

Then there were political attacks: Lilly's short biography of the King caused little stir in England, but a considerable uproar among the expatriate Englishmen collected around Charles II at the Hague; and it was there that Sir Edward Walker, later to become Charles II's Garter King-of-Arms, and who had been Secretary of War to Charles I, wrote his *Full Answer to a Confused Mixture of False, Traiterous and Contradictory Observations on the Life and Actions of the late King Charles*. Walker's book was passed around in manuscript during the 1650s, but not fully published until 1705.

He wrote in the form of a letter to Lilly, whose client he had once been, and who (he claimed) he once believed to be 'a Person of much Loyalty and Integrity and honest Principles'. He began by dealing at length with Lilly's assertion that the King had favoured the Irish rebels. But then,

> having leisure enough, and observing through your whole Discourse a kind of Civility in your Expressions, and some real Truths; yet so enterlayed with frivolous and malicious Imputations, the better to captivate the Willing, and induce the Ignorant to believe whatever you have said is undeniably true; I have thought it a part of the Duty I owe to the Memory and most exemplary Goodness of that most Excellent King, to trace you throughout, and to discover how weak and impertinent your Calumnies are, and how much He was beyond His Enemies in all kinds of Virtue and Honour, nay probably (all Circumstances considered) beyond any Man that lived in this age.

It may be conjectured from this that Sir Edward was about to be as outrageous in his claims for Charles as Lilly had been against him; and in the event, he is perhaps even more so. He makes some good points, however, even if his book (unlike Lilly's) contributes little to what we can know of Charles's character. He ends with a positive threat: Lilly's masters, the Parliamentarians, are, he says, 'Men of Blood, Covetousness, Self-ends, Bribery, Oppression, Corruption, &c., and ... shall be punished for your Rebellion, Treason and Barbarous Cruelty on the Person of our late King. Be your own Judges, for surely a severe Account will be had of His Blood and all that spilt in the most horrid rebellion.' Sir Edward concludes:

> And now, though I pretend not at all to Prophesying, yet methinks I see so far before me as to tell you your own Fate, and that you have been a Person of late Years so full of Self-interest, as that you shall not see the happy Days you mention; for though by your Predictions you have encouraged your Party, and done as much Mischief in stirring up the People as any Man, and yet you know few Men love to

be upbraided with their Beginnings, or to be told by whose means they rise; and although by false Prophesies, Mutinies, Tumults, and at length by open Rebellion, your Masters have got their Power, they will now be too wise by the same means to lose it; so as their Commonwealth being (as they believe) established, they will pluck up the Degrees by which they ascended; and if you leave not writing or give them any more such true Characters as I lately recited, who can blame them to put the Laws in Execution against you, or to banish or otherwise treat you as an Incendiary and seditious Person?

In a sense, Lilly got the worst of both worlds: though he had supported the Parliamentarian cause, on the whole Parliamentarians were temperamentally less sympathetic to astrology than the Royalists; and among the general attacks made on astrology during the 1650s (increasing in vehemence as the years went on) he was often mentioned by name. There was, for instance, *Confidence Dismounted*, a pamphlet published in April 1652 by William Brommerton, 'a well wisher to the Commonweale', which especially attacked Lilly and Nicholas Culpeper, the herbalist (and, one must say, as mild and honest a man as ever lived):

Oh! it grieves mee to think upon that simple deluded multitude, that so runne after this sect of Knaves (for so I may justly terme them) some asking whether they shall be rich and some one question, and some another, and these same cunning knaves will alwayes tell them a good fortune, that they may draw their money from them the more liberally ...

There were several replies to this accusation, among them one from John Gadbury (to become one of Lilly's chief antagonists) showing astrologers to be, irrefutably, 'true servants of God'.

Astrologers certainly had no need to worry unduly about their livelihoods: the ordinary people still showed great confidence in their interpretations of celestial events, however wild they might be, and however diverse. There was, for instance, a general wariness in the early weeks of 1652 about the impending eclipse of the sun in March. The day of the eclipse was referred to as 'Black Monday' by various commentators who speculated about the nature of the events it foretold: Lilly thought it meant the collapse of Scottish Presbyterianism and law reform; Culpeper was one of those who thought it portended the coming of the Fifth Monarchy, and of true democracy. Some other astrologers believed it signalled the collapse of monarchy, or the fall of Rome and the death of the Pope.

Almanac-readers went from pamphlet to pamphlet and took their choice, ignoring only the pamphlet issued by the Council of State, announcing the eclipse as a natural event, foretelling nothing. Those who could afford it loaded their possessions into their coaches and made for the open country outside the city, where they could hope to escape any holocaust; others bought astrological medals or amulets to ward off the coming catastrophe. At Dalkeith the poor threw away all their possessions, 'casting themselves on their backs, and their eyes towards heaven and praying most passionately that Christ would let them see the Sun again and save them.'

In the event, John Evelyn was among the citizens who recorded the passing of March 29th without terrestrial incident, noting merely the occurrence of 'that celebrated eclipse which had been so much threatened by the astrologers, and which had so exceedingly alarmed the whole nation that hardly any would work and none stir out of their houses—so ridiculously were they abused by knavish and ignorant star gazers.'

During the first half of the seventeenth century there was an enormous increase in the public discussion of astrology and the number of astrological publications: not only those directed at the simple and simple-minded, but those meant for the learned, the theorists of astrology, interested in serious argument, and in what might be called the philosophy of the subject. Although there was a growing number of charlatans already to be found in the back streets, the subject was still largely respectable: it was still, after all, being taught at the universities of Bologna and

Salamanca, and was to be taught at the latter university until the eighteenth century (though the Sorbonne had forbidden the teaching of *judicial* astrology in 1619).

There were of course some objections. In his *De la Comparaison de l'Homme avec le Monde*, the French physician Jourdain Guibelet argued that the predictions of astrologers seemed to him to be as ill-founded as those of fortune-tellers, and that they were often produced by the aid of magic and the raising of demons. Yet despite a certain amount of complaint about the theory of the system (why, when so many cheerful people were born under the influence of Mars and Saturn, did astrologers persist in arguing that those are melancholic planets?) he certainly accepted the influence of the planets as self-evident. He is not very persuasive.

Neither is Antonia Merenda, who in 1640 argued from his study in Pavia (where he was a professor of Civil Law) that the prediction of specific events was a diabolical act. Most astrologers agreed with him. He was on sounder ground when he pointed out that it was almost impossible for one to obtain a really accurate birth-time: few clocks kept exact time, and anyway clocks were often only found in convents or monasteries or fortresses, where birth was unlikely to take place, and the system of trotting hastily to the nearest time-piece to discover the birth-time of one's newly born child was not exactly scientific.

There were on the other side those non-astrologers who went to extremes in their persistent support of the theory and what it could do. In 1649, Valentin Weigel's *Astrologie Theologized* was first published in English. In it he took the view that the planets ruled 'all orders, states and degrees of men, distinctions of persons, dignitaries, gifts, offices, and every kind of life as well naturally ordained by God himself as thought of and invented by humane wit ... All these are the fruits of the Starrs.' Through astrology one could obtain complete knowledge 'of all the wonderful and secret things of God'.

In 1631, the enemies of astrology had obtained a new ally in Pope Urban VIII. The Popes had taken equivocal attitudes on the subject during the previous century. Sixtus IV had used astrology to make all important appointments; Alexander VI consulted the astrological prophecies of Cardinal Bianco; Julius II, receiving in Bologna the news of his election, asked an astrologer to calculate a propitious time for his journey to Rome, and for his coronation; Leo X commissioned Luce Gauricus's edition of Ptolemy's *Almagest*, and Clement VII continued to encourage Gauricus to compile his catalogues of astrological horoscopes and other data, until a heavy book fell on to the astrologer's head while he was working in the Pope's library, and killed him.

Urban VIII took a different view, however—mainly because of the somewhat irritating activities of a certain Fr Morandi, of whom nothing is known other than that on the basis of certain astrological calculations he came to the conclusion that Urban would die in 1630. Fascinated by his discovery, he unwisely circulated it to three friends. Abbot Luigi Gherardi of Padua and Francesco Lamponi agreed with him; Fr Raffaelo Visconti thought that as long as the Pope was careful to stay in Rome, he might live until 1643 or even 1644. The latter persuasively set out his arguments in *Un Discorso sulla Vita di Urbana VIII*, which he presented to a number of cardinals and other churchmen.

But Morandi was the better-known astrologer, and it was his opinion that was believed; so in 1630 a considerable number of foreign cardinals journeyed to Rome in the confident expectation of a conclave for the election of a new Pope. Urban failed to see the joke, imprisoned Fr Morandi (who died of a fever shortly afterwards), and on April 1st, 1631, issued a new Bull against astrology. The Bull certainly had its effect in Italy. On April 22nd, 1635, for instance, Giacinto Cantini, nephew of a cardinal, was beheaded, Fra Cherubino da Poligno and Fra Bernardino were hanged and afterwards burned in the Campo di Fiori in Rome, and five other friars were condemned to the galleys, for astrological predictions of the Pope's death, and alleged attempts to bring it about by sorcery.

The Pope's Bull had only an indirect effect in England, and that mainly through the writing of Caesar Carena, whom the Pope appointed as an Inquisitor, and who wrote at length about astrology in his *Treatise on the Office of the Most Holy Inquisition* printed at Cremona in 1636, and reprinted several times and in several languages. His conclusions were on the whole not very unfavourable to astrology.

It was quite proper, he confirmed, for an astrologer to attempt to discover the natural characteristics of a man or woman by a study of the planetary positions at the time of birth (though it was improper to consider the horoscope of Christ, and certainly not that of a Pope). Aquinas had proved to Carena's satisfaction that an astrologer could discover certain facts about one's temperament: 'this conclusion is certain,' he writes, 'nor can there be any doubt about it, because the stars act directly upon the body and its humours.' Prediction, however, was a far less certain business.

As to astrological medicine, this had too honourable and long a history for anyone to dismiss it out of hand. It was quite proper for an astrologer to set up horoscopes at the beginning of an illness, and for the moment when the sick person took to his bed, and to predict the course of an illness. But prediction in other fields was dangerous: it would be quite improper, for instance, to predict that because of the positions of the planets at birth a man was bound to be a sodomite—and apart from being improper, it was forbidden, not specifically by Urban's Bull, but by an earlier one of Sixtus X (in 1586).

The attacks made on William Lilly during the 1650s were rarely based on any desire to prove astrology either fallacious or wicked: most of them came from colleagues, fellow-astrologers who attacked him simply because he was the most successful man among them; his discredit would undoubtedly mean an increased reward for the rest of them, as well as the intellectual kudos that would certainly attach itself to anyone who could demonstrate himself a better astrologer. A smaller number, usually rather better argued, came from the minority (though a growing minority) who were simply against astrology on moral or religious grounds—men such as Thomas Gataker, the puritan divine and critic, a very reputable preacher and lecturer whose commentaries on Isaiah, Jeremiah and *Lamentations* became well known. He was a modest and very honest, forthright man whose first publication, in 1619, had been on the question of the lawfulness of casting lots except when used for divination.

Now, in 1653, he launched an attack on astrologers in general and 'the Scurrilous Aspersions of that grand Imposter, Mr William Lillie' in particular. It makes a substantial book of 192 pages, mainly discussing a text from Jeremiah: 'Thus saith the Lord, Learn not the way of the heathen, and be not dismayed at the signs of heaven; for the heathen are dismayed at them.'

Gataker rebuked Lilly caustically for his 'raving and ranting rhetorick' against the Presbyterians, pointing out that 'in all these dreadful Eclipses and malignant Aspects' he found 'much matter of bad, dismal and disastrous concernment to Princes, Potentates, Priests, Lawyers, Husbandmen &c., but none at all ever to Wizards, Witches, Conjurers, Fortune-Tellers, Sorcerers, Stargazers, Astrologers, &c ...'

It was a very personal attack, on sectarian grounds rather than any other, and Lilly was not much affected by it. Neither was he much affected by the death of his wife Jane, which occurred at the same time. A laconic note in his autobiography records the event: 'The 16th of February 1653/4, my second wife died; for whose death I shed no tears.' Probably a Quaker, she was buried in Walton Church, 'without bells, without ceremony; she never had child, or was conceived,' says a scribbled line in the margin of her horoscope in one of Lilly's notebooks.

He obviously had had little pleasure in her company (the note about her never having conceived may say something about their marital relationship). The Quakers as a sect hated astrology and constantly attacked it, which can scarcely have sweetened the marriage – and Lilly even made a financial loss, for 'I had five hundred pounds with her as a portion, but she and her poor relations spent me one thousand pounds.' A little over a year later, he married again: Ruth Nedham, a year younger than himself, the daughter of a Captain Isaac Nedham of Edmonton; he was to be as happy with his third wife as he had been with his first, and she was to outlive him.

This was in a sense the period of his greatest political influence. He was able to recommend, through John Claypole, a client who happened also to be Cromwell's son-in-law, the appointment of his patron Bulstrode Whitelocke as Ambassador to Sweden, and the appointment of Cromwell as Lord Protector must have given him a sense of security. Moreover, he had a growing number of other extremely influential clients, which included not only the Leveller leader Richard Overton, but Owen Cox, a well-known sea-captain, Lieutenant-Colonel Read, ex-Governor of Poole, Adjutant-General Allen, a leading Republican, and Cornet (later Colonel) Joyce, supposed by Lilly to be the executioner of Charles I. Major-General John Lambert was another client, and later invited Lilly to elect a day on which he could attempt to escape from the Tower during his imprisonment after the Restoration.

Gataker returned to the attack in 1654 with '*A Discours Apologetical*: wherein Lilies lewd and lowd lies in his Merlin or Pasquil for the Year 1654 are cleerly laid open ... and his Malicious and Murtherous Mind, inciting to a general Massacre of God's Ministers, from his own Pen, evidentlie evinced ...'

Gadbury, no friend to Lilly, felt bound to rebuke Gataker for 'scurrilous language, and horrid imprecations, against men whom I know not, as Wizards, Witches, dealers with the Devil, Helhounds, Sycophants, and a thousand more non-Gospel phrases ...' But it was Lilly who again bore the brunt of Gataker's new attack. And attacks in general were building up in intensity and in potential danger. In 1655 he was indicted on the suit of a half-witted woman, at Middlesex Sessions, for having unlawfully given judgment respecting the recovery of stolen goods, and received half-a-crown for it.

The prosecution was under an Act of 1603, 'Against Conjuration, Witchcraft and dealings with evill and wicked spirits,' which laid it down that 'if any person or persons shall ... take upon him or them by Witchcraft Inchantment Charme or Sorcerie to tell or declare in what place any treasure or Golde or Silver should or might be founde or had in the earth or other secret places, or where Goods or Things loste or stolen should be found or become' they should suffer a year's imprisonment for the first offence, with regular six-hour appearances in the pillory on market-day during which they should confess their errors. A second offence was punishable by death. It was a serious charge.

It is difficult to deny Lilly's claim that this was a case put up against him by the Presbyterians; the court was packed with them. Though the law stated quite unequivocally that it was illegal to use astrology as a means to discover such things as where stolen goods had been hidden—it was too obviously an occult practice, and savoured of witchcraft—this was generally disregarded.

The indictment was brought by one Anne East. It accused Lilly, 'not having the fear of God before his eyes, but being moved and seduced by the devil, the 10th day of July, in the Year of our Lord 1654' of telling Mrs East 'where ten waistcoats, of the value of five pounds, of the goods and chattels of the said Alexander East, then lately lost and stolen from the said Alexander East, should be found and become.'

Lilly reports that Mrs East 'was put upon this action against me by two ministers, who had framed for her a very ingenious speech, which she could speak without book, as she did the day of hearing the traverse.' She produced one woman friend who swore that, her son having run away from home, Lilly told her 'he was gone for the Barbadoes', and that she would hear from him within thirteen days, which she did. Another woman swore that, her husband having deserted her, Lilly 'told her he was in Ireland, and would be at home such a time; and, said she, he did come home accordingly.' Lilly was, it seems, being accused of being a successful astrologer.

He agreed in court that he had accepted half-a-crown from Mrs East, but claimed that he had simply told her that her stolen goods would not be recovered and reminded her that she had come to him confused by the conflicting advice of several other astrologers, and pleading for a final verdict. He produced his *Introduction to Astrology*,* pointing out that it had been officially licensed and not suppressed, that astrology was a science not contradicted by scripture, and that he had certainly never used any 'charms, sorceries or inchantments related in the bill of indictment'.

* Presumably, in fact, *Christian Astrology* (see pp. 105, 107).

He also argued that astrology was accepted at the universities—though in fact a publication by John Webster had, only the previous year, deplored the neglect of the subject there, while praising Lilly, Ashmole and others for having taken 'unwearied pains for the resuscitation and promotion of this noble Science'. Four years later freshmen at Oxford and Cambridge were to shout in chorus, in Schools, 'Astrologia non est scientia!'

However, at this point Mrs East seems rather to have lost her head: having recited the speech written for her, she went on to say that after she had visited Lilly she 'could not rest a nights, but was troubled with bears, lions and tygers, &c.' Lilly's counsel was easily able to demolish her, and the case was dismissed.

It had brought him indifferent publicity; and hatched another batch of attacks—the anonymous *Merlinus Democritus*, for instance, which listed a number of spurious events allegedly foretold by Lilly, together with others he did not foresee: 'And likewise in the year 1653 was that great and fatal eclipse of the Moon, a little before which time, William Lilly found a huge Turd at his door; and on coming to Southampton's House to view the effects of it, vow'd to be reveng'd upon the Stars and Planets.'

Ashmole remained a true friend; and the converse was also true, for Lilly was a comforting adviser to his friend during a troublesome period of matrimonial discord. Mrs Ashmole—Lady Manwaring—had long realized that Ashmole had married her for her money, and was becoming extremely irritable. At the beginning of August 1653, Ashmole had set up a horoscope to discover 'what kind of disease it is that now troubles my wife', obviously believing that her ill-temper must be provoked by some motive other than himself. On August 1st, his diary notes:

> About 10 hours before noon a great falling out with my wife about her clothes. This continued long from day to day. Mars and the Moon going to opposition and in fixed signs shew great contention and falling out ... Though Mercury lord of the 5 house is in trine to the ascendant of my radix, yet this year she would not suffer me to enjoy her bed, nor did I more than one time ...

Things quietened down for a while; though not for long. Ashmole assured himself, astrologically, that he would continue to enjoy his wife's fortune (which was what in the main concerned him); and in March 1654 a long-drawn-out lawsuit about the Manor of Bradshaw between the Ashmoles and Sir Humphrey Forster, Mrs Ashmole's brother, was settled in their favour. However much this pleased Ashmole, it had no effect on his wife's temper, for shortly afterwards she stormed out of his house and went to stay with a Mr Witt (who seems to have been a friend of Sir Humphrey). Then began three 'troublesome yeares' between husband and wife, during which she brought some kind of lawsuit against him, the details of which have vanished.

It was during those three years that Lilly and Ashmole became really intimate friends, the former often acting as Ashmole's agent, and attempting to arrange a reconciliation, though he remained wholly on his friend's side, noting in the margin of a paper in the Ashmolean collection:

> Indeed, I do know shee was wholly culpable of that 3 yeares Law Suite which then happened, the Native [i.e., Ashmole] very frequently mooving her for a reconcilement and her returne unto him for Cohabitacon. I my selfe have often done the like, viz: sollicited her to return to the Native. And as Mars is Lord of the Native's 12th house and sixt, so they wear but vulgar & ordinary people who first began the Quarrell about her,

and the whole position was exacerbated by the planetary positions in Ashmole's Chart, which augured 'much damage in his estate by a woaman'.

The two men saw each other as often as possible during these years; when Ashmole came to London, as he did frequently, they would meet perhaps at an astrologers' feast, or privately, for a drink and conversation with friends: a letter survives, for instance, dated January 12th, 1655, from Ashmole 'to my very good freind Mr John Booker in Cree Church Lane':

THE STARRY
MESSENGER;
OR,
An Interpretation of that ſtrange Apparition of three *Suns* ſeene in *London*, 19 *Novemb.* 1644. being the Birth Day of King CHARLES.

The effects of the Eclips of the Sun, which will be viſible in ENGLAND, 11 *Auguſt* 1645. whoſe influence continues in force, from *January*, 1646. to *Decemb.* 1647. almoſt two whole yeares; and cannot but be the fore-runner of ſome extraordinary mutation in moſt Common-wealths of *Europe*, but principally in *ENGLAND*. *With an Anſwer to an Aſtrologicall Judgement. Printed at* Oxford, *upon his Majeſties preſent March.*

By WILLIAM LILLY *Student* in *Aſtrologie.*

*LONDON,*
Printed for *John Partridge* and *Humphry Blunden*, and are to be ſold at the Signe of the *Cocke* in *Ludgate Streete*, and the *Caſtle* in *Cornehill*, 1645.

8. *The Starry Messenger* (1645)
(*British Library Board*)

9. Elias Ashmole, painted by John Riley
(*Ashmolean Museum, Oxford*)

10. William Lilly: an anonymous portrait, c. 1645
*(Ashmolean Museum, Oxford)*

Worthy freind,

These are only to acquaint you that I intend to be this night at the Mairemaid where wilbe other of your freinds, that as earnestly long to see you as will Your reall freind E. Ashmole. Mr Lilly has promised us his Company.

Still, it was a sad time; in the margin of his diary, Ashmole scribbled the pathetic couplet

How sad's that Lyfe, when cruell Fate
Waste all its Houres, 'twixt Love & Hate.

A few days later, he spent twelve days in prison, presumably at his wife's instigation.

In May 1655, he, Lilly and Booker got together to do some thorough work on his 'revolutions' for the coming year—what modern astrologers would call his 'progressions', or laymen a 'forecast'. The notes hint that 'the reconciliacon between the Native and his wife's Brother [Sir Humphrey] may perhaps be effected ...' and Ashmole notes, in the third person, that a particular astrological phenomenon 'seemes to shew the Natives affection to his wife (& his desire of application toward her) which perhaps he might dispose of but for the assistance that she has by Mars lord of the 10. vizt. power or law that seemes to obstruct. Yet the 2d part of the year such hopes may faile her ...'

This is only one example of the extent to which Ashmole used astrology in his everyday life: the entries of his diary rarely omit the astrological reasons for any decision, however minor; the glyphs representing the planets and their positions appear almost daily, marking the receipt of a letter, the visit of a friend, the laying of the first brick of a new greenhouse, the first signs of a cold on the chest. These were not necessarily slavishly copied to denote the necessary cause of events; to Ashmole's curious and enquiring mind they simply provided another bank of evidence of the efficacy of astrological prognostication.

In any event, in the spring of 1655 he and his friends concluded that he 'would have the better in all Contests' with his wife, though she would try to get control of his money – in fact, of course, her own fortune! It is not surprising that Lilly's sympathy was given freely to his friend: he himself had only recently escaped from the tyranny of his unhappy marriage with Jane Rowley, whom he also probably married for her money.

In June, he lent Ashmole the Corner House in the Strand, presumably dropping in from time to time when in town from Hersham. But Ashmole, as the lawsuit dragged on (and by now it was clear that it was going to take a deal of settlement), busied himself increasingly in building up his collection of archaeological and literary remains; posterity owes much to Mrs Ashmole's irritable nature.

But he also continued to concern himself with astrology, making some attempt to quieten down the continual hostilities between rival astrologers. In 1656, John Gadbury dedicated to him the *Astronomical Tables* he and his brother Timothy published, praising in the letter of dedication his 'Knowledge in all Science (Especially in the Mathematiques)', and calling him 'the most fit and Honourable Guardian to protect and keepe a Child of Urania'.* What is interesting is that the authors' letter to the reader acknowledges the help of Lilly and of Gadbury's teacher Nicholas Fiske; that Lilly himself wrote an introductory letter; and that Wharton and Booker were among the astrologers to contribute laudatory verses. A rare moment of stillness, indeed, in astrological contention.

Ashmole's diary continues to note, among various archaeological adventures, Lilly's commentary on his horoscope, and his advice for the future. And in October 1657, he and Lilly together attended the final hearing of his wife's suit against him. Plagued with a toothache, Ashmole was introduced to Sir John Maynard, a friend of Bulstrode Whitelocke's; with the latter's help, Lilly had been able to retain Maynard to represent Ashmole. Maynard was burdened with over 800 sheets of depositions from Mrs Ash-

* Urania, in this context, does not refer to the planet Uranus, which was only discovered in 1781. Astrologers picked up the epithet applied by the Greeks to Aphrodite and Astarte, and applied it to themselves in its 'heavenly' meaning.

mole, but having waded through them was able to point out to the court (where she was claiming alimony) that there was not 'one word proved against [Ashmole] of using her ill or ever giving her a bad or provoking word'.

The following day, Ashmole notes, 'the Lords Commissioners having found no cause for allowing my wife Alimony, did 4 p.m. deliver my wife to me, whereupon I carried her to Mr Lillies, & there tooke Lodgings for us both.' Considering that Mrs Ashmole had just been trying to persuade the court that her husband's intolerable ill temper or adultery had made it impossible for her to live with him, it can scarcely have been a joyful reconciliation.

Lilly, commenting on a note made in the list of 'accidents' Ashmole prepared in 1667 that 'his wife retorned to him', wrote:

> In the 3 yeares contention, I must needs acknowledge the ingenuity of our Native, and his acquired Temperature in the managing of it: in all which tyme though unjustly provoaked, hee ever was willing to receive his wife, without any the least unbeseeming Languag or blaming her; laying all the blame as he justly might, uppon her ill condition Councillors and Abettors.

He also noted that 'the heavens do manifestly declare that Conjunction or second joyning together of the Native and his wife'; and fortunately he was proved correct, for the reconciliation appears to have been as complete as could be expected under the circumstances. Ashmole, in a preface to a book (*The Way to Bliss*) published in 1658, rejoiced that he was now friends not only with his wife, but her brother: 'God, not onely enabled me to endure those impetuous multiplied Stormes, but some few Moneths since, was pleased to sweeten my long-Sufferings with a fair and peaceful Issue.'

The friendship with Lilly was cemented, though the two households were not to grow completely together until after Lady Manwaring's death.

Lilly was flattered to receive, in 1659, a rather grand present from the King of Sweden: a gold chain and a medal which gave him some pleasure, but renewed the splenetic suspicion and malice of his colleagues.

The circumstances of the gift are interesting. England was in general friendly towards Sweden, as the foremost defender of the protestant faith in Europe. In 1654, Cromwell had made the first treaty between the two countries (at a time when Bulstrode Whitelocke was Ambassador), and in 1656 the London Treaty followed—a treaty simply of friendship and trade, though Cromwell was angling for help in religious contentions, and on his side King Charles Gustavus wanted England's assistance in his war with Denmark and Brandenburg.

It may have been with the prompting of Whitelocke, or even the Government itself, that Lilly began to offer his support to the Swedish King in his annual almanacs. The King was mentioned, just, in the 1656 *Ephemeris*, and after he had had several successes against the Poles in that year, Lilly suggested in the following *Ephemeris* that 'a new star' sighted by Tycho de Brahe in 1572 had referred to Charles Gustavus, and predicted more successes.

In the 1658 almanac he went further, predicting

> Severall negotiations on foot to reconcile the Swedish King with Denmark, which people too late may repent their treatcherous taking up of armes against so firm an Ally of the English Lord Protectors, and against a Person so full of honour as Charles Gustavus King of Sweden, both whose fortunes are not to be counterpoised by any single King, Prince, People or Nation of this World at present ...

The following year, the King's gift arrived: the Swedes had translated the 1658 almanac into German and distributed it to their troops (who were mainly German); and by the time the chain and medal reached Lilly, the almanac had gone into Swedish too, with the addition to it of 'another prophesy which comes from a noble and learned man in England'. This was *not* by Lilly, and indeed bears all the marks of having been produced by a political propagandist, and not being astrological in origin at all—though the Swedes had employed some of their own astrologers for propaganda purposes, and the King had awarded a pension to Johann Warner, who had actually accompanied the troops into battle, his almanac in his hand.

Lilly wrote acknowledging the gift (which was valued at £50); the rough draft of his letter exists, and is a good example of seventeenth-century *politesse*, not to say sycophancy:

> What first brought me to honour your Heroick Name, & thence led on the Ingagement of my Pen, in behalfe of yourselfe & Nacion; was the large relacions my only English Maecenas (the right honble the Lord Whitlock) at his retourne from Sweden, gave me of those Princely endowments ... And now give me leave with humble Resolves to engage, that forasmuch as your Majesty's favour, like a Beame cast from that King of Planets, has out of your innate Goodness conveyed Influence upon so obscure & remote a Person, Your Majestie shall thence assuredly draw to yourselfe greater Obligations than hitherto I could manifest, together with the Resolution of sailing after your Owne Ship, & under the Fortune of your own Trophye, through the most perilous Seas, & tryall of all your Concernments.

But it was not to be so. Despite Lilly's prophecies of continued triumphs (in his 1659 *Ephemeris*) Charles Gustavus had what could fairly be called a disastrous year. The 1660 *Ephemeris* gave sympathy and a pious hope of success, rather than a positive prediction of it: 'Notwithstanding the ranting Pamphlets of illiterate fellows, we hope some considerable Victory will be gained by the Sweeds; yea, in or near this month' (January). But in February, Charles Gustavus died; after which Lilly does not mention Sweden again.

The whole episode, despite the chain and medal, was rather a disaster for Lilly, for in a pamphlet published on January 19th, 1659, his rival Gadbury had written of the King (under the pseudonym Merlinus Verax): 'The principal time the illustrious Native ought to provide against, is the middle of 1660 ... but you are to understand, that as the greatest danger in a Bullet is before it touch the mark, so it is in a direction; this Native therefore ought to be securing himself beforehand.' He added a note: 'I write not in hopes of reward: nor out of any disaffection or prejudice to the Magnanimous Prince therein concerned; but only to free Astrologie from the ignorance and unworthiness of some, the scandal and reproach of others; and (if it be possible in so small a room) to yeeld satisfaction to all!'

Whether or not Gadbury was just irritated by the King's gift to his rival (he mentions a gold chain, sometimes several times, in at least five of his current pamphlets), and therefore made a dark prediction of the King's future just to distract attention from Lilly, unquestionably he came best out of the disagreement. Other astrologers were quick to point out how wrong Lilly had been, and one (in an anonymous pamphlet entitled *Pseudo-Astrologus*) warned him not to publish 'another mess of Flatteries, Falsities and Non-sence, in the form of an Almanack' if he wanted to escape more public exposures, 'and suffer his Reputation to run into the Quicksands of a far greater hazard and Danger.'

Unfortunately, Lilly had also forecast in 1659 that the Protector, Richard Cromwell, would 'manifest himself unto the whole world that he hath abilities to govern'. But in May of that year, the Protector was in fact deprived of office, and Lilly was forced to ask, rather weakly, 'the many turnings, and windings, and changes of Government in England in 1659, what Man or Angel could predict?' He had similarly claimed the intervention of the hand of God, or some similar force of Providence, in 1652, as an explanation of his failure to predict the nature of the King's death.

Gadbury, naturally, did not allow himself to be impressed, and in *The Novice-Astrologer* put up a further fine display of scorn, claiming to be able now to put an end to Lilly's quackery, and thus protect the honest astrologers, his friends:

> Since his Errors are so eminently spread and promoted, to the great scandal of Astrologie, and hitherto no one hath offered to question him—I adjudged it convenient (in recompense of his scurrilities) to stop his course at this time, lest in

the height of his folly, he surfeit more dangerously, and run mad beyond the cure of all probable Reason ... I will rip him up, and shew his Nakedness and Folly to the world, somewhat more largely than his own Pen hath been a sufficient index thereof, in his idle and addle fictions for the ensuing year.

Of course it was quite unfair of Gadbury to suggest that it was only Lilly who ever made a false prediction and had to find an excuse for it. Wharton had consistently forecast the King's success, and also claimed the hand of God as an explanation for the Royalist defeat. There was always the possibility, astrologers were constantly pointing out, that God might overrule the planets. Vincent Wing had pointed out that God might 'frustrate the portents of heaven'; and all other astrologers at some time agreed with this view.

Only a few of the attacks on Lilly were overtly political; the others concentrated once more on making him a figure of fun. If he were not disposed of in one way, then he would be disposed of in another. *A letter from the King of Denmark to Mr William Lilly, occasioned by the Death of his Patron the King of Sweden* came out anonymously (for whoever was its author, the King of Denmark certainly was not). Dated from 'Elsenor, March 4, 1660', it was witty and coarse:

You bid your Patron conquer, but alas! he was beaten. You bid him take Copenhagun, but the Royal Knave was sullen, and would not. You bid him live, but he, as if it had been to spite his Astrologer, doth quite the contrary, and dyes ... Thy Name's up, and thou maiest even now go to bed and sleep. But if ever thou appearest again, and writest any thing beyond Prescriptions for letting of blood, and sowing of Pot-herbs, Cursed be thou, and Cursed be all they that reade them. Which is the earnest desire of him that never had any reason to be either Your Friend or Servant.

It seems possible that this attack came from the hand of John Philips, a hack-writer and translator, who was also Milton's nephew. Two months later came another anonymous attack under Lilly's own name, apparently admitting all sorts of errors, and apologizing for them:

> Could any man be so senceless, as to think our Predictions should hold true, longer than our Almanacks should last? If there be any contradictions (and they are but venial sins at most; for no man was ever damn'd for writing contradictions ...) we are confident our meaning was good in them; and we reaped as much advantage thereby as any others did for the most superior truth that ever was predicted ... Tell truth to a natural lyar, he'll but hate you for it; and had we so written always, we had never been master of a Gold Chain, and 100 L. per annum Salary from all Governments since 1646 to poor Protector Dick's —— downfall.

The same month—May 1660—Lilly was accused in another anonymous pamphlet (*Lilly lash'd with his own Rod*) of witchcraft, and of accepting £200 a year from the Rump. The writer points out that while he said there should be no more kings in England, he was quick enough to hail Cromwell as the equivalent of a king.

Talk of pensions from Parliament (however exaggerated and untrue), of friendship with Cromwell, of 'ripping up', was beginning to sound extremely chilly. Cromwell had died in September 1658; his eldest surviving son, 'Tumbledown Dick', had soon been dislodged from the Protectorship; and the weak, divided rule of the soldiers was clearly beginning to lead in the general direction of another civil war—this time between the militia and civilians on the one hand, and the regular soldiers on the other. In March 1660, the 'free parliament' elected under the protection of General Monk called for the restoration of the monarchy.

Lilly's enemies saw a prime opportunity to destroy him: he had never been slow to boast of the assistance he had given Parliament, especially in the early years of the Commonwealth; indeed, leading Parliamentarians had publicly acknowledged it. He claimed to have advised Cromwell himself on the conduct of some of his affairs, and Cromwell had (he said) 'sent one that waited upon him in his chamber, once in two or three days, to hear how it fared with me in my sessions business.' None of this was likely to commend him to the regime poised to take control once Charles II returned to London; and it can safely be assumed that Lilly was not in residence in the Strand when, on May 29th, the King entered his capital with (as Lucy Hutchinson describes)

> an universall joy and triumph, even to his own amazement; who, when he saw all the nobility and gentry of the land flowing into him, askt, Where were his enemies? For he saw nothing but prostrates, expressing all the love that could make a prince happie; and indeed it was a wonder in that day to see the mutability of some, and the hipocracie of others, and the servile flattery of all ...
>
> The Presbyterians were now the white boyes, and according to their nature fell a thirsting, then hunting after blood, and urging that God's blessing could not be upon the land till justice had cleans'd it from the late king's blood.

In view of Lilly's well-known attitude to Presbyterianism, he must have been extremely nervous when he heard of the long list of Presbyterians put into Charles's hand by Monk, from whom the ministers of the new Government were to be chosen.

The rival astrologers closed in, and only a few weeks after the Restoration produced *A Declaration of the several Treasons, Blasphemies and Misdemeanors acted, spoken and published Against God, the late King, his present Majesty; the Nobility, Clergy, City, Commonalty &c. By that Grand Wizard and Imposter William Lilly, Of St Clement Danes; Otherwise called Merlinus Anglicus.*

Lilly, 'the States Balaam, who for hire would curse and bless for the Rump and Oliver according to their respective Instructions and Dictates, upon pretence of Art, wherein he hath no more skill than the Beast his Predecessor rid on,' was accused of urging on and flattering the murderers of Charles I, procuring the King's executioner, slandering the King in his biography of him, praising Cromwell, abusing the nobility and clergy.

The pamphlet winds to a frightening end:

> For that he is looked upon as the only man now in England *guilty* of all our *sufferings*: it is therefore referred humbly to the consideration of this Right Honourable Parliament, whether it be not very just that he should be excepted as to his estate, which is considerable, being the *wages* of his *arch-Villainies*, and he himself kept in such security as the *good people* of *England* may be secured from his *infernal Actings*.

A second pamphlet alleged that 'he being aged 58 years, was imprisoned for pretending to know who cut the king's head off, but being befriended he quickly got off again ...' A third, written as though it was a confession by Lilly himself, ended: 'Because my constant club-fisted friend John Booker hath promised to hang himself, whenever the King comes into England: and since 'tis dishonourable to hang alone, we promise then to swing with him for company: for Monarchie and we can't possibly stand together.'

Soon, the terror began. Lilly, as he sat in his house at Hersham, must have been extremely worried as he read in the *Parliamentary Intelligencer* of the fate of men who were his friends:

> June 14. Resolved that Daniel Axtell be one of the 20 to be excepted out of the general Act of Indemnity and Oblivion, to suffer such pains, penalties and forfeitures, not extending to life, as shall be inflicted on him by an Act hereafter to be made for that purpose.

The *Intelligencer* reported Axtell found guilty, on October 15th, of guarding the court which had tried Charles I; and on October 19th, reported his hanging and quartering, and the boiling of his quarters. Others were arrested, but later released – like Phineas Pain, 'upon misinformation that he was the person that executed his late Majesty'.

Lilly was not to escape completely unscathed. In his autobiography, he writes that his fee-farm rents, valued at £120 a year, 'were all lost by his Majesty's coming to his restoration'. The circumstances of this loss are totally obscure; it may be that some royalist was able, successfully, to claim that Lilly had come by the properties as a result of Parliamentary confiscation. We will never know; and in any event (or so Lilly says) 'the loss thereof did never trouble me, or did I repine thereat.'

In June 1660 he was summoned by two messengers of the Sergeant-at-Arms, to appear before a parliamentary committee for examination as to his claim that he knew who had executed Charles I. Lilly says that the summons was at the instigation of Sir Daniel Harvey, who had been disappointed at the election of 'new Knights for Surrey', when Lilly had campaigned for a successful rival.

Providentially, an old friend, Richard Pennington, happened to be in Westminster on the day of the examination; and persuaded one of the two chairmen of the committee, Richard Weston, to protect Lilly (if rather grudgingly): 'I will do him all the good I can,' Weston said after hearing Pennington speak of the help Lilly had been to him. 'I thought he had never done any good. Let me see him, and let him stand behind me where I sit.'

According to Lilly, and we have no other authority,

> many of the younger members affronted me highly, and demanded several scurrilous questions. Mr Weston held a paper before his mouth; bade me answer nobody but Mr Prinn; I obeyed his command, and saved myself much trouble thereby; and when Mr Prinn* put any difficulty or doubtful query unto me, Mr Weston prompted me with a fit answer.

After giving his evidence (naming Colonel Joyce as the executioner), Lilly was discharged; but the Sergeant (not unusually) kept him in prison for two days, until he and his Messenger were paid off—by six pounds and forty shillings respectively.

Gaining confidence, Lilly accepted the advice of friends, and

* William Prynne, M.P.

actually attended several trials of men he had known—such as Hugh Peter. The *Intelligencer* for September 10th had reported:

> And now we can tell News which all the good Subjects of three Kingdoms will rejoice at; how that great Instrument of Sedition and Firebrand, Hugh Peter, is close prisoner in the Tower of London ... Out of his pocket they took his Almanack, for which he struggled more than for his Bible.

On October 16th, Peter was executed at Charing Cross, the people cheering as he staggered on to the scaffold, and showing their delight by 'several shouts and acclamations, not onely when they saw him go up the ladder, and when the Halter was putting about his Neck; but also when his head was cut off, and held up aloft upon the end of a Spear, there was such a shout, as if the people of England had acquired a Victory.'

The other astrologers were meanwhile busily cashing in on the general feeling of murderous euphoria. The books advertised in the *Intelligencer* show how the tide had turned: 'Cromwell's bloody slaughter-house; or his damnable designs laid and practised by him and his Negro's, in contriving the murther of his sacred Majesty King Charles the first, discovered by a person of honor ...' 'An Epistle written and presented to His Majesty by Arise Evans, who yet liveth ...' A pamphlet celebrating a 'Most Glorious Star' which had appeared at the birth of Charles II: 'Never any Star having appeared before at the birth of any (the highest Humane Hero) except our Saviour.'

Lilly inserted in the *Intelligencer* a brief advertisement announcing that 'No Subject the King hath [is] more joyful of his arrival into the Throne than William Lilly', and otherwise made no noise. Ashmole may have been doing a little quiet work on his behalf behind the scenes, for of course he was by no means in bad odour with the new establishment, and had celebrated Charles's entry into London in a poem entitled *Sol in Ascendente: Or, The Glorious Appearance Of Charles the Second, Upon the Horizon of London, in her Horoscopicall Sign, Gemini.*

There was no indication that the Court as a whole was opposed to astrology: indeed, there were reassuring signs that the opposite was the case. In his speech in Parliament on September 13th, 1660, on the Act of Indemnity, none other than the Lord Chancellor, Lord Clarendon, had said:

> The astrologers have made us a fair excuse, and truly I hope a true one: all the motions of these last twenty years have been unnatural, and have proceeded from the evil influence of a malignant star; and let us not too much despise the influence of the stars. And the same astrologers assure us, that the malignancy of the star is expired; the good genius of this kingdom is become superior, and hath mastered that malignancy, and our own good old stars govern us again; and their influence is so strong, that with your help they will repair in a year what hath been decaying in twenty, and they only shall have no excuse for the star who continue their malignancy, and own all the ill that is past to be their own, by continuing and improving it for the time to come.

It might be suspected that this rather naïve approach by such an intelligent man as Clarendon was simply a rhetorical flourish, except that he refers to astrology quite seriously in his autobiography, on one or two occasions (particularly with reference to 1666, 'a year long destined by all astrologers for the production of dismal changes and alterations throughout the world, and by some for the end of it ...').

Other astrological manifestations were less enthusiastically greeted by the Court, or at all events by the King. John Brown in his *Shortly after the Restoration* (1684) records in some detail Ashmole's story of the encounter between Charles II and Arise Evans, who had been active since before Lilly started to study astrology. It is worth quoting:

> Arise Evans, who then went generally by the name of Evans the Prophet, being troubled with a very despicable and blasted Face, so that it was not only nauseous to view, but very fetid of smell, he coming to Mr Ashmole to request the

favour of his getting him toucht by His Majesty for the same, he utterly refused it, but thinking him a fit person to approach His Majesty's Presence; and being stript of all hope or advantage from him, as also from many others which he had endeavoured to procure: he being utterly denied the attaining the favour resolves with himself (with an assured Faith, that if His Majesty did touch him he should speedily recover) to attend the Kings coming by him in the usual Walke he takes in St James's Park; the King at length coming that way, his Face being covered with a Red Cloath, the which he lifted up till he saw the King near him, which he afterwards letting fall down, cries out *I am 'Rise Evans.*

The King coming nearer him with his Attendants which waited on Him, some of them told His Majesty that he was His Majesty's Prophet; the King coming at him, he kneels down, and cries *God bless Your Majesty*: The good King Charles gives him His Hand to Kiss, and he rubbing his ulcerated and scabbed Nose therewith, which was plentifully stockt with purulent and fetid matter: within two days after his reception of his Majesty's sacred favour, the above-said Mr Ashmole saw this Evans cured, and his ulcerated nose dryed up and healed.

The King may have felt this signal mark of his efficiency as a healer dearly gained. But the account is also interesting for its implicit indication that Ashmole had, to some extent at any event, the King's ear. On June 18th he was appointed Windsor Herald, and four months later Controller of the Excise. No one was now better placed than his old friend to head off any possibly fatal accusation against Lilly, and it was safe for the astrologer to go out and about again (to the distress, no doubt, of his enemies). In Pepys's diary for October 24th, 1660, for instance:

So to Mr Lilly's with Mr Spong,* where well received, there being a Club tonight among his friends. Among the rest

* An instrument-maker, who had constructed at least one astrolabe for Lilly.

Esquire Ashmole, who I found was a very ingenious gentleman. With him we two sang afterward in Mr Lilly's study. That done, we all parted; and I home by coach, taking Mr Booker with me, who did tell me a great many fooleries, which may be done by nativities, and blaming Mr Lilly for writing to please his friends, and to keep in with the times (as he did formerly to his own dishonour), and not according to the rules of art, by which he could not well err, as he had done. I set him down at Lime-street end, and so home ...

So now we see Booker too joining in the general denigration of his colleague. And three months later, there was the most frightening episode of all. Again, Lilly's own account is most graphic:

One Everard, a Justice of Peace in Westminster, ere I was stirring, sent a Sergeant and thirty-four musqueteers for me at White-Hall: he had twice that night seized about sixty persons, supposed fanatics, very despicable persons, many whereof were aged, some were water-bearers, and had been Parliament-soldiers; others, of ordinary callings; all these were guarded unto White-Hall, into a large room, until day-light, and then committed to the Gate-House: I was had into the guard-room, which I thought to be hell; some therein were sleeping, others swearing, others smoking tobacco. In the chimney of the room I believe there was two bushels of broken tobacco-pipes, almost half one load of ashes ...

Among the miserable crew of people, with a whole company of soldiers, I marched to prison, and there for three hours was in the open air upon the ground, where the common house of office came down. After three hours, I was advanced from this stinking place up the stairs, where there was on one side a company of rude, swearing persons; on the other side, many Quakers, who lovingly entertained me.

Lilly managed to get a message out to the Garter King-of-Arms, Sir Edward Walker, who despite their exchange of views about the life and times of Charles I obtained his release, sternly warning Everard that 'it was not His Majesty's pleasure that any of his subjects should be thus had to prison without good cause shewed before'.

Fortunately for Lilly, his enemies the Presbyterians were already beginning to lose their battle against the Cavalier Parliament, through disunity, indecision and lack of a proper cohesive policy. Though the Act for Settling Ministers, supported by the King, had attempted to confirm Presbyterians in their livings, several hundred were ejected between 1660 and 1661; in 1662 the King managed to persuade the Lords to accept a proviso that nonconformists could be retained within the established Church through dispensation or indulgence, but the Commons forced the King to accept the Act of Uniformity later the same year, and by St Bartholomew's Day, August 24th, 1662, almost two thousand nonconforming clergy had been ousted from their livings; more than a thousand of them were Presbyterians.

Lilly would at least no longer have certain impertinent Presbyterians to worry about. But in any event, by now he had sued out a pardon under the broad seal, pledging his allegiance to Charles II, and paying £13 6s. 8d. for the indulgence. 'William Lilly, Citizen and Salter of London', had made his peace with the new regime.

# 8

# The Planets Fade

*... Not far from hence doth dwell*
*A cunning Man, hight SIDROPHEL,*
*That deals in Destiny's dark Counsels,*
*And sage Opinions of the Moon sells;*
*To whom all People, far and near,*
*On deep Importances repair;*
*When Brass and Pewter hap to stray*
*And Linnen slinks out of the Way ...*
*When Butter does refuse to come,*
*And Love proves cross and humoursome;*
*To him with Questions, and with Urine,*
*They for Discov'ry flock, or Curing.*

*Hudibras* II:III (105)

In the second part of *Hudibras*, published in 1664, Samuel Butler pilloried astrology, and in particular an astrologer whom he called Sidrophel. There has been some dispute about the real identity of this character: some critics believed it to be Sir Paul Neal, a self-centred and dogmatic member of the Royal Society, who had allegedly put it about that there was an elephant on the moon when in fact what he had seen was a mouse in the end of his telescope. It is possible: Butler tells a scurrilous story about Sidrophel studying a new and unusual planet which turned out to be a light on a small boy's kite's tail.

Whether Sidrophel was, as some other critics believe, William Lilly, can hardly be proved; there is no real evidence either way. But the poem certainly gives a very good idea of the kind of clientele Lilly had, and the kind of work he did for them—though as might be expected, Butler took an unsympathetic view of those clients and that work, as well as of Sidrophel himself.

The latter, Butler told his readers,

> ... with the Moon was more familiar
> Than e'er was Almanack Well-willer;
> Her Secrets understood so clear,
> That some believ'd he had been there;
> Knew when she was in the fittest Mood
> For cutting Corns, or letting Blood;
> When for anointing Scabs or Itches
> Or to the Bum applying Leeches;
> When Sows and Bitches may be spay'd,
> And in what Sign best Cyder's made:
> Whether the Wane be, or Increase,
> Best to set Garlick, or sow Pease:
> Who first found out the Man i' th' Moon,
> That to the Ancients was unknown;
> How many Dukes, and Earls, and Peers,
> Are in the Planetary Spheres ...
>
> With Lute-Strings he would counterfeit
> Maggots that crawl on Dish of Meat;
> Quote Moles and Spots on any Place
> O' th' Body, by the Index Face:
> Detect lost Maiden-Heads, by Sneezing,
> Or breaking Wind of Dames, or Pissing;
> Cure Warts and Corns, with Application
> Of Med'cines to th' Imagination;
> Fright Agues into Dogs, and scare
> With Rhimes the Tooth-Ach and Catarrh:
> Chace evil Spirits away by Dint
> Of Cickle,* Horse-Shoe, Hollow-Flint;
> Spit Fire out of a Walnut-Shell,

* Sickle.

Which made the Roman Slaves rebel;
And fire a Mine in China here,
With sympathetic Gun-Powder.
He knew whats'ever's to be known,
But much more than he knew, would own ...

Lilly, if taxed, would have said that much of this was in fact outside his experience: but there is no doubt that he claimed to be able to advise most people about most things, by the use of astrology (and no doubt intuition, and perhaps even a certain amount of extra-sensory perception).

As to Samuel Butler, that splendid man had no more interest in astrology than as an admirable (and, it must be acknowledged, very easy) target for his blazing wit. He could be as entertaining on the subject in prose, and no doubt in conversation, as in his doggerel metre. Elsewhere he wrote:

An astrologer is one that expounds upon the Planets, and teaches to construe the Accidents by the due joining of Stars in Construction. He talks with them by dumb signs, and can tell what they mean by their twinckling, and squinting upon one another, as well as they themselves. He is a Spy upon the Stars, and can tell what they are doing, by the Company they keep, and the Houses they frequent. They have no Power to do any Thing alone, until so many meet, as will make a Quorum. He is Clerk of the Committee to them, and draws up all their Orders, that concern either public or private Affairs. He keeps all their Accompts for them, and sums them up, not by Debtor, but Creditor alone, a more compendious Way ...

He is a Fortune-Teller, a Retailer of Destiny, and petty Chapman to the Planets. He casts Nativities as Gamesters do false Dice, and by slurring and palming *sextile*, *quartile*, and *trine*, like *size*, *quater*, *trois*, can throw what chance he pleases. He sets a Figure, as Cheats do a Main at Hazard; and Gulls throw away their Money at it. He fetches the Ground of his Art so far off, as well from Reason, as the Stars, that, like a

> Traveller, he is allowed to lye by Authority. And as Beggars, that have no Money themselves, believe all others have, and beg of those, that have as little as themselves: So the ignorant Rabble believe in him, though he has no more Reason for what he professes, than they.

The general tone of the public attitude to astrology seems already to have been changing: while many intelligent and civilized men still supported it, without doubt there was also a considerable body of opinion shifting away from the whole proposition—in particular where prediction was concerned. On the whole, the general viewpoint was probably still that of such men as William Oughtred, the mathematician and author of *Clavis Mathematicus*, who invented the multiplication and proportion signs, and who (according to Aubrey) 'confessed that he was not satisfied how it came about that one might foretell by the Starres, but so it was that it fell out true as he did often by his experience find'. But many individuals took an opposite view.

The climate had been changing, for various reasons, over the past several decades. Partly responsible was Copernicus's announcement that 'the sun rests immobile in the centre of the world; and that everything which appears as a motion of the sun is in truth a motion of the earth.' This did not, of course, make any real difference to the astrological theory, which rests not on the fact that the earth is at the centre of the solar system, but on the relationship between the earth and the planets, and their interrelationship. As Sir Christopher Heydon put it, 'Whether (as Copernicus saith) the sun be the centre of the world, the astrologer careth not.'

But the layman suspected that, on the contrary, the Copernican revolution had turned astrology topsy-turvy; and the increasing number of astronomical discoveries which were constantly taking place—Halley's growing list of comets, Galileo's discovery of Jupiter's moons—further undermined his faith by suggesting that there were more things in heaven than the astrologers had dreamed of, and that they were therefore unlikely to be even as omnipotent as they had asserted.

The more intelligent astrological writers saw the new astronomical discoveries as challenges, requiring simply (as Francis Bacon believed) a reformation within the science. Sir Christopher Wren, delivering a lecture as Gresham Professor of Astronomy at Oxford, asserted that there was 'a true astrology' which it was possible to set out in a scientific form, and Joshua Childrey argued that all that was needed was that astrologers should prove themselves scientific by taking note of the discoveries of their brothers, the astronomers, and fitting them into their own calculations (just as in later years they were to have to fit in the newly discovered planets, Uranus, Neptune and Pluto).

It was during the seventeenth century that at last, after four thousand years or more, the final split occurred between astrology and astronomy. For centuries, astronomers had automatically been astrologers; and indeed the astrological search for information about man, his character, and the circumstances of his life, had been positively responsible for many astronomical discoveries, and had been part of the driving force which had led astronomy on to ever more far-reaching theories. But now, the astronomers began to take the view that it was not possible to reconcile the new scientific discoveries about the universe with the old astrological theory.

Some of them resisted to the last; but gradually they dropped from their consciousness the idea that the planets could have any effect on terrestrial life. Surprisingly enough, none of them published properly argued reasons for doing so: there was what almost seemed to be a conspiracy of silence—which was to last until the 1960s, when meteorologists once more began to study the effect of the tidal planets upon the sun, and their consequent effects on terrestrial weather: the first sign of a new scientific interest in astrology.

But if the astronomers merely kept silent about their suspicions (except for a few terse comments in the margin of scientific works), the lay public certainly did not. There is a good example of the new, critical, satirical attitude of middle or upper-middle-class people in the letters written by that delicious girl Dorothy

Osborne to her fiancé, Sir William Temple, as early as July 22nd, 1654:

> You little think that I have been with Lilly! In earnest, I was, the day before I came out of town; and what do you think I went for? Not to know when you would come home, I can assure you, nor for any other occasion of my own; but with a cousin of mine that had long designed to make herself sport with him, and did not miss of her aim. I confess I always thought him an imposter, but I could never have imagined him so simple a one as we found him. In my life I never heard so ridiculous a discourse as he made us, and no old woman that passes for a witch could have been more to seek what to say to reasonable people than he was. He asked us more questions than we did him, and caught at everything we said without discerning that we abused him and said things purposely to confound him; which we did so perfectly that we made him contradict himself in the strangest way that you ever heard!

To be fair to Lilly, it was always as easy for anyone to disconcert an astrologer, who set out to do so, as to disconcert a doctor by inventing symptoms or lying about them; and the 1650s, when Lilly was very much under pressure, was a time when he was likely to have been ultra-cautious in talking to any strange client. There is no reason to suppose that, for the most part, clients did not go away satisfied with what they heard—though it must be conceded that the man in the street would have had little means of making his voice heard at this distance of time, even if he considered himself cheated. The broadsheets which occasionally appeared attacking Lilly were either good-humoured lampoons, occasionally mildly obscene, or the work of his professional rivals, and usually humourless and uninteresting at that. One exception is the anonymous pamphlet which came out on November 2nd, 1652, under the title *Lillyes Lamentation*, which is extrovert knockabout stuff with enough wit to make it worth quoting. As usual, the author bases his attack on personal grounds:

'It would make an honest man laugh to see how this fool hath made an Asse of himself since these times of REFORMATION, only to please the *Rich*, deceive the ignorant, & befool himself; one thing indeed he was very excellent at, *to bewitch a mans money out of his pocket* ...'

The author goes on to quote cases in which Lilly had allegedly misled clients. He had told a herdsman that his cows had been stolen and butchered, for instance, when they were later found safe at home. And he has one or two good stories, no doubt apochryphal. Lilly, for instance, once met a countryman and asked the way. He was told:

> If you make not the more haste, you may chance to be wet to the skin before you come there; for there is a shower of Raine a-comming. How dost thou know that quoth Lilly; He, quoth the old man, do you not see yonder Dun Cow; Yes, quoth Lilly; Well, said the old man, when she scratcheth her right eare with her left foot, then be sure it will raine, which thing hath made Mr Lilly so much out of conceit with his own judgement for weather, that he hath turned it all over to his brother Booker.'

And then:

> Mr Lilly walking over Covent Garden one night late, did meet with a light-skirted, silver-lac'd Woman who demanded of him, if he would accept a pint of wine, and he as willing to accept, as she was to proffer, they went lovingly to the Garter Tavern in Long Acre, where after the Figure-Monger had made himself known, shee presently desired him to erect a Figure, to see who should pay for that pint of Wine, so he being busie in the midst of his Calculations, she was imployed at the bottome of his pockets, and in the conclusion left him to passe judgement by himself; so he found the woman was a pickpocket Whore, and he must pay for the Wine himself.

But the anecdote that does ring true (especially in view of the minute examples of what astrology could perform with which

Lilly filled out *Christian Astrology*) is the anonymous author's final one, which tells how a country bumpkin went to see the astrologer about a stolen purse, and found his door-step fouled with human excreta.

> Down came that profound Ass-trologer ... who opening the door and seeing it in that shitten case, began to execrate and curse those beastly Knaves that did it; vowing if he did but know who did him that nasty trick, he would make them Examples to all such Roagues so long as they liv'd; Nay, quoth the Countryman, if he cannot tell who beshit his door, he can as well be hanged as tell me who had my Purse, and so went his way.

Such were the pinpricks of Lilly's own life; but in the larger world there were more serious attacks on astrology, and it was partly in response to them that, during the 1660s, almost the last large-scale attempt was made to produce a rational defence of astrology (until, that is, the first half of the twentieth century). Jean Baptiste Morin's *Astrologia Gallica* was published in 1661 in Paris—a vast work of about 800 double-column pages. While the full book was never published in England, much of it circulated in manuscript, and later on selections were printed (including one made and translated by George Wharton).

Morin was Royal Professor of Mathematics at Paris, a friend of Cardinal Richelieu (to whom his book was dedicated), and an extremely astute and clever mathematician, able to argue on equal terms with Longomontanus (Tycho de Brahe's former assistant, and Professor of Mathematics at Copenhagen). He had developed a brilliant method of determining longitude at sea by the distance of the Moon from a certain star; but is remembered now mainly as the astrologer smuggled into the birth-chamber at Versailles to record the precise moment of birth of the future Louis XVI, and to draw up his horoscope.

Morin had been forced to study astrology when he was a young man (he tells us) by a Bishop whose physician he was. He had a good opinion of himself, asserting that not even Ptolemy had in fact got astrological principles right, and that he, Morin, was the only man ever to do so. The semi-anonymous writer of the preface to the *Astrologia*, one 'G.T.D.G.V.', asserts that in it Morin demonstrates astrology more surely and evidently than Aristotle demonstrated physics or Galen demonstrated therapeutics.

Morin certainly made a good career for himself at Court. He carefully calculated propitious moments for M. de Chauvigny, the Secretary of State, to begin his official journeys on State business; Marie de Medici so admired him that she arranged for him to be appointed as Royal Professor in Mathematics (though Vautier, Louis XVI's physician, failed in an attempt to have his friend made Royal Astrologer). He remained unaffected by three French ordinances against astrology, in 1493, 1560 and 1570, which seemed to be as little observed as the British laws against fortune-telling, and lived in considerable style, able to support himself (and two nieces in a nearby convent) with a pension of 2,000 livres from Mazarin, and 2,000 thaler from the Queen of Poland.

Naturally, Morin had to begin by showing that astrology was in fact a respectable science. The Bull of Sixtus V, he pointed out, condemned only the prediction of fortuitous events and those which interfered with human free will. He went on to explain those passages of the Bible which might seem to the unenlightened to condemn astrology; the devil, he pointed out, had given the impression that astrology had something to do with fortune-telling and the ancient arts of divination. On the contrary, one only had to look at the horoscope of Christ to realize that he had appointed the most propitious moment of his own birth; evidently the science had divine approbation.

The enormous length of Morin's book makes it impossible to summarize adequately; but in it, besides a certain amount of plain silliness, can be found most of the basic seventeenth-century arguments in favour of astrology. The first twelve Books place astrology on a firm natural basis; the last fourteen deal (in almost twice as many pages) with the science itself, beginning by explaining how God had divided the ecliptic into twelve Zodiacal signs according to the natures of the planets and the twelve astrological houses, and revealed all this to Adam, from whom it had come down to modern man.

Morin takes a firm line on some astrological superstitions, such as the casting and selling of trinkets or amulets. Many members of the nobility had tried to persuade him to manufacture these, he says; but he had always resisted them (unlike Ashmole, who spent an enormous amount of time manufacturing them for himself and his friends). This was, if anything, magic; which had nothing to do with astrology. The final sections of *Astrologia* are highly technical, some an exposition of techniques he held in common with other astrologers, some enlarging on his own theories.

Morin was a medical man: he had been physician to a Bishop, an Abbot, and to the Duke of Luxemburg. He complains bitterly that the Paris doctors do not even know how to draw up a correct horoscope, let alone how to use it properly in practice. He goes in some detail into the use of astrology in the treatment of illness, reminding his readers that the Roman Catholic Church, whatever else it had said on the subject, had never disapproved of astrology as a means of diagnosing and treating disease. He was in fact rather enlightened on the subject, explaining that he had ceased to practise medicine out of disgust at the general medical regime of the time—the incessant bleeding of patients, for instance, who often died of it. He did however commend the chemical remedies of Paracelsus, and was a strong believer in alchemy. He was, too, one of the last prominent men to assert the healing properties of gems: the sapphire, he believed, counteracted melancholy, the emerald restrained man from lust and cured epilepsy, leprosy, dysentery and poisoning.

It is the part of *Astrologia* dealing with medicine that seems to have been of interest to Lilly (though there is only one specific reference to it, in his correspondence with Ashmole). Much of the book never saw the light of day in England, or indeed anywhere else after the first and only complete edition. That was little loss, for there is an enormous amount of rubbish in it; but it is interesting to us as yet another example of the extraordinary muddle that the intelligent seventeenth-century scientist could get himself into—accepting alchemy, yet also discussing the elliptical orbits of the planets; dabbling with the theory that disease may be caused by germs, yet believing that God revealed the secrets of astrology to Adam, and that the star of Bethlehem was not a star at all, but a personable Angel carrying a bright light.

The muddle was to persist for some decades yet; even Newton, that dazzling man, was not free from it, maintaining his interest and confidence in some extraordinary theories, while dragging man into the modern scientific age. Lilly had no problems of reconciling modern and ancient science; he was completely of his own, not any future, time.

His private life during the 1660s settled down and became happier and more placid than it had ever been. He was extremely content with his third wife. His apprentice, and later amanuensis Henry Coley, described Ruth Lilly as 'moderately well described by the sign Capricorn ... and Saturn in Libra ... to which may be added the position of Jupiter in Aquarius in the Ascendant.'

The traditional descriptions of Capricorn would have made her prudent and reliable, persevering, perhaps somewhat pessimistic with a sharp sense of humour. Saturn in Libra traditionally indicated a pleasant, lovable character, patient and above all reasonable, again with good judgment. Jupiter in Aquarius would have given her originality and imagination, tolerance and sympathy. (The concomitant failings would have included a certain amount of tactlessness and unpredictability, but Coley did not mention this, choosing to underline the fact that Ruth Lilly had 'a very obliging temper, disposition and deportment, and ... an understanding above the generallity of her sex.' He added that there was 'great sympathy' between her and her husband—for whom, of course, he was writing his notes!)

Lilly remained in touch with his old friends: in fact they sometimes consulted him. In October 1662 he received a letter from John Booker:

> Good Mr Lilly, my younger Son Samuell went from my house on friday last about 4 aclock in the afternoon and hath

> not returned, he tould his mother he would come in by 6 a clock he [useth?] to break his time 2. 3 or 4 howers, but for so many daies doth much trouble us. I bought him a new Suite and Coat and [harness?] this day to have gone to his Mr I had provided for him, my wife is affraid some misfortune or imprisonment is come to him, I have sent my sonne John to the Barbadoes, where God keep him, and now am I perplexed with another ... was ever man so vexed with his children males as I have late been?

The complaint has a peculiarly modern ring. Lilly could only assure his friend that there was no danger to his son's person.

The friendship with the Ashmoles continued, and the few letters of Lilly's that Ashmole kept and filed provide some side-lights on his life and character. Evidently, he was continuing to suffer from time to time from indifferent health. In 1662 he had treated himself for 'a coagulated choller and fleam in the small guts' (a fairly severe intestinal complaint). He put himself to bed, and (as he wrote to his frend):

> I now neither spitt, have any gryping in the gutts, nor desire of vomitt, from a 12 houres fitt, its come to a small parcell of tyme: it very quietly stole on mee this Saterday, at 3 I entered my bed took a cordiall to sweat, did sweat till 8 as pleasant as any man in the world, from 3 till 8, just as your letter came, I had a small heat in my hands, nothing violent or troublesome; but Sir believe me had I been under the Doctors hands about 6 weeks hence I might have been wors than I am: I shall have I conceive 2 fitts more, very small ones ...

His interest in medicine was as keen as it had been when he had nursed his master's wife through terminal cancer forty years earlier; and it was soon to become even keener.

In the meantime, he became during 1663 and 1664 church-warden of Walton-on-Thames. The church records for this period have vanished, and there is only a short note in his autobiography, pointing out that during that time he 'settled as well as I could the affairs of that distracted parish, upon my own charges; and upon my leaving the place, forgave them seven pounds odd money due unto me.' Walton was not the only parish in financial trouble after the Civil War; and Lilly seems to have remained connected with the Church Council for some years after his retirement as warden.

In 1665 we glimpse the astrologer finding it necessary to guard against too much freedom of speech. Ashmole had been asking him about a prophecy Lilly had printed in his *Collection of Ancient and Modern Prophesies* of 1645, which said that about 1666 'the influence and efficiency of the third Conjunction of Saturne and Jupiter in Sagittarius then impending' would 'produce no small alteration in the Church and Common-wealth of England'. With 1666 now approaching, various admirers of Lilly's had been speculating about his meaning. But he was not to be drawn, for in 1662 an 'Act for preventing the frequent Abuses in printing seditious treasonable and unlicensed Bookes and Pamphlets' had been passed, and could well be applied to any more specific interpretation of the Saturn/Jupiter conjunction—or even to so broad a one as he had already printed. He told his friend:

> After much study, I find it not convenient to enlarg more than is yet printed: if I am not commanded by his Majesty or one of those 2. my great friends [i.e., Ashmole himself or Sir Edward Walker, now a friend again] there being as many Negatives as affirmatives—and a Statute or Act not to medle in such things: if I am commanded its possible I might do much good. I am not willing to runn myselfe upon a Rock now in my old age ...

He was wise. Two years later his colleague, the not altogether reputable John Heydon, found himself imprisoned and (it is said) tortured for being in possession of the King's horoscope. An unsigned letter ordering him to set up the chart was thought to have come from the second Duke of Buckingham. Pepys noted in his diary (March 3rd, 1667): that one of the reasons for the Duke's arrest was

> that he hath been endeavouring to have the King's nativity calculated; which was done, and the fellow now in the Tower about it—which itself hath heretofore, as he says, been held treason, and people died for it—but by the Statute of Treasons, in Queen Mary's times and since, it hath been left out.

As a matter of fact, the casting of the monarch's horoscope had never been treasonable (though during Elizabeth's reign an Act had made it a felony). In Imperial Rome, possession of the Emperor's horoscope had certainly been a sufficient crime to be punishable by death. Heydon escaped with his life; but Lilly must have heard all about his ordeal, and remained sufficiently cautious.

By this time, Ashmole and his wife had become really close friends of the Lillys; Lilly even permitted himself to tease the irritable Lady Manwaring in an occasional postcript ('my most harty respects unto honest Elias—himselfe & his lady, wishing shee wear a widdow, that I might a little cheat her ...').

Lilly was not above using Ashmole, or attempting to use him, to make his own position in society more secure. In 1666, for instance, he wrote to tell his friend that 'amongst my manuscripts I found an old greasy booke, written or coppied in H. the 8th his tyme, in which I find many prophecyes ... [which] may do his Majesty service.' The prophecies were a lot of jargon about an Eagle coming from the East which should overthrow many castles; and Lilly suggested that they should be 'putt in the London Gazette by which meanes it will pass all over England if not the whole world ... I am confident it would putt much courage into his Majesty's subjects.'

Charles himself, interested in astrology and the occult, might or might not have concurred. The effort on Lilly's part was to ingratiate himself. Ashmole did not approve of this particular scheme, despite Lilly's final comment that 'I well know how to humor the people in such like business, but I submitt to your judgement intending to proceed or acquiess as you direct, but would be very willing to serve his Majesty with my penn, as it shall be thought Convenient. The English of all nations are most taken with Prophesies.'

That letter was written from Hersham. By 1665, Lilly seems to have moved out of London permanently, and may even have sold the house in the Strand, which is certainly not mentioned in his Will. The reason for his complete move to the country may not be unconnected with the 1665 plague, which decimated the population of the city, and from which many men had fled. One might have hoped that Lilly, with his interest in medicine, might have ventured into London to nurse the sick, as he had remained some forty years earlier to guard his master's goods. But the terror of the time was such that it is difficult to blame any man for not placing himself deliberately at the centre of the sickness.

Astrologically, there had been several prophecies of plague: it would have been strange if there had not, for it must have been increasingly obvious for years that renewed and perhaps more serious recurrances of the disease would occur. Aubrey remarks that in the *Britannia* of the antiquary and historian William Camden, was 'a remarkable Astrologicall observation, that when Saturn is in Capricornus a great Plague is certainly in London. He had observed it all his time, and setts downe the like made by others before his time. Saturn was so posited in the great plague 1625, and also in the last great plague 1665 ...' Lilly had also printed, in *Monarchy or no Monarchy* (1651), among the other figures, a woodcut of shrouded bodies lying ready for burial, while beneath them two grave-diggers were about their work. This too was claimed as a direct prophecy of the plague.

Be that as it may, plague came; and historians writing soon after the event threw some light on the part astrologers played in the panic of the time. Defoe gives perhaps the most graphic account of this, and although *A Journal of the Plague Year* is of course a work of fiction, such pamphlets as have survived confirm his view that

> Books frightened [the people] terribly, such as Lilly's Almanack, Gadbury's Astrological Predictions, Poor Robin's Almanack, and the like ... Astrologers added stories of the

> conjunctions of planets in a malignant manner and with a mischievous influence, one of which conjunctions was to happen, and did happen, in October, and the other in November; and they filled the peoples heads with predictions on these signs of the heavens, intimating that those conjunctions foretold draught, famine and pestilence ... Some endeavours were used to suppress the printing of such books as terrified the people, and to frighten the dispersers of them, some of whom were taken up; but nothing was done in it, as I am informed, the Government being unwilling to exasperate the people who were, as I may say, all out of their wits already.

Defoe was certainly not exaggerating the popular credence of the better-known astrologers. In his old age, the diarist John Evelyn was to recall that 'fifty years ago ... many were so terrified by Lilly that they durst not go out of their houses.' But it was the real cheapjacks that made a killing. Defoe wrote:

> These terrors and apprehensions of the people led them into a thousand weak, foolish and wicked things, which they wanted not a sort of people really wicked to encourage them to, and this was running about to fortune-tellers, cunning-men, and astrologers to know their fortunes, or, as it is vulgarly expressed, to have their fortunes told them, their nativities calculated, and the like; and this folly presently made the town swarm with a wicked generation of pretenders to magic, to the black art, as they called it, and I know not what; nay, to a thousand worse dealings with the devil than they were really guilty of. And this trade grew so open and so generally practised that it became common to have signs and inscriptions set up at doors: 'Here lives a fortune-teller,' 'here lives an astrologer,' 'here you may have your nativity calculated,' and the like ...
>
> With what blind, absurd and ridiculous stuff these oracles of the devil pleased and satisfied the people I really know not, but certain it is that innumerable attendants crowded about

their doors every day. And if but a grave fellow in a velvet jacket, a band, and a black cloak, which was the habit these quack-conjurers generally went in, was but seen in the streets the people would follow them in crowds, and ask them questions as they went along.

There had been quacks before the plague, of course: in *The Wise-Mans Crown* John Heydon had complained only the previous year that 'the late years of the tyranny admitted stocking-weavers, shoemakers, millers, masons, carpenters, bricklayers, gunsmiths, potters, butlers, &c., to write and teach astrology and physic.' And it should not be forgotten that the serious astrologers were also at their work (though Defoe and fellow-sceptics would not of course have recognized the fact), making some attempt for instance to discover whether it might be possible by astrological means to predict major outbreaks of plague. The method of doing this (and one which Lilly would have used to arrive at his private opinion that 1665 was a likely year for the next outbreak) was simple: the dates of previous major outbreaks were collected, and the planetary positions at those times compared. If there was a correlation, it was assumed to be significant.

As to the astrologers' role as doctors, however, it must be admitted that it is unlikely that Lilly would have been able to do much good had he gone into the city during the plague. Such medical treatment as he might have prescribed would probably have been useless. Among the annotated books in his library was *A Treatise of Mathematical Physicke, or Briefe Introduction to Physicke, by Judiciall Astronomy*, written by 'G.C., Gent.' and published in 1598, which as treatment for the plague suggested that sufferers 'should put their legges in warme water, & be let blood in the vaines, which lead from the heart and head,' and that they might also 'use vinegar in their meates, and to wet their chamber floores with Vinegar.'

Many people put their faith in astrological trinkets, and tobacco and dried toads were among the efficacious remedies prescribed by the quacks. The truth was that no one knew what caused the plague, and no one knew a cure for it.

In the early stages of the epidemic, before he retired to Hersham on June 27th, Lilly wrote,

> very many people of the poorest sort frequented my lodging, many whereof were so civil, as when they brought waters, *viz.* urines, from infected people, they would stand purposely at a distance. I ordered those infected, and not like to die, cordials, and caused them to sweat, whereby many recovered. My landlord of the house was afraid of those poor people, I nothing at all. He was desirous I should be gone. He had four children: I took them with me into the country and provided for them. Six weeks after I departed, he, his wife, and man-servant, died of the plague.

With so many people casting around for an occult reason for so terrible a visitation, it is not surprising that Lilly's *Monarchy or no Monarchy*, published fourteen years earlier, should be recalled. In it he had published nineteen plates of 'heirogliphics' 'which in Aenigmaticall Types, Formes, Figures, Shapes, doth perfectly represent the future condition of the English Nation and Commonwealth for many hundreds of years yet to come.'

The plates show various scenes: Parliament lounges idly by while an invasion takes place; a strange animal, backed like a weasel, attacks a crown; a heavenly band of angels plays music. But it was to four of the plates in particular that attention was paid in the late 1660s. Two, printed on the same page, show the ravages of plague. Three bundles lie on the bare earth, one of them open to display an emaciated corpse; and below, two grave-diggers busily split the ground to receive two coffins, while over a church in the background four strange and ominous birds wheel. The other two show, first, a city in flames by an obviously important river; and second, a number of men throwing water on to a flaming bonfire, into which fall the Gemini twins. Gemini is the zodiacal sign associated with the city of London.

On this basis alone, it would have been mildly eccentric to have accused Lilly of predicting either the plague or the Great Fire of London—though it has very often been the habit of astrologers to claim to have foretold particular events when all that has been foretold has been a vague occurrence which might or might not have been anything to do with what actually happened. Both plague and fire were common occurrences in seventeenth-century cities. Plague had recurred frequently throughout Europe in the fifteenth, sixteenth and early seventeenth century (for the century and a half before 1660, there had been only about a decade during which some cases of plague had not occurred in London). There was no reason for the plague to die out suddenly.

But elsewhere, Lilly had been more particular. In a pamphlet of 1648, he had pointed out:

> In the year 1665 the Aphelium of Mars, who is the general signification of England, will be in Virgo, which is assuredly the ascendant of the English monarchy, but Aries of the Kingdom. When the absis therefore of Mars shall appear in Virgo who shall expect less than a strange catastrophe of human affairs in the commonwealth, monarchy and kingdom of England. There will then, either in or about those times, or near that year, or within ten years, more or less of that time, appear in this kingdom so strange a revolution of fate, so grand a catastrophe and great mutation unto this monarchy and government as never yet appeared of which as the times now stand, I have no liberty or encouragement to deliver my opinion—only it will be ominous to London, unto her merchants at sea, to her traffique on land, to her poor, to all sorts of people, inhabiting in her or to her liberties, by reason of sundry fires and a consuming plague.

And in his own copy of *Monarchy or no Monarchy*, he had written beneath the woodcut illustrating the plague, the words 'mortalitas circa 1665'; while under the one of the fire, he scribbled 'expectes hoc in 1693 vel vitius; forsan 1666 vel 1667'. It seems more than likely that someone saw this private copy some time after the fire—perhaps Lilly even showed it to someone, for he cannot have failed to have been rather proud of his accuracy, and was never one to hide his light under a bushel.

In October 1666, a month after the last flames had died down, and Pepys, walking to St Paul's Wharf, had seen 'all the town burned, and a miserable sight of Pauls church, with all the roofs fallen and the body of the quire quite fallen into St Fayth's—Paul's School also—Ludgate—Fleet Street—my father's house, and the church, and a good part of the Temple the like,' a committee sat to attempt to discover the cause of the fire.

Rumour was of course rife, and it would in a sense have been a comfort to find that the city had been intentionally fired, rather than that the whole calamity had been an accident. But perhaps occult forces had been at work? The diary of Pepys shows that all sorts of suspicions were held, and that superstition was as usual responsible for many wild conjectures. The diarist encountered Sir George Carteret (Treasurer of the Navy and Vice-Chamberlain of the King's Household), and discussed with him Nostradamus's prophecy of the burning of London, 'some of whose verses are put into Booker's Almanack this year'; and Lady Carteret told how 'abundance of pieces of burnt papers were cast by the wind as far as Cranbourne; and among others she took up one, or had one brought to her to see, which was a little bit of paper that had been printed, whereon there remained no more nor less than these words: "Time is, it is done."' When news of the fire reached Prince Rupert, he thought first not of incendiaries, but of Mother Shipton, the Yorkshire prophetess. 'All the Prince said was, that "Now Shipton's prophecy was out."'

Lilly had not been alone in predicting disastrous fires (if indeed that is what he had done in his hieroglyphic). Two years earlier, he had received a letter from Francis Bernard, a physician and astrologer (later James II's chief doctor), claiming that he could predict major outbreaks of fire by examining the horoscopes of cities. The difficulty was of course in choosing the moment for which to set up the chart: later astrologers were to use the time of the signing of the charter, if that was available. But for London?

Bernard had the simple idea of examining the events of the city's past, and from them 'rectifying' a chart until it seemed on examination to fulfil all the conditions of history. He had examined, he said, all the major fires in London whose dates he could discover (starting with the fire which had destroyed London Bridge in 1212), and could now predict fires in the city with considerable accuracy.

But he had not as yet published his theory: Lilly *had* published his hieroglyphic, and his name—that of the major prophet of his time—naturally came up in the committee. It is a mark of how careful astrologers had to be (as of their readers' credibility) that he found himself in deep water. Pepys noted in his diary for December 13th, 1666:

> W. Hewer dined with me, and showed me a Gazett in Aprill last (which I wonder should never be remembered by anybody) which tells how several persons were then tried for their lives, and were found guilty of a design of killing the King and destroying the Government; and as a means to it, to burn the City; and that the day entended for the plot was the 3rd of last September. And that fire did endeed break out on the 2nd of September—which is very strange methinks—and I shall remember it.

The report had appeared in *The London Gazette* for April 29th, 1666: at the Old Bailey Sessions, 'an old army colonel', one John Rathbone, with seven other 'officers or soldiers in the late Rebellion', were charged with conspiring to kill the King and overthrow the Government.

> The better to effect this hellish design the City was to have been fired, and the portcullis let down to keep out all assistance; and the Horse Guard to have been surprised at the Inns where they were quartered, several ostlers having been gained for that purpose ... the third of September was

pitched on for the attempt, as being found by Lilly's Almanack, and a scheme erected for that purpose, to be a lucky day, a planet then ruling which prognosticated the downfall of Monarchy.

The eight men had been found guilty, and executed; and now, with the *Gazette* case in mind, as well as the hieroglyphics, the committee sitting to investigate the cause of the fire sent a note to Lilly, who happened to be in London at the time: 'Ordered, that Mr Lilly do attend this Committee on Friday next being the 25th of October 1666, at two of the clock in the afternoon in the Speaker's Chamber; to answer such questions as shall be then and there asked him.'

Lilly was extremely worried. 'I was timorous of Committees,' he writes, 'being ever by some of them calumniated, upbraided, scorned and derided.' He immediately went for comfort to Ashmole, who accompanied him to Westminster and the Committee's sittings. Ashmole knew a good number of the committee-men, and took 'great pains and care, in speaking unto many worthy members of that Committee your acquaintance, that they should befriend me and not permit me to be affronted, or have any disgraceful language cast upon me.'

Ashmole, a respected man, was heeded, and Lilly was able to record that 'I conceive there was never more civility used unto any than unto myself.'

The committee did not bring up the matter of the trial of Rathbone: on examination, Lilly's 1666 almanac proves not to mention anything about the possible downfall of the monarch; the original rumour may have arisen not only because of the usual vagueness of his utterances, but because September 3rd, as the anniversary of Dunbar, and of Cromwell's death, was always a fateful day to fanatics.

*Monarchy or no Monarchy* was, however, a different matter; and it seems that the committee may even seriously have suspected Lilly of firing the city in order to obtain for himself the credit for forecasting the event; there is a sense in which one would not put it beyond him. Sir Robert Brook, the chairman, pointed out that he had seemed to predict the fire in his publication of 1651. Lilly was careful to make his reply politically sympathetic to the committee:

> After the beheading of the late King, considering that in the three subsequent years the Parliament acted nothing which concerned the settlement of the nation in peace; and seeing the generality of people dissatisfied, the citizens of London discontented, the soldiery prone to mutiny, I was desirous, according to the best knowledge that God had given me, to make enquiry by the art I studied, what might from that time happen unto the Parliament and nation in general.

He had consulted the planets, and

> thought it most convenient to signify my intentions and conceptions thereof, in Forms, Shapes, Types, Heiroglyphics, &c., without any commentary, that so my judgment might be concealed from the vulgar, and made manifest only unto the wise ... Having found, Sir, that the city of London should be sadly afflicted with a great plague, and not long after with an exorbitant fire, I framed these two hieroglyphics as represented in the book, which in effect have proved very true.

Sir Robert asked whether Lilly had foreseen the precise year of the fire. 'I did not,' Lilly said; 'or was desirous. Of that I made no scrutiny.' So evidently, whether or not an informant had seen his private notes, the committee certainly did not have his copy of the book under discussion before it. Lilly had, he said, spent some time attempting to discover by astrological means whether in fact there had been a plot to fire London, 'but cannot or could not give myself any the least satisfaction therein. I conclude, that it was the only finger of God; but what instrument he used thereunto, I am ignorant.'

The committee having dismissed him with thanks for his evidence, and his reputation having if anything gained by the incident, Lilly was properly grateful to Ashmole for his protection. (There had been, after all, some danger; Robert Hubert, an unfortunate addlebrained French watchmaker who had 'confessed' to starting the fire, was hanged for it, though he was fairly obviously innocent.) Two months later, he sent his friend a parcel of books by way of acknowledgment, and 'as many thanks for your civility as motes in the sun'. The parcel contained some works of Baronius, alchemical books of Heinrich Khunrath, on anatomy and surgery by Hieronymus Fabricus ab Aquapendente, a Latin history (perhaps Saxo Grammaticus), and the offer of two more, if Ashmole did not already possess them. 'I more esteem your love and generous spirit than all these, were they many more,' wrote the astrologer.

Mrs Lilly added her present: some permaines and pears. And a few days later, on February 11th, 1667, Lilly sent his friend yet another present: a manuscript notebook containing astrological and autobiographical notes. In it, Lilly wrote:

> This manuscript, was my collection from several persons when I first studied astrology, and is every line of it my own handwriting; from hence I collected with my own experienced observations *Christian Astrology*, the second book thereof, the first part is entirely my own, and so is the Method of all the three books. There are many excellent judgments herein, not at all printed. All these this 10th of February 1666/7 I present unto Elias Ashmole Esq., a true Mecaenas to all honest and learned Sciences; as a testimony of my love unto him. Anglicus—or—William Lilly.

In his autobiography, after recalling his appearance before the Fire committee, Lilly remarks (disconcertingly for the biographer) 'Since [that] time no memorable action hath happened unto me, my retirement impeding all concourse with me.'

But that was not entirely true.

# 9

# Our Prophet's Gone

*Our Prophet's gone; no longer may our ears*
*Be charm'd with musick of th' harmonious spheres.*
*Let sun and moon withdraw, leave gloomy night*
*To shew their Nuncio's fate, who gave more light*
*To th' erring world, than all the feeble rays*
*Of sun or moon ...*

GEORGE SMALLRIDGE,
*An Elegy upon the Death of*
*William Lilly the Astrologer*

Lilly's true character emerges more strongly during the last twelve years of his life than during the previous sixty-five. Very few really personal notes are to be found in his autobiography, or in his notebooks and records; from them we learn about his professional life and character. But in the Ashmolean collection and among the letters to Ashmole kept in the British Museum, we find the most personal utterances Lilly has left us, all dating from his last years.

His friendship with Ashmole became one of the most important things in his old age; and this relationship deepened after Ashmole's second wife's death in 1668. His note of the event in his diary is as terse as Lilly's record of *his* second wife's death. '1 April, 2H a.m. the Lady Manwaring, my wife, died.' We do not even know where she is buried, or whether Ashmole bothered to go to the funeral. Any reconciliation which had taken place after the recriminations and quarrels of earlier years seems to have been cool; it is worth wondering (there is no evidence either way) whether the couple were living together at the time of her death. The friendly note struck in an earlier letter from Lilly was nowhere repeated.

In any event, four months after Lady Manwaring's death, Ashmole paid his usual annual visit to Blyth Hall in Warwickshire, the country home of Sir William Dugdale. He had met Sir William in 1655, at the height of his troubles with his wife, and they had become firm friends. Sir William had an unmarried daughter, Elizabeth, thirty-six years old (the late Mrs Ashmole had been seventy; Ashmole himself was fifty). Presumably Ashmole had a serious talk with Sir William about Elizabeth; he went straight from Warwickshire to London, to buy a house in Shear Lane, and on November 3rd, 1668, noted in his diary: 'I married Mrs* Eliz. Dugdale, daughter to William Dugdale Esquire Norroy King of Armes, at Lincolnes Inn Chapell.'

Ashmole would scarcely have taken such an important step without consulting the planets, and it seems likely that he asked Lilly about the wisdom of the marriage he was contemplating. Lilly may not have been too enthusiastic, for in the second part of his analysis of his friend's horoscope, which he had delivered on October 16th, he had written that he did not think Ashmole would at present entertain 'a woman shee friend', but that he would probably marry when he was fifty-two or fifty-three. Even if he knew of Ashmole's intention towards Miss Dugdale, he certainly cannot be accused of pressing the match.

Interestingly, he went on to paint a sketch of the woman he thought would be Ashmole's third wife. She

> should bee of a middle stature, round visage, having a mole on her left cheeks, one other uppon her breast, of a lovely feature indifferent fleshy or Corpulent, or inclining thereunto, loving hospitality or to live handsomely, of a good fortune ... shee may bee more than 30ty, or about 35 or 36 yeares of age ... It's very probable a third wife shall bury

* A courtesy title; Elizabeth had not previously been married.

> him, yet will shee bee very flegmatic, and accidentally inclined to the spleen and griefe.

She would also be 'instabilem in veneriis et amoribus'.

Elizabeth Ashmole did outlive her husband; and Warwickshire was certainly north of Ashmole's home—another probability Lilly had noted. All the same, it seems doubtful that his sketch was very accurate, though the third Mrs Ashmole does seem to have been in some respects a little unstable. She was certainly naturally of a serene and pleasant disposition, and not only was Ashmole happy with her, but she liked both Lilly and his wife, and the two couples came greatly to enjoy each other's company. The letters from Lilly to Ashmole and his 'Gallant', as he called Elizabeth, are full of the kind of good humour, private jokes and nicknames which mark the letters of intimate friends.

It seems to have been during the late 1660s that Lilly made another friend, and acquired an assistant, in Henry Coley, an astrologer thirty years younger than himself, and who has always been described as his 'adopted son'.

Coley had been born in Oxford in 1633, and lived in Baldwin's Gardens, Gray's Inn Lane, where he had practised astrology since about 1660. He probably met Lilly first at one of the astrologers' feasts; but the development of their friendship is difficult to chart. Certainly by 1670 he was known to Ashmole, and presumably by that time his intimacy with Lilly was considerable.

As to their precise relationship, it seems unlikely to have been as close as has been suggested. Lilly certainly called him 'son': but then, he called his physician and friend Thomas Agar 'son' too; he called Sir William Dugdale 'Father', called Ashmole 'brother', and even called one of his servants 'sister'! Coley was not mentioned in his will, and though he probably gave the younger man verbal permission to continue to publish 'Lilly's Almanack' after his death, this was probably no more than a reasonable recognition of the work Coley was to do for him during the next decade.

The old man showed his assistant kindness, persuading Ashmole to entertain him and introduce him to influential people who might be helpful to him ('what if you sent for Mr Coley to dine with you?' he wrote one day in 1673, hearing of a dinner-party); but there were to be disagreements and petty quarrels too. No, however much Lilly may have regretted that he had no children, he hardly regarded Coley as a son in any sense other than one of courtesy and friendship.

Neither Coley nor Ashmole were strangers to the household at Hersham, which by this time was a substantial one. The deeds which might have given a clue to the rate of growth of Lilly's estate have vanished; but from his will (dated 1674) we know that during the 1660s and 1670s he bought Conyers Close, next to Hurst Wood; then Roberts Lane Close (about fifteen acres), Leacroft Wood, and Ilmores Close (about twenty-two acres). He had a sizeable holding—over sixty acres of land.

Far from the single servant who had come with them to Hersham years before, by the 1670s he and his wife employed at least six: a staff headed by the invaluable Henry Rogerson, an educated man who could write a good letter, and who was one of the witnesses of his master's will. Besides Rogerson there was his daughter Ann, a man called Gabriel, two girls, Mary Wilson and Susan, and 'sister Mollo', who sounds like a cook-housekeeper, on easy terms not only with Lilly and Ruth, but with Ashmole and Elizabeth (to whom she is always, if one can trust Lilly's letters, sending her love).

Then there were at least two horses (called, in 1675, Rozinante and Major Brown), a cat called Tab, and two dogs called Smutt and Ginny (the latter constantly cited as making Tab's life a misery, and who on one occasion badly injured himself 'in pursuit of Venus her pleasure').

Lilly and his wife made friends in the neighbourhood; they are mentioned in the correspondence of Robert Semple, guardian of the house that Frances Howard, Duchess of Somerset, rented and occasionally occupied at Walton. In November 1670 we find Semple complaining that he has 'spent the last lb of Mr Lilly's butter', and a few weeks later he is worried about the clerk to Walton Church, and that 'at the vestry on Thursday Mr Andrews will put him out of his place, Mr Twyne and Mr Clark being also his adversaries'.

Lilly was obviously still a member of the Church Council, for Semple hopes the clerk 'will come off better than was expected, because both Mr Lynn and Mr Lilly are likely to stand his friends ...' We do not know the outcome of the fracas, but it seems to have arisen out of malice, and may well have been resolved in the clerk's favour.

Lilly was well known to the Duchess—perhaps she was a client?—for in May 1671 Semple writes:

> Yesterday morning Mr Lilly and his wife upon an urgent occasion sent a man on horse-back to desire me to let them have 6 pigeons, but for the money offered I told the servant I never in all my life took any for pigeons and would take none of his master who had been so good a neighbour to my Lady, if it were for all the pigeons in the house.

There was by now no necessity for Lilly to work too hard: always careful with his money, he had time to devote himself to the interest, allied to astrology, which became in his last years as important—medicine. He spent most of 1670 completing his studies, while the Ashmoles contributed to his physical comfort. In a letter of April 25th, thanking them for their hospitality to Ruth (who had just been visiting them), Lilly writes:

> Ruth she sayd—Esq: and his Lady would have given me Cloth for shirts for thee—I sayd, you weare a foole you took them not: no fool, sayd Ruth, their kindness wear so great I was ashamed, not knowing how to gratifie them—I thank you for your kindness therein; I am sure to fare the wors for my wife's modesty; but that I verily believe shee did it out of pure nobleness of spirit— ... I conclude with my harty affection to your selfe and my brave noble Gallant and say, that I am your old loving freind William Lilly.
>
> I am a better man than I was, my wife perusing the letter, tells mee the cloth is come, happy man am I that speed so well, and blessed be my noble Gallant that so loves mee, and

long live Doctor Elias, that takes such care of his very old freinds . .

Occasionally, Lilly acted as host for small supper-parties—such as that in May 1670, when he and Ashmole met with Thomas Agar, and they spent the evening discussing medicine (Agar practised nearby). And he and his wife were constantly exchanging visits with Mr and Mrs Ashmole. This had started in 1669, when Elias and Elizabeth twice came to Hersham. No doubt then, and during the year, the two men discussed the step Lilly was contemplating. By now he knew a great deal about medicine, and wished to spend the rest of his life practising it. On October 8th, 1670, Ashmole 'moved my Lord Archbishop of Canterbury for a Lycence for Mr Lilly to practise Physick, which he granted'.

Since 1511, and a statute of Henry VIII, officials of the archdeacons had been issuing licences to provincial doctors, surgeons and midwives, for the practice of medicine. Not all doctors had these certificates: some evaded examination by 'expert persons' — usually local physicians — which was generally necessary. But by the early years of the seventeenth century, two-thirds of the doctors in London were licensed.

London medicine was supervised, in a somewhat desultory way, by the Royal College of Physicians, founded in 1518 for the purpose. The city did not do well under this arrangement, for the College jealously restricted the number of licences it granted, and it has been reckoned that the ratio of patients to doctors was probably not less than five thousand to one. Outside the city, the situation was a little better, for the Church was rather more free with its licences. And besides the physicians there were also the apothecaries and surgeons. The former would often diagnose illnesses and prescribe for them, as well as preparing the medicine. Then there were also the quacks: by 1669, one pamphleteer pointed out that there was 'scarce a pissing-place about the city' without its poster advertizing some cure-all.

Lilly was never a quack in medicine: he took it extremely seriously, and had done so all his life. Apart from his nursing of Mrs Wright, when he first came to London, he had from time to time made notes of his clients' illnesses, and his opinions on them; and he would meticulously send to a qualified physician any client who seemed to need professional attention. In 1650, for instance, Miles Beveridge wrote to him thanking him for 'a patient you sent me from Bromley', and discussing the horoscope Lilly had sent with him. 'By God's blessing she is recovered only troubled with the wind ...'

Doctors such as Lilly fulfilled a distinct purpose at a time when the poor could scarcely afford any kind of medical treatment (some more conventional doctors charged as much as a pound a day for their attention). He certainly knew enough about his subject to pass the test of examination by the 'two Physitians of the Colledge in London' who advised Dr Gilbert Sheldon to permit him to practice. Ashmole writes:

> Hereupon he began to practise more openly, and with good success, and every Saturday rode to Kingston, where the poorer sort flockt to him from severall parts and received much benefit by his advice and prescriptions, which he gave them freely and without money; from those that were more able he now and then received a shilling, and sometimes an halfe Crowne, if they offered it to him, otherwise he demanded nothing: and in truth his Charity toward poore people was very great, no less than the care and paines he tooke in considering and weighing their particular Cases, and applying propper remedies to their Infirmities, which gained him extraordinary credit and estimation.

Any kindness shown to the sick in seventeenth-century England was sure to gain a physician credit and estimation: of all the uncomfortable features of the life of the time, the discomforts and dangers of being ill, and the even greater discomforts of being cured, must have been the worst.

The plague was probably the greatest source of fear: but syphilis, which Columbus' crew had brought back from the New World, was by now raging terribly, its symptoms so fearful, its effects so awful, that even lepers declined to share a house with its victims. Smallpox too appeared with great regularity. Other diseases, less noxious, preyed on the mind. But perhaps the most worrying feature of the scene is exemplified by a note of Aubrey's—that George Villiers' mother, the Countess of Bucks, 'died of a dropsi *and Phisick*'. As Robert Boyle said, many people came 'to apprehend more from the physician than the disease'. There was no telling a good doctor from a bad, a knowledgeable from an ignorant; and how good the good physicians were remains in doubt, for this was a time when most minds were closed to new ideas and to anything savouring of radical experiment or thought: William Harvey told Aubrey that 'after his Booke of the Circulation of the Blood came out, he fell mightily in his Practice, and 'twas beleeved by the vulgar that he was crackbrained'.

Most doctors had their own ideas about cures: many hugged to themselves their secrets, and some sold them for considerable sums. One woman received £100 from Bart's for a certain cure for leprosy which she promised to leave the hospital at her death. Many doctors were so uncertain of the methods they used that they might have as profitably observed the habit of their colleague Dr Napier, who, Aubrey reports,

> was no real doctor but a divine (rector Lindfordiensis) and practised Physick, when a Patient, or Quaerent came to him, presently went to his closet to pray. It appears by his Papers that he did converse with the Angel Raphael, who told him if the Patient were curable or incurable ... his Knees were horny with frequent praying.

The note of comedy fades when one remembers the dreadful sufferings of the sick. Pepys left no account of his being cut for the stone; Evelyn has described such an operation, and it was horrid. In people with a low threshold of pain, and especially with children, the result of even quite minor operations was often permanent damage to the mind. Aubrey wrote of Charles II's son by Barbara Villiers that 'the Duke of Southampton (who was a most lovely youth) had two fore-teeth, that grew out very unhandsome. His cruel Mother caused him to be bound fast in a Chaire, and had them draw'n-out; which has caused the want of his understanding.' A humbler child, in a cottage at Broad-Chalke, had a thumb amputated with a chisel and mallet. 'The Girl was then about seven yeares old: and was a lovely child. Immediately after the thumbe was struck-off, the fright and Convulsion was so extreme that she lost her understanding, even her Speech; she lived till seventeen in that Sad condition.'

Some cures of common illnesses were less unpleasant: a cure for the thrush, Aubrey noted, was to 'take a living Frog, and fold it in a Cloth, that it does not go down into the child's Mouth: and putt the Head into the Child's Mouth till it is dead. And then take another frog.' More amateur cures were even simpler: Sir Jonas Moore, the mathematician, cured sciatica by 'boyling his Buttock'.

Astrological physicians, or medical astrologers, were unlikely to terrorize their patients quite as fiercely as professional physicians. They relied greatly on innocent if often crude herbal remedies, though they certainly advised their peers on the time when patients should or should not be bled, and when an operation was not advisable because a patient might bleed too freely during it (it is interesting that in 1973 an American medical journal published research claiming to show that patients on the operating table bled more freely when the planets were in certain positions). The alliance of astrology and medicine, though by the 1670s it had ceased to be absolutely inevitable, was still extremely strong (Richard Napier, John Lambe and William Salmon were only three of Lilly's astrological colleagues who also held physicians' licences).

It was still popularly believed—as in Hippocrates' time—that a knowledge of astrology was absolutely necessary to any doctor who wished to command a complete medical technique. Nicholas Culpeper put the general view when he pointed out that 'none else [than astrologers] are fit to make physicians'. If not all doctors agreed with him, certainly all astrologers did. Morin, for instance, firmly believed that the moon was the cause of critical days in the progression of an illness, and advised the drawing-up of a horoscope at the first sign of a disease, because diseases were generated naturally from their seeds and had their own symptoms, movements and periods.

Abdius Trew, in his disputations on astrological medicine published in Altdorf in 1663, argued that it was essential to consult the horoscope of a patient who fell ill—but also that of a convalescent, for the planetary indications which brought on the illness might return and cause a relapse. The movements of Mars and Saturn ('the evil planets') should be consulted before administering purgatives; it was probably safe to do so when the moon was moving away from the planet which encouraged a particular illness towards one which would discourage it—from Mars to Venus in the case of cholera, for instance, or from Saturn to Jupiter or Venus in melancholy or phlegm. Clysters* were best applied when the moon was moving away from Saturn. Trew went on to give comprehensive advice about the movements of the planets which strengthened or weakened the effect of medicines on particular parts of the body. And they were *very* important in cases of surgery.

Medicine, in Trew's book (and the books of most other astrologer-physicians) meant of course herbal medicine. In this, the general argument was, and usually is in astrology, a simple one: Culpeper set it out in his *English Physitian, or An Astrologo-Physical Discourse of the Vulgar Herbs of the Nation.* (Though he dealt with herbal treatments, the argument was similar when an astrologer spoke of, say, fractures or wounds).

Describing how his book is to be used, he writes:

> First consider what Planet causeth the Disease; Secondly, consider what part of the Body is afflicted by the Disease, and whether it lie in the Flesh, or Blood, or Venticles ... Thirdly, consider by what Planet the afflicted part of the Bodie is governed. Fourthly, you have in this Book the Herbs for Cure appropriated to the Several Diseases, and the

* Enemas.

> Diseases for your ease set down in the Margin, whereby you may strengthen the part of the Bodie by its like, as the Brain by Herbs of Mercury, the Breast and Liver by Herbs of Jupiter, the Heart and Vitals by Herbs of the Sun, &c ...

So, if one had the gout, one picked hemlock, roasted the root in the embers of the fire (wrapped in wet paper) 'until it be soft and tender, and then applied to the gout in the hands or fingers.' (Hemlock root 'applied to the privities' also diminished lechery; if one licked one's fingers, it indeed terminated it).*

But astrological medicine had many other branches than the herbal. There was for instance 'judgment of the urine'—by which, so many years before, Lilly had gained the confidence of Bulstrode Whitelocke. By setting up a 'figure' for the moment he received a sample of urine from a patient, the astrologer could predict the course of the illness, and provide treatment. Astrology apart, some doctors believed it was possible to advise treatment on sight of the urine alone (the Royal College put an end to this custom).

Lilly, apart from the knowledge he had collected during his years of astrological practice, also studied the publications of his colleagues. *A Treatise of Mathematicall Physicke, or Briefe Introduction to Physicke*, was certainly one of the books Lilly studied during the years of his intensive preparation for medical practice. Its astrological associations are evident and strong.

It contains, for instance, a table showing what planet in which sign represents any part of the body (for instance, the sun in Cancer represents the feet; Venus in Leo, the belly, thighs and knees). This was most important in observing the progress of a disease, and in treating it. The astrological houses also had their meanings ('The thyrd house governeth the shoulders, armes, and handes ...').

The author gives rules for discovering the true nature of the sickness:

* Culpeper enlarged on his astrological medical theory in his *Semeiotica Uranica*, a textbook of astrological medicine, with an Appendix on Urinalia.

> The kind and qualities of the sickness is taken from the nature of those significators which eyther of themselves are very weake & impotent: or else corrupted of evill planets, or doe labour in both the sayd discommodities together, and are both weake and infortunate, and also afflicted of malevolent starrs.

There were rules for discovering whether the sickness would continue; whether the patient would recover or not; and which signs in a particular case presaged death. Particular diseases were associated with particular zodiacal signs: an emphasis on Gemini tended to encourage 'all Diseases and Infirmities in the Arms, Shoulders, Hands, corrupted Blood, windiness in the Veins, distempered Fancies, &c.' Then there were the planets, which had their associations: Mars was the planet 'of Chronical Diseases, imparteth such as proceed of red Choler, hot Apostemations, overflowings of the Gall, Jaundice, Madness, Frenzies, hot Gouts, Exulcerations, Fistulaes, Carbuncles, Agues, Burnings, Vomiting of Blood, etc. ...'

Sometimes the astrological associations faded: particularly in those parts of contemporary medical books which treated of surgery or anatomy—though even there it peeped out from time to time, as in Culpeper's *A Directory for Midwives* (1651), which was an attempt to treat the subject sensibly, and to teach often ignorant women about the mechanics of conception, pregnancy and birth. In the middle of a reasonably straightforward description of the male genitals, we find: 'The Delights or Desires of Venus ... cause the Yard to stand; and that's the reason venerial sights and venerial tales will do it (it need be no stranger to any, that Venus (being a planet cold and moist) should add heat to those parts, that the Moon (being colder and moister than she) should burn by night ...').

In his comprehensive *Complete Herbal*, Culpeper not only gave directions 'to the vulgar', but also to astrologers, the latter often extremely technical: 'Fortify the body with herbs of the nature of the Ascendant, 'tis no matter whether he be a Fortune or Infortunate ... Let your medicine be something anti-pathetic to the Lord of the Sixth ... If the Lord of the Tenth be strong, make use of his medicines ...' And so on. It is quite clear that, as he puts it, Culpeper genuinely regarded a physician without astrology as being 'like a lamp without oil'. No doubt Lilly agreed: indeed, he was ambitious to write his own astrological medical textbook, but never completed it. In a foreword to Richard Saunders's *Astrological Judgement and Practise of Physicke* (1677), he was to write that in view of his age and infirmity 'it cannot be expected that I should oblige the World with anything of the Subject, which I once had thoughts to have attempted.'

For different reasons, it is as difficult to evaluate Lilly as doctor as it is to evaluate Lilly as astrologer. In both cases, he certainly gave wide satisfaction. There is no reason to believe that as a physician he was any better than the mass of his contemporaries. The prescriptions he gives in his letters to Ashmole are harmless, but unlikely to be more than mildly palliative, or at the worst to provide any more violent purging than any seventeenth-century patient would expect. His prescriptions are for fairly simple purges—taken 'in the pap of an apple' or in a posset; they were a cure-all, and the Stuarts seem to have been as fixated on the movements of the bowels as the Elizabethans; Ashmole's diary is full of notes about his 'motions', and there are some instances of rather unpleasant practical jokes based on purgatives. Sometimes, one is glad to note, they backfired (if that is the appropriate verb), as when in April 1675 Ruth Lilly attempted to 'cozen her mayd with some purging ale, wherein shee had some syr. spine cervine.' But (Lilly told Ashmole) 'shee mistooke, and drunke that her selfe, so that sunday she shitt abomination at least 7 or 8 tymes if not more ...'

It was a joke everyone, even possibly the maid, would have taken in good part; friendships in the seventeenth century were partly made of such stuff. In the case of the Ashmoles and the Lillys, however, simple affection was the basis of the relationship. The men twitted each other about their ladies, and were constantly threatening seduction, Ashmole for instance protesting at Lilly's youth (he was in fact fourteen years younger than the astrologer); and Lilly in return assuring his friend that 'my Gallant will take no exception at my youth, it's onely your Lemmon colored stockings' (Malvolio's apparel already a common allusion?).

Mrs Ashmole was pregnant at the time of that allusion, and the Lillys were 'more than ordinary desirous to hear of your Lady, and how it is with her. Shee must bee near her tyme. God send her a safe delivery, els I shall want a Gallant, for nobody but shee will bee troubled with such a Youth as my selfe ...' But the child, like all Ashmole's children, was still-born. Nine months later (in April 1671) Lilly was inviting his friends to Hersham again:

Eminentissime Patrone, salutem in christo—

Last munday 3 April Susan our mayd was to come to London to buy her selfe some necessaries, by whom I wrote an especiall letter to my Gallant (not to you, Sir Esq) which letter is so sweetly, so amorously, so affectionately pennd, contrived, digested, that your selfe uppon sight thereof must needs get one payre of yellow stockings. It comes to her unaltered this day by my servant, for Tuesday proving fayre, the Lady Susan was impeded, and sett to the washing bowle...

I hope after so long an expectation, so many promises, so numerous engagements made but not performed as yet, you will not now defraud me and my wife of my Gallant's company. (These Courtiers never performe their words probatum per te: meum Mecenatem: fuge Diabole). Thes are meer miserable evasions, frauds, connycatchings—I am confident nothing would so recover my poor Gallant as Hersham aire, and the sight of her Gallant. My wife is the best nurse of this world—avant, Satan, this is your own deceit, nulla fides in Ashmodelibus! Oh, monstrum horrend!—let my Gallant bring Medicaments away with her. The very ayre of our hungry place is sufficient to cure—To be serious, I conceive the ayr you are in is too close for her; she is, I am certain, persuaded of our harty love and kindness unto her. Ego dico, et uxor dicit et vult dicere, that my dear Gallant shall have all the curtesies our poor house can or may or might afford.

'Sir Esq., how do yo?

'Well I thank you. But how do y ——

'Our very hart affection and sister Mollus is remembered unto my good Gallant and your Selfe.

Your old lo: freind William Lilly.

By this time Lilly seems to have been working more steadily as medical man than as astrologer. In several letters to Ashmole he complains (humourously, for he certainly was not in need of money) of the low fees he received, and of the impossible feats expected of him. In July 1671, just back from Kingston (wrapped in a warm cloak, a present from his Gallant, against the chill of a late summer evening) he wrote: 'An aged woman, 85, sent me 4d to preserve her to 105. I am perswaded I shall cozen her, but I took her groat, fearing I should get no more that day; but 2s came afterward. You see how I thrive.'

And the following month:

> Love my Gallant above all earthly creatures ... her Cloak constantly worn to Kingston is a propitious one, as to Astrologicall questions: last Saturday, Item 10s, Item 5s, Item 1s, for Physick 6d. Oh, blessed Saint Elizabeth, her cloak! Wear I a Papist, I would reserve reliques out of it. Our harvest weather is extream rainy and uncertain. Last afternoon his Majesty passed by my house to Gilford, there to hunt some Staggs. Had hee called, I would have offered him a cupp of sack, but no other Commodity ...

Ashmole and his wife spent the summer of 1672 with the Lillys, and the two men worked at attempting to recover some of the manuscripts of John Dee. Interest in Elizabeth's 'magician' had fallen off badly after his death, and in the 1670s he was still considered mainly as a magician rather than as the experimental scientist he really was. On August 20th there was a splendid windfall. One Samuel Storye, Ashmole's manservant, appeared on the doorstep with a parcel in which were the manuscripts of no less than five lost mystical works by Dee, written in the man's own hand. Storye had got them from a warder at the Tower of London, and they had been found by the warder's wife in a secret drawer of an old cedar chest her former husband had bought.

The manuscripts were not, unfortunately, of great interest to us, being accounts of Dee's conference with various angels (he had been drawn into these by his companion Edward Kelly); there were angelic instructions for the making of a holy table, invocations, instructions for finding the powder of the philosopher's stone. The angels had ordered that the MSS should be burned; but instead, they went into Ashmole's collection.

During 1673 Ashmole was almost as active as Lilly as an astrologer. Lilly had been having a somewhat difficult time with his almanacs: the *Anglicus* of 1672 had been 'macerated, obliterated, sliced and quartered', and was to be censored for some years to come. Ashmole, on the other hand—more in sympathy with the Court—was often consulted for astrological advice, and more often than not in his turn consulted Lilly (though not always taking his advice). He was, of course, by now Windsor Herald and Treasurer and Registrar of the College of Arms, as well as being Comptroller of Excise; his interest in astrology was well known. It was natural that anyone in Court circles who wished for astrological advice should turn to him. Early in January 1673 he sat for two hours with the Lord Treasurer, Lord Clifford, who a few days later wrote asking for astrological judgments on the question of the King's Declaration of Indulgence to dissenters, and how it would go in the Commons.

In October of the same year, the difficulties between King and Commons were put to Ashmole by Sir Robert Howard, Clifford's friend. Ashmole put the question in turn to Lilly, and his copy of it ('Whether the house of Commons shall have good Successe in these proceedings to setle the Protestant religion and the Interest and property of the nation; and whether they and theyr King shall unite in A good Correspondency') bears Lilly's notes, showing the extent to which Ashmole leant on his friend in preparing the reply—though it is clear he was far more inclined to favour the King's cause than Lilly.

But Ashmole's most notable client during 1673 was Charles himself, who at the end of October asked Ashmole about future relations with Parliament. Ashmole drew up a horoscope for the time of the King's speech to Parliament on October 27th, and compared it with Charles' birth-chart. There would be, he suggested, 'a notable harmony & unity between the King and Parliament within a few daies,' and Charles would 'be able to dispose of and controle the House of Commons in all things shall please him.'

This time, Ashmole did not mention the question to Lilly until after he had given his own answer. He did send his friend a copy of the question and answer on October 30th. Lilly wrote:

> Charissime Patrone et Ptolemee,
>
> I have seriously weighed and considered your profound judgement upon the figure sent mee, and I am very glad of the honor His Majesty did you, but more satisfied at your prudent and well grounded answer about the success—which certainly will correspond with your grave judgement ...

In the event, what good feelings there were between Charles and the Commons were more a result of Charles's modification of his original views (or, at least, demands) than of his ability to 'dispose of and controle the House'. Ashmole kept his counsel; Charles' consultation seems to have remained as secret as that of any less majestical client.

Again, the Ashmoles spent the summer at Hersham, where he and Lilly did some more research into the life of Dr Dee, going over to Mortlake to gather some reminiscences of the old man's life there, looking over his house and garden, and visiting his grave in Mortlake Church. They had an evening or two with Sir Edward Walker, now completely reconciled with Lilly, testing a dozen or so bottles of Ashmole's home-made ale; and towards the end of the year, Lilly sent his friend a copy of the 1674 *Anglicus*, which the latter evidently helped to edit or amend (as did Henry Coley).

Coley was by now playing an increasingly important part in helping Lilly with astrological work—in particular, with the almanacs—for now began the series of illnesses from which the astrologer was to suffer during the final seven years of his life. In the summer of 1674 (Ashmole later wrote) 'a violent humour discovered itselfe in red spots all over his Body, with little Pushes* in his head. This, in the Winter following was seconded by a distemper, whereof he fell sick, & was let Blood in the left foote, a litle above the Ankle.'

That was on December 18th; the blood-letting did little good, for the following day he 'had a great paine in his left Leg which lasted 24 houres, & put him into a great Feaver'.

Christmas 1674 was not a happy one. On December 20th,

> a humour† descended from his head by his left side from 8 a'clock at Night till the next Morning, & then staying a while in the calfe of his Leg, at length descended toward his Toes, the anguish whereof put him into a Feaver. This humour fixed in two places on the top of his left foote (one in that where he was let blood two daies before) which (upon application of Plegets‡) growing ripe, they were lanced by Mr Agar ... after which he began to be of ease, his Feaver abated.

At least Lilly had a friend to nurse him, in Mr Agar, who seems at least to have been no worse a doctor than the average. On January 4th, Ruth (in one of the few letters of hers to survive) was able to tell Mrs Ashmole that 'my husband hath had no feaver these 2 dayes, and hath rested well these 2 last nights, which gives mee hope concerning him'. A week later, the servant Henry Rogerson told Ashmole that his master's 'legg mends very well and godbethanked is in very good ease', though Ruth was now ill with a bad cold.

By February they were both well on the way to recovery, and Lilly was able to give some attention to supervising the boiling of a gift of peas Ashmole had sent. 'They are most excellent—I boyled some in a bag yesterday. Henry made pottage, never any

* boils; pimples. † fluids ‡ compresses

prooved better ... [they] are worth all the Patacoons* in Portugal.' His recovery was also hastened by the consumption of seven barrels of oysters: 'I find they agree best with me.'

Ashmole had his own troubles. In January, Elizabeth had miscarried again. 'Make much of my Gallant,' Lilly wrote from his own sickbed; 'wee are hartily sory for her, what shall Sir Giles do for an other ...?' (He signed himself 'Sir Giles without a crutch'.) And 1675 was not to be a good year for Ruth Lilly's health. In February she suffered from a pain in the head, and vapors ... in her Stomach and Region of the hart ... in one leg shee hath little pain, in the other *much* pain at some tymes since Sunday; I find her cheerfull and very little complaining.' Elizabeth Ashmole volunteered to come to Hersham to nurse her, but Lilly demurred: 'My Gallant shall be welcome at all or any tyme or tymes, but there's no cause (except shee come for ayre) as yett to put her to such a trouble as adventuring to Hersham. Let it bee warmer weather first. This is plain dealing, and truth, I protest.'

Within a month, Ruth had recovered sufficiently to contemplate with equanimity a gift of 'excellent Sprats' Ashmole had sent Lilly, who wrote:

> My wife had a mind to eat twenty, but having the day before disturbed her stomack, she onely eat 2 spratts. The oysters wear very good, for the daintyes I onely thank my good Gallant. Ruth I hope will amend when warmer weather comes; shee walkes, shee talkes, shee eats—but her greatest want is naturall sleep, which I hope in tyme will come.

He put her on a diet, that same month, but was sure that 'nothing but warm weather will cure her'. (Winter in a large house on low-lying land near the Thames must have been a damp, dank experience in the mildest of weather). The Ashmoles showered the Lillys with gifts: barrels of oysters, jumbals (sweet cakes), sprats, herrings, crabs, roses, and on one occasion a sturgeon,

* Spanish silver coins

were sent to Hersham; and between April and June, Ruth Lilly being much recovered, Elizabeth Ashmole came on a visit. Lilly had been most persuasive. Ashmole was himself going to the Dugdales at Blyth Hall, but though 'its most rigorously cold—I peep out but rarely—Ruth not at all,' Elizabeth would be 'as welcome to us, as at Blyth Hall. I have one hundred storys to tell her, and I hope shee hath some for mee.'

She spent about seven weeks at Hersham between mid-spring and midsummer. It was evidently a very happy time. There was plenty of fresh food. At the beginning of the year there were five calves and eighteen young pigs in Lilly's yard; swarms of bees in the orchard; three dozen bottles of sack lay in the cellar, and he had laid in a pound of Spanish tobacco and a pound of sweet-scented Virginia, together with a selection of pipes—'long, middle-sized, short ones' (Elizabeth enjoyed a pipe); and there were two barrels of Colchester oysters, into which he and Sir Edward Walker made great inroads one evening in March, when they remembered Ashmole, an absent friend, 'in clarret and sack XXty tymes'.

On other evenings, Lilly, Ruth and their guest would sit quietly before the fire playing at Noddy (a card game closely related to cribbage), drinking ale, gossiping:

> My Gallant hath seen young Caleb Cheesman: hee hath both Pox and measells. She likes him well! My servant Ginny* is wounded, in following his lechery. We all drink your health continually. My Gallant beats me constantly at Noddy, though I am the better gamster. You would laugh to see her choller, when my wife tutors me at play ...

And, later, 'Hear is nothing but quarrelling, viz whether I do cheat my Gallant most, or her Ladyship mee, at our cardship ...'

It was during 1675 that Lilly engaged in the last of his great public altercations: this time with John Gadbury, an astrologer himself much given to quarrelling. It must be admitted that in

* The dog.

this case Lilly seems, mischievously, to have started it. In 1674, he published a pamphlet (which cannot now be traced) in which he slyly and obliquely attacked Gadbury by pointing out that someone with Scorpio strong in his birth-chart tended at least to be a criminal, a reprobate, full of ingratitude, and with a tendency to perjury, lying, lechery, ambition, arrogance and falsity. Gadbury had Scorpio rising, and by all accounts had at least some of the faults of that sign; he fell out even with his friends.

He was furious, and defended himself in *Obsequiam Rationabile* 'against the malicious and false attempts of that Grand (but Fortunate) IMPOSTER William Lilly'.

> Sir! be ye dignified or distinguished by what Names or Titles soever, it is ye that are rendered by Mr Lilly his black pen, the most wicked, vile and dangerous People in the whole World. Ye are the hated Generation that he hath advised all People to beware of. Ye see that sort of men that are, by him, stigmatised to be both naturally and necessarily the most destructive to human Society; and this meerly for the sake of your innocent Horoscope, although it be sufficiently known that the Heavens do only incline, and that but gently too. Ye are the Species of Mankind (in Mr Lilly his righteous eyes) which are born to be Plagues of the Age ye live in. It is ye that must carry the Red Cross of Mr Lilly his malice, and a lord have mercy upon us, in your foreheads, that all men which see you may for your Signs Sake flee and avoid you ... Ye are all equally concluded (with me) under Mr Lilly's egregious Scandal against Scorpio; yet I have great reason to believe that Mr Lilly hath levelled that his malicious and Envious Dart against *me* in particular, than (it may be) against any of you ...

And he wound up, since he had a page to spare, with a verse, concluding:

> Now let me (being Astrologer) presage
> The like Catastrophe to those that rage

And Rave 'gainst harmless Scorpio, (tooth and nail)
As if the Heavens the Equals were, to frail
And envious man (a Bubble!), who to day
Doth storm like Thunder, tomorrow's turn'd to clay.
On then Aquarians! with your Envious breath
(As at poor Scorpio) try to out-rail Death.
Go on too Pisceans! with your Slipping tricks,
You'll want a Motion for to baffle Styx.
The Fatal River warns ye, make your Peace,
Ask Heaven's Pardon, and your Envy Cease.

Lilly must have been delighted that his rival had risen so readily to the bait. He had always disliked Gadbury, writing evidently in a temper on one of the latter's broadsheets that he was 'beggerly brought up, putt to a pettifogger, turnd away for lying, putt to Nichol, a poore taylor in Oxford by charity or the parish ... was calld sawcy & lowly Jack,' and 'in London turn'd Ranter, & Atheist—thrust himself into a pulpit being drunk at London Wall.'

He replied to *Obsequiam Rationabile* in a pamphlet issued under the pseudonym of Bentivolio Philo-Huff-Lash.

When first I saw J. Gadbury's Pamphlet, his rhetorical outcries to all persons, Gentle or Simple, of the Tribe of Scorpio, & the Frightfull Stuff wherewith he alarms them to awake, look about them, & be active for their security &c., made me apprehend some horrid Plot on foot worse than Faux's Treason, the Sicilian Vespers, and Parisian Massacre, I applauded his good nature in cautioning them against such unknown and ghastly dangers, that they might wear swords and daggers, pocket pistols, and coats of mail whenever they went abroad, and sleep a nights armed back and breast, and in headpieces musket proof ...

But upon a calm and impartial examination I find our Author is only Don Quixoted with pride and malice, and thence takes to Windmills of his own addle Crown for inchanted Castles and affrighted Mormos; so that I dare assure

> all the Scorpionists between Dover-pier and Berwick-upon-Tweed that if they will but keep the King's peace and have a final portion of Grace, or so much as a competent Dose of right Reason about them, they may still (notwithstanding anything Mr Lilly has written) live in safety, and die in their beds without putting themselves to the untoward trouble of cutting their own throats or the charge of preparing halters.

Game, set and match to W. Lilly. But it was his last incursion into controversy; for one thing, his eyesight was beginning to fade. In July 1675, he told Ashmole 'my eye is bad; the blister runs'. And after a violent vomiting fit in November that year, he took to his bed for a while, and Ashmole noted that a

> dimnes in his Eyes ... after occasioned him to make use of Mr Henry Coley as his Amanuensis to transcribe (from his dictates) his Astrologicall Judgements for the yeare 1677, though the Monethly Observations for that yeare were written with his owne hand sometyme before, though by this tyme he was growne very dim sighted. His Judgements & Observations for the Succeding yeares till his death ... were all composed by his directions, Mr Coley coming to Hersham the beginning of every Sommer, & staied there till by Conference with him he had dispatched them for the Press—to whome at these oppertunities he comunicated his way of Judgement & other Astrologicall Arcanas.

Lilly himself, in the preface to his 1677 *Anglicus*, commended Coley to the reader as an 'Industrious and no less Ingenious Artist' who would 'continue what so many years we have carried on for the Honour of Astrology'. In 1676, he contributed a Foreword to Coley's most ambitious work, the *Clavis Astrologiae Elimata* (dedicated to 'the most eminently accomplish'd in all ingenious literature, Elias Ashmole'.):

> I am now neer 74 years of Age compleat, and after much sickness and Indisposition of Body in my Old Age (especially

these two years last past) I am now by the blessing of God upon the means used, reasonably well recovered again; and it was all along my intention (had I not been unhappily prevented and discouraged) to have freely communicated to the world (for the benefit of all honest and grateful Sons of Urania) what many years since I promised in my *Introduction to Christian Astrology*. But this Author (being the only Publick Person that I have hopes of) hath now with no small pains and Industry, saved me that labour, in presenting the world with this most compleat piece of astrology ...

Coley had recently been working on a translation of Guido Bonatus and Cardan which was published under Lilly's name. Lilly explains in an Introduction that this took the place of a revised edition of his *Introduction to Astrology* (by which, as usual, he meant *Christian Astrology*). 'The laboriousness of that Work, considering our Age and many Infirmities of Body, with the Discouragements we have already met with from some ungrateful persons, caused us to lay aside ... these intentions.'

It seems likely that Lilly kept a careful eye on the translation, for his own style seems discernible in many of the Cardan aphorisms, at least:

If you prune your Vines when the Moon is at full in Taurus, Leo, Scorpio, Sagittarius, neither wormes nor birds will infest your Grapes.

If in a Woman's Nativity Mars shall be under the Sun Beams, she will be apt to play the Harlot with her Servants and meane Fellows, but if Venus be there, then she will trade discreetly with Nobles and Gallants of Quality.

Mars is seldom joyned with Mercury for Good, for he makes people naughty and Imprudent, yet industrious in Art, whence it comes to pass that the best Artists are too often the worst men.

Lilly's letters to Ashmole become less and less frequent as his sight fails: in April 1677, he ends one short note (thanking Ashmole for eggs and strong ale) 'My eyes permit no more ... very very bad sight.' He was of course treating himself for this—with, for instance, a distillation of 'Fennel, Vervin, Eybright, Endive, Betony, red Roses, Maidenhair each 3 handfulls, bruised and steeped a whole day in white wine ...' But to no avail.

The Ashmoles cheered him with visits and with gifts; and the Lillys on their side sent gifts of their own—including beehives and four swarms of Hersham bees, whose arrival so delighted Elizabeth Ashmole that she 'cutts capers like a Maid-Marion & feeles not the Ground she goes on'. But understandably Lilly was getting a little tetchy, quarrelling from time to time with Coley (who in the summer of 1677 was reduced to using Ashmole as an intermediary). This may have been because of his delay in providing 'copy' for the 1678 almanac: a letter of July 17th apologizes to Lilly for this. Coley has, he says, 'been extraordinarily ill of a cold' and 'constantly visited all day with schollers and querants', but working by night and candlelight he hopes to complete the work soon. He hopes to hear

> that yourselfe & my mother Lilly are now in reasonably good health after so long & odious sickness & indisposition ... I hope your eyes continue reasonable well. Mr Elvard of Bristol has been in town this last Terme and tells me his powder will do strange things as to your recovery of sight if you please to make use of it ...

Coley must have been as busy by this time as Lilly had been at the height of his career. An advertisement in the *Anglicus* for 1682 announces that 'at his house in Baldwins-Gardens' Coley 'will teach arithmetic, geometry, trigonometry, navigation, astronomy, the use of the Globes ... and the art of Astrology in all its parts.' This marks one of the earliest advertisements to appear in an almanac: there are others, including one for Dr Lockier's Universall Pill, and one which states that from John Reve at the Naked-Boy by Fleet Bridge, one might obtain 'Trusses of all sorts easie. None such made in England as these be. Ruptures or Broken Bellies. No Cure No Money.' Soon, Old Moore's almanac was to begin printing pages of such advertisements, which still make up a large bulk of twentieth-century almanacs.

The 1682 almanac was the last which Lilly substantially wrote: it included a judgment on the 'terrible comet' notable 'especially for the length of its Taile', which Ashmole had seen on December 21st, 1680, and which Lilly had forecast, astronomically. It promised, he now stated, 'tribulations, sorrows and afflictions ... fierce tempests, both at Sea and Land ... strange treacheries, unnatural barrenness or dryness of the Earth, corrupt Aires, with Pestiferous qualities reigning therein ...' *Plus ça change ...*

If these horrors were to occur, they were not to trouble William Lilly. There were ominous signs after dinner on March 25th, 1681, when it was noticed that the left side of his mouth 'was drawn aside, but recovered again'. Five days later, 'towards evening a dead palsy began to seize his left side'. Two days later, he took to his bed. Ashmole visited him on June 4th, and found him almost speechless, and very difficult to understand (though he knew his friend). Ashmole wrote in his continuation of Lilly's autobiography:

> The eighth of June, he lay in a great agony, insomuch that the sweat followed drop after drop, which he bore with wonderful courage and patience (as indeed he did all his sickness) without complaint; and about three o'clock the next morning, he died, without any shew of trouble or pangs. Immediately before his breath went from him, he sneezed three times.

Lilly was buried in Walton Church on June 10th. Ashmole arranged the funeral, and helped to lower his friend's coffin into the grave on the left side of the chancel, where later he set up a black marble stone. Then the will was read, which the astrologer had made seven years earlier. It was simple enough.

> Rendring my soule into the hands of God, my body I leave to be buried at the discretion of Ruth Lilly my wife. My

> worldly estate I thus dispose it. I give and bequeath unto Ruth Lilly my wife, during her naturall life, all that parcell of ground called Hurst Wood, containing by estimation eighteen acres, be it more or lesse, and all the profittes thereof ...

He then listed the other pieces of land he owned: Conyers Close, Roberts Lane Close, Leacroft Wood and Ilmores Close; after Ruth's death, all these were to go to Carleton Whitelocke, 'sonn of Sir Boulter Whitlock, Kt.' Something of a surprise: not only that Lilly should have misspelt Bulstrode Whitelocke's name (a far less careful view of spelling was taken by Lilly and his contemporaries than we now have), but that he should never have mentioned Carleton Whitelock in any of his letters to Ashmole, or as far as one can see in any of his MSS notes. But the fact that no one seems to have been at all surprised by the contents of the will seems to indicate that the news was no news either to Ruth Lilly or to Ashmole. Whether Henry Coley (not mentioned in the will) was equally calm about it is not revealed.

'My brother Robert Lilly,' still in Diseworth, received £5, 'William Lilly his sonne the summe of twenty shillings', and 'my sister Susan Beufoy' ten shillings. So much for the Lillys. There seems to have been little family feeling: the brother and sister are barely mentioned in the autobiography. Though £5 was not a negligible sum in the 1680s, it still seems a little odd that a childless man should so have ignored his blood relations. There may have been positively bad blood between them.

The servants were remembered. 'Ann Rogerson, the daughter of Henry Rogerson,' was to receive £5 (though in fact Lilly had handed over that gift three years before his death, and had carefully noted the fact on the manuscript of the will). Mary Wilson, 'at the day of her marriage,' was to receive no less than £20 'for a peece of plate'; and each of the other servants were to receive 20s. Five pounds was to be distributed to 'the poore of Walton towne' and an equal sum to 'the poore of Hersham and Burwood'. No doubt they missed Lilly: Ashmole noted that 'his charity and kindness to his poor neighbours was always great and hearty'

Little remains to be told. Ashmole bought Lilly's library from his widow for £50, 'he having oft tymes in his lyfe time exprest that if Mr Ashmole would give that summe, he should have them.' Ruth Lilly wrote to him, a few days later:

> This is in particular to returne me thanks for thy kindness in my concerne. I have likewis sent the halfe crowne disbursed on my account. I have also sent a relique of my husbands, viz. a cape, which I hope thou will be pleased to accept as a remembrance of him.

The indications seem to be that the Ashmoles kept in touch with Ruth: she certainly visited them in November of 1681, and while she makes no further appearances in Ashmole's diaries, it would be pleasant to think that they remained friends.

The marble gravestone which Ashmole placed on his friend's grave cost him £6 5s. 6d. He had done the same for John Booker, fourteen years earlier, and had also bought that astrologer's library: both libraries, more or less intact, are in the Ashmolean collection. At the end of his completion of Lilly's autobiography, which he started on the fourth anniversary of his friend's death, he set an epitaph composed by George Smallridge, later Bishop of Bristol. Not unnaturally, Smallridge saw Lilly's death as being in perfect accord with heavenly signs:

> He must be gone, the stars had so decreed;
> As he of them, so they of him, had need.
> This message 'twas the blazing comet* brought;
> I saw the pale-fac'd star, and seeing thought
> (For we could guess, but only LILLY knew)
> It did some glorious hero's fall foreshow.
> A hero's fal'n, whose death more than a war
> Or fire, deserved a comet ...

The elegy seems enormously overblown, of course; can it seriously have been supposed, as Smallridge suggests, that

* i.e., the comet of 1680.

Now swords may safely come
From France or Rome, fanaticks play at home.
Now an unseen, and unexpected hand
By guidance of ill stars, may hurt our land;
Unsafe, because secure; there's none to show
How England may avert the fatal blow.

It is certainly true that fewer people were taking Smallridge's view about the real efficacy of astrological prediction—especially perhaps horary prediction. In France, in 1682, there was a major attack on astrology as one of the chief remaining superstitions which science must drive from the minds of modern men. Pierre Bayle argued that the astrological theory was ignominious to human nature, based on caprice, and so open to attack that it was an extraordinarily difficult feat to write anything at all on the subject without mortally wounding it! France's new attachment to philosophy had begun to drive such superstitious nonsense from the country, and it could not vanish too soon.

It is interesting now to note that one of Bayle's most vehement attacks was on the notion that the position of the moon and other planets affected terrestrial weather; this is perhaps the only tenet of astrology now almost universally accepted by astronomers. And he was almost alone in his antagonism to it; even at the time when he published, John Goad, then headmaster of Merchant Taylors' School, was simultaneously arguing in London that the planets certainly affected the weather on earth, and might, he thought, have their effect on earthquakes (a theory developed and partly supported, in the twentieth century, by the work of Dr Rudolf Tomaschek).

But though astrological medicine survived for some time, and though experimental method was to offer some basic (though often over-simple) support for the astrological theory in general, hostility was growing fast; the attitude of Kepler and Francis Bacon—that there were interesting elements in the theory which deserved serious study—was giving way to complete condemnation, a condemnation which was to take forms as various as the satire of Swift and the vituperation of Voltaire.

Six years after Lilly's death, Newton was to publish his *Principia*, making the study of the skies a disciplined science. As Arthur Koestler puts it*:

> The wild dance of shadows thrown by the stars on the wall of Plato's cave was settling into a decorous and sedate Victorian waltz. All mysteries seemed to have been banished from the universe, and divinity reduced to the part of a constitutional monarch, who is kept in existence for reasons of decorum, but without real necessity and without influence on the course of affairs.

Astrology joined God, in the eyes of science, as an extraneous, mildly interesting but unprovable hypothesis.

Lilly's unquestioning acceptance of the proposition that the positions of the planets at the time of, say, a theft, enabled one to determine the height, colouring and dress of the thief, and where and how he had hidden the stolen goods, was never to return. Other theories which he expressed in *Christian Astrology* are remarkably similar to theories which Jung picked up and examined half a century ago, and to other theories which are now being examined by scientists in Europe and America.

On some levels Lilly's career was a joke; on others, of historical, social interest. His life was eccentric, sometimes foolish, devious, sometimes brave and sometimes self-seeking. It cannot be said to have been dull; and perhaps, after all, not so entirely founded on a false proposition as the Victorians supposed. The universe, as J. B. S. Haldane put it, 'may be not only queerer than we suppose, but queerer than we *can* suppose.' Lilly would have recognized and respected that proposition, and in his way did something to support it as an outward-looking and valuable one—the only one for an astrologer, and it may be the only safe one for a scientist.

* In *The Sleepwalkers*, p. 509.

# A Note on Sources

The starting point for any life of William Lilly must be his own autobiography, written at the suggestion of his friend Elias Ashmole, and preserved in manuscript in the collection of Ashmole's books and papers now in the care of the Bodleian Library in Oxford. The autobiography was first published in 1715, going into a second edition in the same year. A third edition in 1774 also included Ashmole's own *Life*; I have used the more accessible 1822 edition (though the book was again reprinted, in a fifth edition, as part of a series of autobiographies published in 1826).

Lilly is occasionally slapdash—about dates and titles, for instance. He can usually be corrected with the help of contemporary printed material, including his own almanacs.

The most comprehensive collection of these is in the Thomason collection in the British Museum; there are copies to be found in the Bodleian and elsewhere, however. In the Bodleian also is a collection of manuscript material, including a number of Lilly's notebooks, in which he recorded the astrological charts drawn up for his clients, and some details about them and the questions they asked, as well as his answers. Then there are the diaries of Ashmole, which record his first meeting and subsequent friendship with Lilly. These have been meticulously edited by C. H. Josten, to whom anyone studying the period must be indebted.

Among the other sources I have consulted the following books are included. Asterisks mark those which were of greatest interest.

Abernathy, George R. 'The English Presbyterians and the Stuart Restoration', *Transactions of the American Philosophical Society* (London, 1965)

Aubrey, John. *Brief Lives*, ed. Oliver Lawson Dick (London: Secker & Warburg, 1949)

*Ashmole, Elias. *Notes and Correspondence*, ed. C. H. Josten (Oxford: Clarendon Press, 1966)

Bald, R. C. *John Donne* (London: Oxford University Press, 1970)

Blatcher, Marjorie (ed.). *Report on the Manuscripts of the Marquess of Bath at Longleat*, Vol. IV (London: H.M.S.O., 1968)

*Brinsley, John. *Ludus Literarius*, ed. E. T. Campignac (Liverpool University Press, 1917)

*Butler, Samuel. *Hudibras* (1664)

Clarendon, Earl of (Edward Hyde). *A History of the Great Rebellion* (1667)

*Commons Journals*, Vols. VII, VIII

Deacon, Richard. *John Dee* (London: Frederick Muller, 1968)

Defoe, Daniel. *A Journal of the Plague Year* (1722)

Donne, John. *Sermons*, ed. Logan Pearsall Smith (Oxford University Press, 1919)

Godfrey, Elizabeth. *Home Life under the Stuarts* (London: Grant Richards, 1903)

Hoskins, W. G. *Essays in Leicestershire History* (Liverpool University Press, 1950)

Hutchinson, Lucy. *Memoirs of Captain Hutchinson* (London: Oxford University Press, 1973)

Jenkinson, Wilberforce. *London Churches Before the Great Fire* (London: S.P.C.K., 1917)

Koestler, Arthur. *The Sleepwalkers* (London: Hutchinson, 1959)

McCaffery, Ellen. *Astrology, its History and Influence in the Western World* (New York: Scribners Sons, 1942)

Macdonald, A. *A History of King's School, Worcester* (privately pub.)

Osborne, Dorothy. *Letters to Sir William Temple* (London: Folio Society, 1965)

*Parliamentary History*, Vol. III

Pearl, Valerie. *London and the Outbreak of the Puritan Revolution* (London: Oxford University Press, 1961)

Pepys, Samuel. *Diary*, ed. Latham, R. and Matthews, W. (London: Bell, 1970)

Plant, Marjorie. *The English Book Trade* (London: Allen & Unwin, 1965)

Plomer, H. R. 'English Almanacs and Almanac-makers of the 16th and 17th centuries', *Notes & Queries*, 6th series, XI and XII.

Raleigh, Walter. *History of the World* (1614)

Rowse, A. L. *The Elizabethan Renaissance* (London: Macmillan, 1971); the reader's attention is also directed to this author's *Simon Forman* (London: Macmillan, 1974)

*Thomas, Keith. *Religion and the Decline of Magic* (London: Weidenfeld & Nicolson, 1971)

*Thorndike, Lynn. *The History of Magic and Experimental Science* (Columbia University Press, 1941)

*Tillyard, E. M. W. *The Elizabethan World Picture* (London: Chatto & Windus, 1943)

Traill, H. D. (ed.). *Social England* (London: Cassell, 1895)

Trevelyan, G. M. *England under the Stuarts* (London: Methuen, 1904)

Walker, Sir Edward. *A Full Answer to a Book Entitled Monarchy or no Monarchy* (1705)

Watson, J. Steven. *A History of the Salters' Company* (London: Oxford University Press, 1963)

Wedgwood, C. V. *The Common Man in the Great Civil War* (Leicester University Press, 1957)

—— *The Great Rebellion* (London: Collins, 1965)

Wharton, George. *Works*, ed. John Gadbury (1683)

*Whitelocke, Bulstrode. *Memorials of the English Affairs* (1682)

# Index